Current Perspectives in Psychology

Posttraumatic Stress Disorder

Malady or Myth?

Chris R. Brewin

YALE UNIVERSITY PRESS   NEW HAVEN & LONDON

Set in Adobe Garamond type by The Composing Room of Michigan, Inc.
Printed in the United States of America by Vail-Ballou Press.

Library of Congress Cataloging-in-Publication Data

Brewin, Chris.
    Posttraumatic stress disorder : malady or myth? / Chris R. Brewin.
        p.   cm. — (Current perspectives in psychology)
Includes bibliographical references and index.
    ISBN 0-300-09984-3 (alk. paper)
    1. Post-traumatic stress disorder.   I. Title.   II. Series.
RC552.P67 B745 2003
616.85′21—dc21   2002155619

A catalogue record for this book is available from the British Library.

The paper in this book meets the guidelines for permanence and durability of the
Committee on Production Guidelines for Book Longevity of the Council on
Library Resources.

10 9 8 7 6 5 4 3 2 1

*To my sister, Jill Brewin, whom I knew for only two years.
Her short life and death have been a lasting influence on my work,
not always in ways that I have understood at the time.*

Contents

Series Foreword

Current Perspectives in Psychology presents the latest discoveries and developments across the spectrum of the psychological and behavioral sciences. The series explores such important topics as learning, intelligence, trauma, stress, brain development and behavior, anxiety, interpersonal relationships, education, child-rearing, divorce and marital discord, and child, adolescent, and adult development. Each book focuses on critical advances in research, theory, methods, and applications and is designed to be accessible and informative to nonspecialists and specialists alike.

In this book, Dr. Chris Brewin presents the latest findings on stress and trauma. Trauma is an unfortunate experience of everyday life and can arise from exposure to war, crime, natural disaster, accidents, physical and emotional abuse, and loss. The sources of trauma and their impact on individuals, communities, and countries give this book broad personal and social relevance.

Reactions to trauma vary widely. One of these reactions, posttraumatic stress disorder (PTSD), can have multiple psychological effects and result in impaired functioning, often for many years. This book goes beyond mere description of the disorder and its many interesting clinical features, providing in-depth discussions of controversies over the nature, existence, and consequences of PTSD. It also features an account of the political and social factors that led to the classification of such reactions to trauma as a psychiatric disorder, and of the much-debated subject of false memory.

Another strength of this book is its comprehensive view of the biological, psychological, and social processes associated with traumatic stress. Reactions to war and rape, two of the areas that are the most well investigated, include processes involving self-blame, anger, criticism from others, and lack of social support, all of which can influence and exacerbate the impact of trauma. Brewin covers advances in key areas of research about the underlying processes related to trauma, such as hopelessness, loss of identity, memory, thoughts, and emotions in general. This kind of research draws from not only studies of victims but also laboratory studies of the brain, fear conditioning, and memory.

This book is an engaging as well as scholarly treatise on the importance of trauma and its devastating effects. We are fortunate to have Dr. Brewin as an author. His contributions to theory, research, and clinical work make this a volume at the highest level of scholarship.

ALAN E. KAZDIN
Series Editor

Acknowledgments

For helping me to understand the often confusing and contradictory literature on trauma, my thanks must first go to the patients suffering from posttraumatic stress disorder with whom I have worked over the past ten years. Through their courage and their willingness to explore and share intensely personal and distressing experiences, I have been able to hear firsthand how much and in what complex ways traumatic experiences may impact the psyche.

I am also enormously grateful to the many friends and colleagues who work in the world of trauma and/or memory and who have unstintingly shared their views and insights with me. Among these I would particularly like to mention Jackie Andrade, Richard Bryant, Claude Chemtob, David Clark, Martin Conway, Anke Ehlers, Edna Foa, Jennifer Freyd, Ann Hackmann, Allison Harvey, Steph Hellawell, Emily Holmes, Deborah Lee, Richard McNally, Phil Mollon, John Morton, Roger Pitman, Patricia Resick, Martina Reynolds, Suzanna Rose, Michael Rugg, Paula Schnurr, Jonathan Schooler, Arieh Shalev, Stuart Turner, and Kerry Young. All the members of the British Psychological Society's Working Party on Recovered Memories gave generously of their time to furthering understanding of this complex topic. I very much enjoyed working with them and learned much from them.

Several important meetings have contributed greatly to generating new ideas, breaking down barriers, and furthering the discovery of common ground among people with different views. In 1996 Don Read and Stephen Lindsay organized a NATO Advanced Study Institute on "Recollections of Trauma: Scientific Evidence and Clinical Practice," and in 1998 Jennifer Freyd and Anne de Prince organized a conference titled "Trauma and Cognitive Science: A Meeting of Minds, Science, and Human Experience." Both of these meetings focused on the scientific background relevant to understanding recovered memories of trauma. Also in 1998, Douglas Bremner and Philip Saigh organized a research conference on posttraumatic stress disorder at Lake George in upstate New York. All these were landmark events and I was privileged to participate in them. The International Society for Traumatic Stress Studies and its sister organizations throughout the world provide a regular forum where researchers and practitioners can meet and share ideas, and they have taken a much-needed lead in developing best-practice guidelines for the treatment of posttraumatic stress disorder and in providing resources for professionals and the public in the wake of traumatic events such as the terrorist attacks of September 11, 2001.

Finally, I express my deep gratitude to my wife, Bernice Andrews, who first sparked my interest in the relation between trauma and depression. Our joint work has shaped much of the thinking behind this book, and she has been an unfailing source of research expertise, practical support, and canny insights into human nature.

1

Saviors and Skeptics

No diagnosis in the history of American psychiatry has had a more dramatic and pervasive impact on law and social justice than posttraumatic stress disorder.

—A. A. Stone, "Post-traumatic Stress Disorder and the Law:
Critical Review of the New Frontier"[1]

In the aftermath of the airplane hijackings and the destruction of the World Trade Center on September 11, 2001, it is tempting to think that although the world may have a lot to learn about the prevention of terrorism, our health providers at least understand its psychological impact and how to care for the survivors, relatives, emergency workers, and all those who have been drawn in to the circle of destructive chaos that surrounds any disaster. But the chaos extends to understanding the effects of trauma, with a long-drawn-out struggle between two opposing views. The version of the story from the "Saviors" is that after years of neglect, the special suffering brought about by psychological trauma has at last been recognized, in the form of posttraumatic stress disorder, or PTSD. Victims of war, oppression, child abuse, marital violence, robbery, natural disaster or disaster of human origin, life-threatening accidents, and other overwhelming events have in common a mental and physical response that is caused by the traumatic incident and has nothing to do with any personal weakness or vulnerability. For the first time, it is recognized that PTSD may haunt them for the rest of their lives unless it is treated or, better, prevented.

But as the quotation that opens this chapter hints, there is an opposing story from the "Skeptics." Numerous articles and books continue to question the introduction of PTSD to the psychiatric canon.[2]

Nor are these concerns published in obscure places or by critics who habitually reject the entire psychiatric enterprise for labeling individuals as deviant and permitting society to control them by means of drugs and incarceration. Ever since the formal recognition of PTSD in 1980, the world's leading medical journals have regularly published articles by influential opinion makers that have questioned the legitimacy of the diagnosis and the very existence of supposedly typical traumatic reactions. These critiques have also, again almost uniquely, been echoed in the popular press.

In fact, the study of traumatic stress and its effects has been disrupted by an unprecedented oscillation between long periods of neglect and high-profile, public controversy ever since its origins in the middle of the nineteenth century. Fierce disagreements have bordered on the fanatical about the existence of long-term psychiatric disorders attributable solely to severe stress and about the need to make special provisions for soldiers and civilians exposed to war zones, survivors of concentration camps, or victims of disaster. For most of the past 150 years it has simply been assumed that people exposed to these events will be distressed, even profoundly distressed, but that they will recover naturally given time. Today, we expect that survivors of major terrorist attacks, such as in Oklahoma City or on September 11 in the United States, will be offered counseling. But children thousands of miles away in other countries are also suffering from posttraumatic stress after watching the images on television.[3] Then there are the survivors of events such as beatings and car crashes that affect thousands of people every day. Do they all deserve or require similar help? Or does widespread counseling have the effect of creating a "victim culture" and undermining a person's natural resilience in the face of adversity? There is profound disagreement about who exactly needs help, what help should be offered, and whether counseling, "psychological debriefing," or other new forms of therapy are effective.

Other claims made by those who have campaigned on behalf of trauma victims have attracted an unprecedented level of professional and public skepticism. One issue has been whether memory for traumatic events is different from "ordinary" memory and, if so, in what way? During the 1990s the idea that traumatic events might be completely forgotten and then suddenly remembered later occupied acres of newsprint. For instance, because of these apparent recovered memories, defendants were indicted on murder and assault counts, grown-up children sued their parents for long-forgotten abuse, their parents sued the children's therapists, and finally some of the children sued the therapists as well. Although many of these battles were fought in the courtroom, the questions challenge our basic understanding of what memory is and how it works.

Some psychologists, psychiatrists, and other mental health professionals have become highly emotionally involved in these arguments about trauma, PTSD, and memory, and many accusations have arisen about tainted motives, coupled with exclusive claims for scientific legitimacy. Usually, zealots and mythologizers are contrasted unfavorably with those whose perspective is based on objectivity and science. Unfortunately, both sides attempt to occupy the same rhetorical vantage point, which makes for a high degree of confusion among onlookers. The good news is that after twenty years of intensive research, an immense amount of information is now available with which one can evaluate these arguments and competing claims. The field of traumatic stress therefore provides an almost unrivaled opportunity for assessing the extent to which scientific research is able to settle enduring controversies between the Saviors and Skeptics and produce original insights into the processes responsible for human suffering.

In this book I want to use the existence of these controversies both to reflect upon the social forces that have shaped the study of traumatic stress and to help us understand the nature of trauma itself. The very passion of the debates requires some discussion, presented below in this chapter, of why traumatic events appear to affect not just individuals but the whole of society. Chapters 2 and 3 will tackle the criticisms leveled at PTSD and evaluate them in light of recent scientific studies. Then I will present my own ideas about how to understand the effect of trauma by focusing on the core psychological processes of identity and memory in Chapters 4 through 6. In Chapters 7 through 9, this material will be brought to bear on controversies involving recovered memory and trauma treatment, and Chapter 10 will synthesize our emerging social and scientific knowledge in the form of *[handwritten margin notes: trauma of (V) — revelation of cognitive-dissonance that could not be denied — the revelation that deeply held beliefs + values may not be true — requiring potentially a complete reorientation of a person's life]*

a new and sometimes surprising understanding of traumatic stress and its effects. But first, we need to explore what trauma is, what constitutes PTSD, and what all the arguments are about.

What Is a Trauma?

In the early part of the twenty-first century, the word *trauma* usually refers to almost any very distressing incident. As with most terms that have become common currency, professional usage is more restricted than the metaphorical way in which the word appears in the media and in ordinary conversation. From the Greek for *wound,* the word was first used at the beginning of the twentieth century in the sense of a mental shock. Sigmund Freud used the analogy with a physical wound to write of a traumatic event penetrating a kind of mental skin designed to protect a person from excessive stimulation from outside: "It seems to me that the concept of trauma necessarily implies a connection of this kind with a breach in an otherwise efficacious barrier against stimuli . . . another problem arises instead—the problem of mastering the amounts of stimulus that have broken in and of binding them, in the psychical sense, so that they can then be disposed of."[4]

As this quotation indicates, Freud thought that the breaching of the barrier by overwhelming sights, sounds, and other forms of stimulation that could not be organized, classified, and contained produced psychological symptoms such as hysterical paralysis and loss of function. He particularly associated the emotional condition of sudden fright with mental shock.

After many years during which few psychologists interested themselves in trauma, Ronnie Janoff-Bulman put forward in an important and insightful book the related idea that trauma is an event that shatters people's assumptions.[5] She suggests that the majority of us hold core assumptions that, though they may be illusory, help to sustain us in our everyday lives and motivate us to overcome difficulties and plan for the future. The three assumptions she regards as the most significant are these: the world is benevolent, the world is meaningful, and the self is worthy; that is, other people are in general well-disposed toward us, reliable rules and principles exist that enable us to predict which behaviors will produce which kinds of outcomes, and we ourselves are personally good, moral, and well-meaning. Being attacked by a complete stranger without any provocation, being involved in a serious traffic accident when we have been obeying the rules of the road, and putting our own survival ahead of anything else when our life is threatened are all situations that have the potential to be traumatic in that they may contradict deeply held and probably unexamined beliefs about the world and ourselves.

Similar but even more basic assumptions have been suggested by Derek Bolton and Jonathan Hill in a philosophical approach to the question. They proposed that for people to act in the world, they must have a set of (probably unquestioned) core beliefs: that the self is sufficiently competent to act, that the world is sufficiently predictable, and that the world provides sufficient satisfaction of needs. Traumatic incidents are highly unpredictable and unpleasant and produce feelings of intense helplessness, thereby challenging these core beliefs. Bolton and Hill suggest that in some cases this produces intense conflict because the experience of the trauma appears to contradict the person's core theory, but according to the theory the experience cannot really be true:

> Another way of putting the problem is that core convictions and the trauma cannot both be believed, but must be each believed. Solution of this problem requires drastic mental measures. Both cannot be believed at the same time, with the same mind. One kind of solution is dissociation . . . in third-person memories or dreams of the event, in remembering without affect, in memories experienced as unreal, in forgetting the worst times. These are ways of believing that the trauma was experienced, and believing that it was not, at the same time. The alternative is persistent reexperiencing, alternating with persistent forgetting/denial, thus achieving beliefs in each side of the contradiction at different times. There is in posttraumatic stress reaction a failure to integrate the trauma into the system of belief about the self and reality.[6]

For all these writers, trauma is defined in theoretical terms as some kind of internal breach or damage to existing mental structures.

An alternative approach that focuses more on the character of the events than on their effects has been adopted in the series of Diagnostic and Statistical Manuals (DSM) published by the American Psychiatric Association.[7] As part of the initial definition of PTSD proposed in 1980, the third edition of the DSM (DSM-III) suggested that a traumatic event consisted of "a recognizable stressor that would evoke significant symptoms of distress in almost everyone" and was "outside the range of normal human experience." Two kinds of events that the DSM committee had particularly in mind were taking part in combat and being the victim of marital violence. In contrast, they emphasized that marital conflict alone and simple bereavement were not to be considered as traumatic events.

Since 1980 many different kinds of traumatic events have been studied. Among people involved in the military, these have included being exposed to gunfire, engaging in combat, handling dead bodies, and witnessing grotesque violence or its effects. Civilian events have included being exposed to natural disasters, such as earthquakes, hurricanes, and floods; being exposed to disasters of human origin, such as fires, explosions, and radiation leaks; being exposed to physical or sexual assaults and terrorist attacks; being involved in serious accidents; and witnessing extreme human suffering and death. Bonnie Green examined the specific features that were consistently related to psychological problems across different types of events and proposed that they could be summarized as follows: experiencing a threat to one's life or bodily integrity, receiving severe and/or intentional physical harm or injury, being exposed to the grotesque, experiencing the violent or sudden loss of a loved one, witnessing or learning of violence against a loved one, learning of exposure to a noxious agent, and causing death or severe harm to another person.[8] Many of these features were included in the expanded definition of a traumatic stressor provided by the next edition of DSM, the DSM-IIIR, published in 1987.

In the most recent version, the DSM-IV, published in 1994, the committee responsible for PTSD acknowledged the problem with defining events in purely objective terms. Their solution was to require traumatic events to have certain objective characteristics, such as involving actual or threatened death or serious injury, but also to have those events produce reactions of either intense fear, intense helpless-

Table 1.1. DSM-IV Diagnostic Criteria for Posttraumatic Stress Disorder

---

Criterion A (Stressor): The person has been exposed to a traumatic event in which both of the following were present:

> (i) the person experienced, witnessed, or was confronted with an event or events that involved actual or threatened death or serious injury, or a threat to the physical integrity of self or others
>
> (ii) the person's response involved intense fear, helplessness, or horror. Note: In children, this may be expressed instead by disorganized or agitated behavior.

Criterion B (Reexperiencing): The traumatic event is persistently reexperienced in one (or more) of the following ways:

> (i) recurrent and intrusive distressing recollections of the event, including images, thoughts, or perceptions. Note: In young children, repetitive play may occur in which themes or aspects of the trauma are expressed.
>
> (ii) recurrent distressing dreams of the event. Note: In children, there may be frightening dreams without recognizable content.
>
> (iii) acting or feeling as if the traumatic event were recurring (includes a sense of reliving the experience, illusions, hallucinations, and dissociative flashback episodes, including those that occur on awakening or when intoxicated). Note: In young children, trauma-specific enactment may occur.
>
> (iv) intense psychological distress at exposure to internal or external cues that symbolize or resemble an aspect of the traumatic event
>
> (v) physiological reactivity on exposure to internal or external cues that symbolize or resemble an aspect of the traumatic event

Criterion C (Avoidance): Persistent avoidance of stimuli associated with the trauma and numbing of general responsiveness (not present before the trauma), as indicated by three (or more) of the following:

> (i) efforts to avoid thoughts, feelings, or conversations associated with the trauma

---

continued

Table 1.1. Continued

    (ii) efforts to avoid activities, places, or people that arouse recollections of the trauma

    (iii) inability to recall an important aspect of the trauma

    (iv) markedly diminished interest or participation in significant activities

    (v) feeling of detachment or estrangement from others

    (vi) restricted range of affect (e.g., unable to have loving feelings)

    (vii) sense of a foreshortened future (e.g., does not expect to have a career, marriage, children, or a normal life span)

Criterion D (Arousal): Persistent symptoms of increased arousal (not present before the trauma), as indicated by two (or more) of the following:

    (i) difficulty falling or staying asleep

    (ii) irritability or outbursts of anger

    (iii) difficulty concentrating

    (iv) hypervigilance

    (v) exaggerated startle response

Criterion E (Duration): Duration of the disturbance is more than one month

Criterion F (Distress or Impairment): The disturbance causes clinically significant distress or impairment in social, occupational, or other important areas of functioning

---

Source: American Psychiatric Association, 1994; reprinted with permission.

ness, or intense horror (Table 1.1). Effectively, this was a return to a more psychological definition of a traumatic event. The practical difficulties in measuring trauma will be discussed in more detail later in this book.

Who are the victims of trauma? The answer is "most of us." Surveys have been carried out in the United States to document the likelihood of a person experiencing or witnessing physical assaults, sexual assaults, accidents, disasters, or other incidents involving the risk of death or serious injury. Generally, between 70 and 80 percent of people will experience one of these events over the course of a lifetime.[9] In the U.S. National Comorbidity Survey, one of the largest studies of its kind, 35 percent of the men and 25 percent of the women reported more than one major traumatic event in their lives thus far.[10] These figures clearly contradict any notion that traumas are "outside the range of normal human experience." Perhaps a better way of putting it is that they are usually outside the range of the individual person's normal experience.

Of the events likely to lead to PTSD (apart from combat), rape has been studied the most. Questionnaire surveys of women in the United States, Canada, and New Zealand found rates of about 15 percent for rape and an additional 12 percent for attempted rape,[11] with higher rates reported in studies that used detailed, in-person interviews. In National Family Violence Surveys, 28 percent of respondents reported at least one incident of violence in their current relationship.[12] Around the world, the rate of contact crimes such as physical assault, sexual assault, and robbery experienced by urban dwellers over a five-year period ranges from 15 percent in Western Europe and Asia to more than 30 percent in Africa and Latin America.[13] Worldwide, the effects of wars and disasters have created another huge pool of trauma victims. The International Federation of Red Cross and Red Crescent Societies estimates that 40 million people have been killed in wars and conflicts since World War II, that 16 million refugees and asylum seekers left their countries each year between 1990 and 1995, and that disasters affect the lives of another 128 million.[14]

Diagnosing PTSD

Traumatic events have been linked to an increase in numerous psychiatric conditions, including anxiety, depression, substance abuse, dissociative disorders, and psychosomatic disorders, but as we have seen, the prototypical, most frequently discussed, and most controversial condition is PTSD. The DSM-III committee that initially described the new diagnosis of PTSD in 1980 was faced with a difficult job because little formal research existed on which the diagnosis could be based.[15] In practice, the criteria were based on the large numbers of informal studies describing the aftermath of a person being in combat, surviving the Holocaust, or being exposed to other extreme stressors. Particularly influential was the work of the psychoanalyst and researcher Mardi Horowitz, who was one of the first to conduct experimental studies of responses to stressful stimuli in the laboratory. His 1976 book *Stress Response Syndromes* put forward a model that described how people adjust to events that overwhelm mental defenses.[16] This involved a pattern of intrusive, reexperiencing symptoms alternating with avoidance and emotional numbing, two interlinked processes designed to enable change in mental structures to occur gradually in a manageable way.

By the time the next committee was preparing to revise the DSM-III, much more information was available. Theoretical formulations emphasizing reexperiencing and avoidance had proved useful, and this led to the development of sets of symptoms in these two categories.[17] In addition, several studies reported high levels of physiological arousal and concentration difficulties in traumatized people. These observations led to the introduction of a third category of hyperarousal symptoms. Crucial in the development of the new diagnostic criteria was the work of the Veterans Administration, which funded research on combat veterans, most of them U.S. soldiers returning from Vietnam. Although there was other relevant research, for example, on the bereaved and on disaster victims, military research provided the bedrock for much of the initial shaping of the diagnosis of PTSD.

As we have already noted, the traumatic event has to have certain essential characteristics, such as experiencing or witnessing death, serious injury, or a "threat to physical integrity" (Criterion A, Table 1.1). Rape, for example, would violate someone's physical integrity even if no injury were caused. Threats are included to allow for events in which a person expects severe pain, injury, or death even if these do not transpire.

To qualify for a diagnosis of PTSD, a person must report at least one of the reexperiencing symptoms (Criterion B, Table 1.1), such as intrusive memories or traumatic dreams. Another reexperiencing symptom involves reliving the event vividly in the present, the so-called *traumatic flashback*. This particular symptom is one of the reasons why it has been claimed that memory for trauma is different from memory for ordinary events. PTSD also requires at least three symptoms in the avoidance and numbing category (Criterion C), such as the avoidance of reminders of the event, loss of interest in previously valued activities, and the inability to feel love or happiness. Included among this group is amnesia for aspects of the event, which critics have charged contradicts the claim that traumatic events leave exceptionally strong memory traces. The diagnosis also requires at least two arousal symptoms (Criterion D), such as having problems sleeping and being constantly on guard. Finally, the symptoms must cause significant distress or impairment in the person's work or social life and must last for at least one month (Criteria E and F).

Skeptical Challenges

The inclusion of PTSD in the DSM-III brought out numerous robust challenges to the new diagnosis. Some were skeptical of the idea that a traumatic incident was intrinsically different from a supposedly non-traumatic incident, such as a bereavement or the breakup of a relationship.[18] What was the justification, these Skeptics wanted to know, for this special status, and how was the clinician to tell what was "outside the range of usual human experience" or "markedly distressing to almost anyone"? Was it not the case that in PTSD the *event* was distinctive rather than the *response,* which was simply an ordinary stress reaction already described elsewhere in the DSM? Skeptics were unhappy with the implication that the traumatic event was a sufficient cause of disorder on its own rather than, as in other psychiatric disorders, acting in concert with personal vulnerabilities and the nature of the social environment.

One reason for the skepticism was the suspicion that the decision to include a new diagnosis in the DSM was based as much on political as on scientific concerns. After all, it was not as though anyone was claiming that a new disorder had suddenly been discovered. Critics were well aware that changes in the DSM were in part a response to lobbying on the part of Vietnam veterans and their clinicians, who described a syndrome that did not fit neatly into any existing category. Recognition of this disorder would have profound implications for both the psychiatric treatment veterans might expect from the Veterans Administration and also for their entitlement to an award for service-connected disability. Other groups also backing the new diagnosis included representatives of battered women, who also had a strong motivation to promote the recognition of hidden suffering and disability brought about by traumatic experiences. Whatever the scientific justification, there was no question that changing the DSM must inevitably have a political dimension.

Taking a more historical and cultural perspective, others argued that the concept of traumatic memory was an invention of nineteenth-century psychiatry and that before this time no traces could be found of a traumatic neurosis corresponding exactly to PTSD.[19] Similarly, it has often been proposed that the traumatic flashback had no previous psychiatric currency but originated in the movies. The sociologist Jerry Lembcke noted that flashbacks in Vietnam war films of the 1960s were not the usual device whereby an earlier episode is spliced into a narrative.[20] Rather, they were mental events, portraying the memory of disturbed veterans. This has led to the claim that filmmakers were responsible for the creation of this supposed trauma-induced psychological phenomenon.[21]

More radically, Lembcke suggested that the legitimization of the PTSD diagnosis was greatly influenced by high-profile media articles, for example in the *New York Times,* that advertised difficulties experienced by homecoming Vietnam veterans. He suggested that the medicalization of veterans' anger and distress had the convenient function of repairing negative images of the war and focusing attention on the men who fought it rather than on the politicians who promoted it. Further, it enabled the authorities to pathologize the radical political behavior of veterans opposed to the war, and thereby discredit it, while at the same time appearing concerned for veterans' welfare. For Lembcke, then, PTSD was more a cultural and political construct than a description of a mental disorder.

A critique of PTSD from a very different political perspective appeared in 1998 with the publication of *Stolen Valor* by B. G. Burkett and Glenna Whitley. Burkett, himself a Vietnam veteran, put forward the thesis that the soldiers who fought in the war had been uniquely and unfairly vilified by society and by the media for supposedly taking drugs and committing atrocities while they were in Vietnam, and then for being aggressive, antisocial, and unemployable after they returned. Much of the research they report in the book confirms that Vietnam veterans did not have more problems than the veterans of previous wars, and additionally shows that large numbers of self-proclaimed

Vietnam veterans who received widespread media coverage for their supposedly war-related problems in fact never served overseas or were never members of the elite combat units with which they pretended to have served.

Burkett and Whitley also charged that PTSD was a product of the anti–Vietnam war protest movement that came to prominence in the 1970s and that had many supporters within the psychiatric profession. According to the antiwar view, soldiers were not just exposed to danger but were taking part in a morally indefensible activity that would inevitably lead to severe problems in adjustment and to mental breakdown. This could not be adequately recognized with labels such as "shell shock" or "combat fatigue" that had been used in earlier, less morally ambiguous wars. Burkett and Whitley argued that antiwar spokespeople were critically involved in the discussions and political activities that led to the creation of the new PTSD diagnosis, and that "the diagnosis of PTSD shifted the disorder's cause from the patient (and his individual psyche) to the cause (the war), and in so doing became the textbook definition of 'Vietnam veteran.'"[22]

Among their other contentions were that the prevalence of PTSD among Vietnam veterans has been grossly overestimated and that the Veterans Administration colluded in a process that produced undeserved funds both for the organization and for veterans making fraudulent claims: "Like the inclusion of PTSD in the DSM-III, the continuing push to show that Vietnam veterans are severely afflicted by PTSD—which advocates say can manifest itself twenty years after the triggering incidents—is political, not scientific."[23]

Science and politics became even more enmeshed in the debate over the so-called *false memory syndrome.* The coining of this syndrome and its widespread and persistent propagation throughout the mass media were very largely due to campaigning groups such as the False Memory Syndrome Foundation (FMSF) in the United States and its international counterparts. One of the foundation's great advantages was that parents accused of abusing their children gave interviews and put their cases forward with the full support of the organization behind them, whereas the accusers and their therapists were rarely willing to go public with their side of the story, even if journalists thought to ask them to do so. Naturally, this led to one-sided coverage.

Politically, the FMSF appealed particularly strongly to social conservatives eager to uphold the integrity of the nuclear family and to reinforce traditional notions of personal responsibility. Many regarded the dramatic spread of psychotherapy with its tendency to focus exclusively on the well-being of the individual as a threat to the stability of marriages and families, whose idiosyncrasies should be tolerated for their contribution to social cohesion and to the successful transmission of the values of loyalty and obedience to proper authority. In contrast, an excessive focus on the rights and feelings of the individual, as exemplified, for example, by the PTSD diagnosis and the psychotherapy movement, was held to be socially divisive and to promote victims rather than heroes who would meet adversity and conquer it.

A critical ingredient to the success of the campaign was the involvement of eminent scientists and clinicians who publicly supported the FMSF position. A great deal was made of how scientific knowledge about memory was inconsistent with the claims of some therapists that traumatic events could be completely forgotten, only to emerge years later. The lack of scientific evidence for clinical concepts such as repression and dissociation was often repeated, with the implication that these therapists were deluded peddlers of fantastic, implausible theories about how the mind worked. Also disputed were clinical claims that because memory functioned differently in conditions of extreme stress, conclusions based on laboratory experiments were largely irrelevant.

Other disputes between Saviors and Skeptics have not attracted the same degree of headline coverage but have occurred, sometimes fiercely, within professional circles. The proliferation of counseling and therapeutic services offered by commercial organizations has opened them to the charge that the interventions they market are not necessarily supported by evidence of effectiveness. Skepticism has focused in particular on a procedure known as *critical incident stress debriefing,* or more generally psychological debriefing, which is offered to people involved in a traumatic incident within a few days of it occurring. Attendees are asked to recall the event in considerable detail, focusing on facts, thoughts, and innermost feelings. Typically, everyone who was present at the incident is encouraged to attend the debriefing, and some employers make such attendance a condition of employment. Many public and private-sector organizations have been persuaded that this procedure is beneficial and that they have an obligation to supply it. Recently, some studies have suggested that the procedure could actually be harmful, thereby making employers, emergency services, and counseling organizations vulnerable to lawsuits.

Saviors and Skeptics can also be found among therapists who treat PTSD, with the advocates of newer and briefer types of therapy, sometimes referred to as *power therapies,* contrasted with those favoring more traditional therapeutic approaches. Chief among the power therapies is eye movement desensitization and reprocessing (EMDR). The use of EMDR has proliferated at an astonishing rate, with thousands of mental health professionals now trained in the method and an international network of groups supporting its practitioners. Whereas its advocates point to promising outcome studies that suggest it is an effective treatment, its detractors have complained that it has no scientific basis and have likened it to mesmerism.[24]

It is hard to escape the conclusion that the subject of trauma attracts passionate advocacy and passionate skepticism in a quite disproportionate measure. In no other area of mental health are the debates so public or so bitter, or the scientific credibility of experienced and committed practitioners impugned in such a forthright manner. Perhaps the professional disputes reflect some deeper unease with the subject that infects normal habits of respect for alternative opinions. Is it possible that even talking about trauma and its effects arouses emotions that polarize opinion and cloud otherwise lucid minds? To answer this question we need to consider societal reactions to traumatic events.

Society and Trauma

The events of September 11, 2001, along with numerous other disasters, accidents, and terrorist outrages, offer some clues to our general ambivalence about traumatic events. September 11 offered novel, shocking pictures and ideas that captured the imagination by force. Absorption in the events was followed by intense interest in the human stories of those who escaped, those who died, those who were bereaved, and those who had to face the unimaginable consequences. In most societies there was a widespread empathic response to the sudden incursion of death into so many otherwise ordered lives. From a Western perspective, it was hard to comprehend how anybody could fail to respond to the magnitude of the event with pity and horror.

When accidents, disasters, crimes, or outrages happen, the emotions felt toward the victims are strongly influenced by judgments of whether or not those involved could have prevented the tragedy happening or whether they in some sense shared a measure of culpability.[25] Media coverage tends to be more sympathetic when the event is unexpected and strikes ordinary people who are going about their ordinary business and with whom it may be easier for others to identify. Less sympathy tends to be expressed when people are perceived to have contributed even indirectly to their own misfortune. Likewise, there tends to be less sympathy when disaster befalls a group with whom people identify less, perhaps because, like members of cults, members of such groups are seen as having placed themselves outside the mainstream or as having rejected society's core values.

There are also strong expectations about recovery from trauma. Like the bereaved, trauma victims are expected to recover their psychological equilibrium and resume their normal lives within a matter of weeks or months. According to much lay thinking on the subject, victims of misfortune should eventually return to their pre-event psychological state. These beliefs about recovery have also been part of medical thinking, as before DSM-III no officially classified disorder was seen as being caused by a long-term failure to overcome stressful life circumstances. Thus, although trauma survivors can initially elicit sympathy for having been involved in the event in the first place, they can also be blamed for not recovering quickly enough, a process over which they typically are seen as having control. Particularly if a survivor has no evident physical injuries, the event may come to be seen as an excuse for his or her avoiding personal, social, and familial responsibilities.

Interestingly, as we will see below, one of trauma victims' most frequent complaints is that they will never be the same again, that their experiences have changed them permanently, and that they feel other people who have not lived through a similar trauma are unable to understand them. Reporting the results of numerous comparisons of victims' versus nonvictims' basic assumptions, Janoff-Bulman commented:

> Those who had survived a traumatic life event generally viewed themselves and the world less positively than those who had not been victimized. They recognized that bad things happen more often than they had thought, that people can be monstrous, that events may be more random, less just, and less controllable than they had thought. They realized that being a decent person was not protection against bad outcomes, or they maintained a belief that the world is just but no longer perceived themselves as decent and good. Regardless of the particular pattern of basic assumptions affected, to them, the world was no longer unquestioningly regarded as safe and secure. They had "walked through a door," and what they found on the other side was threatening.[26]

In effect, the existence of an identifiable trauma tends to bring into play the lay theories about recovery of onlookers who were not present but who have something to do with the primary victims. In this respect, PTSD and bereavement are different from more "mysterious" conditions such as agoraphobia or obsessive-compulsive disorder that rarely have a sudden onset. Although traumatic events are typically outside the onlookers' range of experience, their assumptions have not been overturned to the same extent. It is commonplace for the bereaved and for trauma survivors in general to describe a gradual pressure from others to overcome their distress and return to previous routines, a pressure that grows as time goes by. Likewise, it is notable that the intense media interest in the traumatic incident itself and how people felt while it was happening is rarely matched by any corresponding interest in the slow and often painful process of recovery.

Hostility may sometimes be expressed at groups in society who are expected to be immune to trauma, such as the police and the armed services. In Britain there was an outcry when police officers who had been present at the Hillsborough football stadium when dozens of people were crushed to death attempted to gain compensation for posttraumatic stress. There were several complicating factors. The courts had previously ruled that relatives of the dead, who in some cases had witnessed the events at the stadium on television, were not eligible for compensation because they were not actually present at the scene. Other police officers with responsibility for crowd control had also been accused of being culpable in the disaster. Above all, however, was a view that this was what police work involved and that it was wrong for public funds to be spent compensating officers for simply doing their job.

In the end the officers lost their case for compensation. Among the significant features the case highlighted were the public preconceptions that police officers should be able to act effectively during horrifying, grotesque incidents and show no ill effects afterward. Little curiosity was expressed about how the police were trained to prepare for such events or about whether they had in fact received any relevant training. Nor did anyone draw attention to the inherent contradiction in demanding that the police should be simultaneously sensitive and compassionate in some circumstances, for example, when dealing with the public, but immune to emotion in others, such as when overcoming their own feelings of horror and revulsion. Similar contradictions are increasingly being experienced by members of the armed services as they take on peacekeeping roles involving close liaison with and guarding of civilian populations.

It is clear that society's response to the trauma victim inevitably contains a moral element that is based on succeeding judgments of controllability and responsibility. As Janoff-Bulman has pointed out, even victims of completely uncontrollable traumas are likely to arouse discomfort in others, particularly when they fail to make a speedy recovery. For such people, the victims "are manifestations of a malevolent universe, rather than a benevolent one. . . . People do not want to acknowledge that life can be tragic. We spend our lives preserving positive illusions about ourselves and the world. These same illusions, which are shattered in victims by the experience of traumatic life events, are threatened in others by the acknowledgment of such victimization."[27]

The illusion of invulnerability is a central aspect of terror management theory, which proposes that awareness of the inevitability of one's own death carries with it a potential for high levels of anxiety. As a protection against this, people have a cultural worldview that provides an explanation for existence, a set of standards for what is valuable, and a promise of immortality to those who live up to these standards. Immortality may be either literal, in the form of some kind of afterlife or reincarnation, or symbolic, through connections to entities that are more powerful and long-lasting, such as families, nations, churches, science, or the arts.[28]

When people are obviously confronted with reminders of their mortality, they tend to exaggerate their invulnerability or deliberately suppress thoughts of death. In contrast, indirect reminders of one's own death, such as reading about killings or disasters, produce a compensatory strengthening of the worldview, an increased sense of national identity, and an increased use of cultural items such as flags and scriptures. Numerous studies have shown that making death momentarily more salient leads to a variety of subtle reactions of which a person is likely unaware, such as increased liking for people who support one's worldview and increased hostility toward those with alternative worldviews.[29] The message from this research is that, when thoughts of death are salient, the mere existence of people with different beliefs threatens our primary basis of psychological security. In some cases the people expressing different beliefs will not be obvious targets, such as foreign terrorists, but will be those who are most affected by the disaster, such as the victims or those caring for them.

In the presence of victims, as in the presence of all stigmatized groups, people feel ill at ease. Harber and Pennebaker reported that listening to videotaped interviews with Holocaust survivors recounting their horrifying experiences during World War II produced changes in the listeners' autonomic nervous system, such as increases in skin conductance levels.[30] Even people who are actively trying to support trauma victims are prone to switch the topic of conversation to something more neutral, press their own perspective on the victim, or avoid the victim altogether.[31] After the 1989 Loma Prieta earthquake, Harber and Pennebaker noted that many people wanted to talk about what had happened to them, whereas other Bay Area residents wore T-shirts printed with the slogan "Thank you for not sharing your earthquake experience." For the listener, the trauma narrative may arouse pity and a corresponding desire to help, feelings that become unpleasant if they are coupled with helplessness about being able to make any difference to the victim.

A fascinating anecdotal account of the threat posed by trauma victims was given by Shoshana Felman, who described a class she taught on trauma and testimony.[32] The first part of the course was based on literary sources, but toward the end she showed the class videotaped testimonies of two Holocaust survivors. Faced with the requirement to respond to these testimonies, the class experienced panic, loss of direction, and a sense of being cut off from other people. Students talked incessantly to their friends about what they had witnessed while simultaneously feeling that the experience was so profound as to be beyond words. The article provides an important insight into why people might ordinarily want to block out horrifying stories and defend themselves against too personal an engagement with trauma victims.

Another well-established phenomenon that may assist in the maintenance of the onlookers' illusions and help them to keep a psychological distance from trauma is the tendency to blame victims for their misfortunes. Less common in the case of disasters, these reactions have frequently been noted in cases of rape, assault, and interpersonal crimes. It is thought that one of the main functions of victim-blaming is to preserve the onlooker's sense of invulnerability. This is supported by *hindsight bias,* the tendency for someone to assume, once something is known to have happened, that it could and should have been anticipated. Thus, rape victims are blamed for what they were wearing or where they were walking, for fighting back or not fighting back, or for being unable to read the minds of the men who later attacked them. Interestingly, hindsight bias is so pervasive that not only onlookers but also victims often blame themselves for not acting differently, even when it was not reasonable for them to have been able to anticipate what would happen.

These various processes may not only help to explain why controversies about trauma are so emotion-laden, but also why historically, posttraumatic reactions are repeatedly recognized and then forgotten. The cycle whereby knowledge of combat stress and how to treat it was laboriously gained in one war only to be forgotten during peacetime, leaving the next war's combatants inadequately provided for, is common to many cultures and has been described by numerous writers.[33] One of the pioneers of trauma research in Israel, Zahava Solomon, has speculated on why the sufferings of Holocaust survivors and Israeli combat veterans were ignored for so many years. She suggested a number of influences: a society that felt vulnerable to attack and needed to extol strength rather than acknowledge weakness, a pre-eminence given to psychoanalytic theories that were rooted in internal fantasies rather than external realities, and a fundamental human difficulty in comprehending and acknowledging our own vulnerability. As Solomon noted, the first two influences are less universal, leading her to place most emphasis on the third.[34]

Conclusions

The sheer extent of trauma and the plight of victims are powerful forces that have in many countries led to strenuous and in some cases heroic efforts to recognize and meet the needs of trauma victims. The gradual uncovering of children's experiences of physical and sexual abuse has been shocking both to society and to the professionals who have been in a position to listen and to attempt to respond. Hearing the stories of trauma tends to produce profound pity and a strong urge to make amends, to heal wounds, to punish wrongdoers. Saviors have been, and are still, much needed.

In this context of overwhelming need, the Skeptic's voice is often unwelcome. Arguably, it is not too fanciful to wonder whether the amount of skepticism that pervades the field has something to do with the fact that trauma readily arouses unpleasant emotions in onlookers and reminds them of their own past misfortunes. Skeptical challenges to the validity of PTSD and recovered memories of trauma may be related to a more general societal tendency to manage these unpleasant states by downplaying the existence of trauma, denying that it can have devastating and long-lasting effects, or asserting the unworthiness of the supposedly traumatized.

Perhaps in professional circles it is also the uncritical following that Saviors can sometimes acquire that triggers an automatic response from the Skeptics to any received wisdom that does not have a firm foundation. Whatever the reason, it is precisely the extent of the need of people who have endured traumatic events and the vulnerability of people who have often endured multiple further instances of incomprehension and unthinking callousness after a trauma that make it necessary to ensure that any actions we take are soundly based. We must ask whether the medical and psychological concepts we employ are adequate, whether our assumptions about trauma are accurate, and whether our interventions work. Above all, we must be open to the possibility that what is intended to help may also harm. For that reason, the Saviors and the Skeptics are both necessary. In this book we explore when, and why, each is right. In the process we will construct an account of posttraumatic stress that makes sense in scientific as well as in human terms.

2

Posttraumatic Stress Disorder
Discovery or Invention?

The researcher struggles to distinguish between the phenomena that obey his will, because they are his unintended creation, and the phenomena that arise spontaneously, because they originate in nature, and *resist* his manipulations.

—Allan Young, *The Harmony of Illusions*[1]

In this chapter we will investigate some of the major criticisms of PTSD. Part of this will involve understanding more about the nature of a psychiatric diagnosis and how it is that so many fundamental arguments can exist about what should be a cornerstone of professional knowledge. The main problem is that psychiatric diagnoses are not associated with a clear biological cause or condition, as are many purely medical conditions. There is no particular bacillus, deteriorating area of tissue, or other physiological marker that is always present in these illnesses and that can resolve diagnostic disputes. Rather, diagnoses are based on recognized constellations of signs that the observer can see (such as agitation) and symptoms that the patient can report (typically mental events such as intrusive memories, or emotional experiences such as sadness).

In effect, then, the psychiatric diagnosis depends on a professional consensus of observations, initially based on patients currently in treatment. This leaves enormous scope for historical and cultural forces to shape what kinds of patient are deemed to have an illness and be in need of treatment in the first place, which of their symptoms and signs are systematically noted, and on what basis clinical observations are to be grouped together. The first two editions of the DSM were heavily influenced by psychoanalytic principles, but the DSM-III introduced a quite different approach, in which disorders were to be simply described, independent of any specific psychological or biological theory. Moreover, the descriptions were to be backed up by scientific studies. In recent times one of the most notable casualties of changing views about mental disorder has been homosexuality, which was considered an illness in early versions of the DSM-II but was declassified as a mental disorder by the American Psychiatric Association in 1973.

It is important to realize that attitudes toward diagnoses vary enormously, even among those mental health professionals who routinely use them. For some, they are categories that will eventually be found to correspond to specific forms of biochemical or anatomic pathology. This is the classical medical or disease model, which identifies disease with damage or malfunction that must be corrected with surgery, drugs, gene therapy, or similar interventions. For others, diagnoses simply help to identify constellations of symptoms, signs, and biological changes that indicate a particular response to excessive demands on a person. These demands typically come from prolonged stress or from events that are traumatic, that damage trust in self or others, or that destroy aspirations for the future. For yet others, including many psychologists and psychotherapists, diagnoses reflect the effects of specific mental patterns of assessing reality, interpreting the past, and anticipating the future.

Endorsing a diagnosis, therefore, may not say anything about the mental health professional's adherence to more biological or more psychological models. Moreover, when it comes to treatment, other considerations may determine what is considered appropriate. Diagnosis does, however, frequently act as a gateway, both to treatment and to compensation for civil or criminal injuries, which may not be available in the absence of a recognized psychiatric condition. The inclusion of a new diagnosis has profound economic implications for service providers, insurance companies, and governments as a whole new class of patient becomes eligible for treatment. It is against this background that we must evaluate the claims that the inclusion of PTSD in the DSM-III was a mistaken, politically motivated decision. Three arguments of the Skeptics will be evaluated: that PTSD is a recent invention with no historical parallel, that it unnecessarily medicalizes normal human reactions to trauma, and that it is not clearly distinct from existing disorders.

A Dip into History

One of the most frequently voiced criticisms of PTSD has been that it did not exist until it was invented for reasons of political expediency in the late 1970s. In one sense, of course, this is unanswerable because this was when the precise constellations of symptoms and boundaries for the syndrome were first proposed. A major handicap is that scientific medicine and scientific psychology are largely inventions of the nineteenth century. Before that time, neither was supported by the rigorous observation and hypothesis testing that we take for granted today. Despite the absence of any culture of systematic observation, we could still look for informal evidence that the individual symptoms of PTSD were familiar to, and were described by, earlier writers, whether or not in a medical context. And from the nineteenth century on it would be reasonable to look for descriptions of the key components of PTSD. For example, we should be able to find evidence for a vivid reliving of a trauma approximating to the flashback, even if that particular term was not in use.

The nineteenth century witnessed an increasing interest in nervous disorders, which tended to fall under the two main headings of *neurasthenia* and *hysteria*. Reading James Beard's authoritative text on neurasthenia published in 1890, the modern reader is struck by the dozens of physical and mental symptoms that were considered diagnostic of the disorder.[2] Clearly, the utility of the concept was thought to lie more in its inclusiveness than in its precision. Beard provided case examples of many conditions we would now regard as distinct anxiety disorders, such as panic, agoraphobia, social phobia, and obsessive-compulsive disorder. Among the numerous symptoms of neurasthenia, we can find many that are today considered diagnostic of PTSD, such as morbid fear, hypervigilance, insomnia, irritability, and inability to concentrate. Beard believed that neurasthenia was an insidious and chronic disorder, whereas hysteria, characterized by convulsions and paroxysms, was a more acute and violent condition that could resolve as quickly as it appeared.

Notably, Beard's treatise omits any mention of the reexperiencing or avoidance symptoms of PTSD, and indeed omits to discuss traumatic events at all. For the vast majority of nineteenth-century doctors, neurasthenia and hysteria were regarded as conditions with a physical cause in lesions of the nervous system. This belief in physical causality was coupled with two other assumptions that were inimical to psychological inquiry. One was an attachment to a Darwinian notion of hereditary weakness conveying vulnerability to disorder, and the other was a classic Victorian morality centered on duty and will. Many of the most influential medical men were not so much indifferent to psychological approaches as antagonistic to them, because "they encouraged morbid introspection and egoism, heightened suggestibility, and aggravated existing deficiency of willpower."[3]

In this climate it was hardly surprising that there was little interest in the phenomenon of posttraumatic stress. Nevertheless, one of the great triumphs of Victorian engineering, the railway, indirectly produced the first systematic study of traumatized people—in this case, by a railway accident. Writing in 1883, Herbert Page commented: "We know of no clinical picture more distressing than that of a strong and healthy man reduced by apparently inadequate causes to a state in which all control of the emotions is well-nigh gone; who cannot sleep because he has before his mind an ever-present sense of the accident; who starts at the least noise; who lies in bed almost afraid to move; whose heart palpitates whenever he is spoken to; and who cannot hear or say a word about his present condition and his future prospects without bursting into tears."[4]

Many of Page's contemporaries regarded such symptoms as resulting from physical lesions to the brain, spinal cord, or peripheral nervous system, and such patients were often referred to a suffering from "railway spine." Despite the frequent absence of any demonstrable physical injury, they concluded, consistent with the approach to medicine prevailing at that time, that there must be subtle forms of neurological damage. Page's position was remarkably close to modern views. He attributed his patients' symptoms to "general nervous shock," which he defined as "some functional disturbance of the whole nervous balance or tone rather than structural damage to any organ of the body."[5] The main cause of the nervous shock was extreme fright.

He thus managed to articulate a psychological account of patients' reactions to trauma that did not abandon the physiological level of explanation.

Similarly, in France Pierre Janet had for some years been studying the effects of traumatic events on people with hysterical symptoms.[6] Janet believed that in some individuals a constitutional weakness led to a particular response to stress in which ideas and behaviors became separated from consciousness. The result of this "dissociation" was a loss of memory for the traumatic event coexisting simultaneously with a variety of symptoms such as hysterical paralysis, blindness, or mutism. He saw these dramatic responses as adaptive in the face of acute trauma but prone to continue indefinitely and to lead to a wide variety of bodily disorders if the dissociated memories were not reintegrated into conscious experience.

The firm belief in an organic psychiatry that lay behind the widespread unwillingness to endorse a psychological account of distress after railway accidents and other traumas also meant that most doctors were unprepared for the psychological casualties of World War I. The early stages of the war saw the same debate over an organic versus a psychological account of "shell shock," which was initially attributed to the physical effects of proximity to an explosion. To Charles Myers and to many other psychologists and doctors serving at the front, it rapidly became clear that the term was a misnomer because the same symptoms were frequently evident in soldiers who were remote from any explosions. "Shell shock" thereafter tended to refer to a mental reaction "where the tolerable or controllable limits of horror, fear, anxiety etc. are overstepped"[7] and was differentiated from "shell concussion." Harold Wiltshire, a doctor serving at Number 12 General Hospital in France, similarly attributed most cases of shell shock to horrible sights, losses, or fright from an explosion, particularly when the soldier feared he would be buried by the blast.[8]

What symptoms did doctors treating cases of shell shock at the front or in the military hospitals see? Rows described a series of patients treated at the Red Cross Military Hospital in Maghull: "In some cases the physical expression of a special emotion, such as fear or terror, persists for a long time without much change. This condition is usually associated with an emotional state produced by the constant intrusion of the memory of some past incident."[9] Among the other common symptoms he noted were irritability, apprehensiveness, and nightmares, but he also noted perspicaciously: "They know that they are irritable, that they are unable to interest themselves or to give a maintained attention to a given subject. . . . All this is very real to them and leads to a condition of anxiety which is increased by their not being able to understand their condition; they worry because they fear how far this sort of thing may go."[10]

Another World War I doctor, Millais Culpin, noted dissociative states linked to extreme terror, in which soldiers were partially detached from reality, as well as terrifying dreams and dreadful memories. In treatment, he observed the astonishing power of the traumatic memory: "The patient was made to close his eyes, visualise his first experience of fighting, and describe what he saw . . . if success was obtained he seemed to be living his experience over again with more than hallucinatory vividness, ducking as shells came over or trembling as he took refuge from them."[11] He also provided good accounts of avoidance, describing a man who "wittingly tried to forget war horrors" and concluding, "The evasive statements and arguments by which the shell-shocked soldier tried to avoid discussion of his real troubles are of the same nature as the denials and evasions of patients in civil life."[12] Indeed, like many military doctors at the time, Culpin became convinced that shell shock was indistinguishable from civilian reactions to traumatic events.

Without an appreciation of the dominance of organic psychiatry in the nineteenth century, and the absence of any science of psychopathology, it is hard to realize the enormous impact of the writings of Sigmund Freud and the intensity of the resistance they aroused at the time. For the military psychologists and psychiatrists, however, their wartime observations provided strong support for Freud's highly controversial theories concerning the unconscious and the repression of unacceptable mental contents. Of course, they did not support his theories about sex. As one writer put it, their experiences "confirmed the truth of Freud's theories about the nature of the machinery concerned in the production of symptoms, though they did not prove the truth of his more fundamental principles concerning the driving force of that machinery."[13]

Normality versus Pathology

One danger in linking psychiatric disorder to a stressful event is that normal human reactions can get medicalized and labeled as pathological. Not surprisingly, people have objected that any so-called symptoms are part of the normal process of adjustment. According to this "commonsense" argument, the more extreme the event, the longer the time people will need to recover from it. This will be particularly true of events involving severe threats of death or serious injury for which most people are ill-prepared. Like other Skeptics,[14] Summerfield argued that PTSD has more to do with society and politics, and with the development of a compensation culture, than with medicine: "An individualistic, rights conscious culture can foster a sense of personal injury and grievance and thus a need for restitution in encounters in daily life that were formerly appraised more dispassionately. Post-traumatic stress disorder is the diagnosis for an age of disenchantment. Today there is often more social utility attached to expressions of victimhood than to 'survivorhood'.... Once it becomes advantageous to frame distress as a psychiatric condition people will choose to present themselves as medicalised victims rather than as feisty survivors."[15]

This argument is strengthened by the fact that the impact of a trauma is typically much wider than would be suggested by considering only the period of the event itself. For example, someone involved in a serious motor vehicle accident might have to deal with all of the following: severe physical injury cutting short a planned career; painful, prolonged medical treatment and residual chronic pain; death of someone close; intense anger directed at another driver; long delays in obtaining any compensation; frequent requirements for medical reports and examinations; anxiety-provoking attendance at police and court proceedings; worries because of loss of income; difficulty in maintaining a social life; and insensitive and hurtful comments by friends, relatives, and strangers.

Likewise, refugees from oppressive political regimes routinely have to deal with an accumulation of testing and demoralizing events: pain and illness arising from torture and ill-treatment; uncertainty about their asylum status and fears of being sent back to their country of origin; lack of knowledge about their family and friends and fears for their safety; problems communicating with social services and difficulty in understanding rights and procedures; social isolation; unfamiliar language, food, and customs; and unsuitable housing, where they may be exposed to excess noise or additional threats. Small wonder that traumatic events do not involve just intense fear, helplessness, and horror, as specified by the DSM, but are also often accompanied by other powerful emotions such as sadness and loss, betrayal, humiliation, and, particularly, anger.[16] The trauma victim, then, may often be overwhelmed by multiple difficulties and frustrations arising from a single event, several of which may be associated with fear and helplessness in their own right, raising the legitimate question of whether the "symptoms" are in fact normal reactions to abnormal circumstances.

This argument has been made before, in the context of severe mental illness. Some sociologists have repeatedly charged psychiatrists with labeling human eccentricities, such as hallucinations and delusions, as symptoms of illness and with being agents of social control who use diagnoses such as schizophrenia to justify depriving people of their liberty. In the case of PTSD no loss of liberty is involved, but labeling posttraumatic responses could still be regarded as an unwarranted intrusion by mental health professionals into essentially private reactions with which people will find their own ways of coping. Perhaps a closer analogy is with the diagnosis of an abnormal grief reaction, a state that psychiatrists believe represents a clear-cut departure from normal grief, and one that requires intervention if it is to be resolved.

Medical Skeptics of the diagnosis, such as Field, have also charged that posttraumatic symptoms such as intrusive thoughts and memories of the event are completely normal reactions and not evidence of psychopathology.[17] Rather than these reactions naturally fading over the course of time, Field suggests that they are kept alive by the litigation in which patients may be involved. The succession of legal and medical reports, and the anticipation of having to appear in court, constantly refreshes the memories and the unpleasant emotions that accompany them. It is certainly true that intrusive thoughts and memories are part of normal life and are not in themselves indicative of anything pathological.[18] There is little evidence, however, that after a trauma the intense reexperiencing of the event (flashbacks) is prominent for any length of time in people who do not have PTSD.[19] The litigation argument has historically been popular with certain experts who regularly appear in court on behalf of defendants charged with negligence. For many years personal observations by distinguished doctors about the role of compensation in "accident neurosis" (what we now call PTSD) were almost all the courts had to go on. Certainly, the sheer difficulty and frustration involved in making compensation claims does lead often to intense anger and rumination about injustice. Defendants will often deny liability and try to distort the facts of the case, and it appears to be in no one's interest except the claimant's to settle the case quickly. Not surprisingly, this tends to exacerbate the claimant's symptoms. Once systematic follow-up studies with accident victims were conducted, however, it was clear that the end of the court case was not generally followed by the symptoms' going away, refuting the argument that the compensation claim itself is the main culprit in delaying recovery.[20]

For the Skeptics, posttraumatic reactions are a normal response that dissipates with time. But there is an onus on them to make at least some suggestion about how long should be allowed for this process to be complete. One justification for the original introduction of the PTSD diagnosis was that, like abnormal grief, it represented a longer-term failure to adapt to what had occurred, and one that could be helped with psychiatric or psychological intervention. In 1987 the DSM-IIIR specified that the symptoms had to be present for at least one month after a trauma, and DSM-IV further specified that significant distress had to be attached to the symptoms or people's work or social relationships had to be impaired. In practice, the symptoms usually do cause significant distress. But is there any evidence that after a trauma unpleasant symptoms do in fact persist for a long time in the absence of intervention?

Surveys documenting the natural course of PTSD indicate that immediately after a traumatic event, for example, a physical or sexual assault, many people show sufficient reexperiencing, avoidance, and arousal symptoms to meet the diagnostic criteria.[21] In the case of rape, this may be as many as 94 percent of victims. The numbers drop off rapidly over the first three months and tend to stabilize thereafter. People who still meet the symptom criteria after three to four months, and definitely after six to eight months, are likely to have chronic symptoms that will not improve further without intervention. When the authors of the National Comorbidity Survey asked their respondents more informally about the persistence of PTSD symptoms, they found a gradual decline that began to flatten out after the first year. More than a third of their sample were still suffering from symptoms many years later.[22] From these studies it seems that of all those who are eligible for a PTSD diagnosis after the first month, many will continue to recover naturally but a subgroup will be at risk of developing long-lasting problems. At three months, if symptoms have not already begun to decrease, the probability of a person recovering naturally is much diminished and as time goes on, becomes extremely small.

This is one reasonable justification for thinking that some pathological process is at work. The minimum duration of symptoms of one month laid down in the DSM-IV may lead to people being diagnosed with PTSD who are recovering naturally but could be defended on the grounds of permitting those at risk of longer-term problems to be identified. Another justification for the new diagnosis was provided by the observations that the onset of PTSD was sometimes delayed by months or even years after the trauma and could follow a long period of a person being symptom-free. This is not readily explained by the idea that symptoms are a natural short-term reaction to stress.

Other research shows that PTSD is associated with a number of biological changes suggestive of something more than a normal reaction. Several studies have compared Vietnam veterans suffering from PTSD with veterans who also saw combat but did not develop PTSD. The majority, but by no means all, of the PTSD group showed stronger peripheral physiological responses, such as higher heart rate and blood pressure, when they were presented with reminders of Vietnam.[23] PTSD patients have also been found to show greater pain tolerance under these conditions, suggesting a more pronounced release of endogenous opiates in the brain. Brain imaging studies conducted with Vietnam veterans and survivors of childhood sexual abuse also indicate that those who are currently suffering from PTSD have different levels of activity (regional cerebral blood flow) in certain parts of the brain when they are exposed to trauma reminders.[24]

Among the possible problems with these studies is that defining groups on the basis of the PTSD diagnosis alone does not take into account the existence of other ongoing problems that could be adding to arousal levels, such as family criticism, housing problems, and financial threats. The experimental results could be produced by these independent consequences of PTSD, rather than by the disorder itself. This is unlikely, however, because PTSD patients do not show greater physiological reactivity to stressful events that were not the cause of the PTSD or to general stressors such as having to do mental arithmetic.[25] Another potential problem is that the amount of stress experienced by the PTSD groups could have been more than that of the non-PTSD comparison groups. As we will discuss in more detail in the next chapter, there are a lot of practical difficulties in accurately measuring the degree of stress, particularly because of the strong subjective element in how people respond to threat and danger. Thus, in some studies the groups may not have been particularly well-matched. It is still striking, however, that group differences were found despite the fact that the traumas occurred twenty or in some cases forty years previously, which again is inconsistent with the idea that PTSD is a normal short-term reaction to stress.

Alongside the idea that PTSD is a normal response to stress, it is sometimes argued that it is a response unique to European and North American culture and is therefore not a form of universal pathology.[26] These Skeptics draw attention to the crucial role played by social context in determining what is and what is not traumatic, how people cope with their suffering, and how they seek help. They criticize the concept of PTSD as being too rooted in individual mental experience, ignoring alternative ways of an individual showing distress, such as through psychosomatic symptoms, and ignoring the collective impact of events such as famine or civil war on entire societies.

Although it is undoubtedly true that the concept of PTSD is limited, the kind of careful scientific study that would support these arguments is largely absent. It is striking that even these Skeptics report that intrusive memories and avoidance symptoms are commonly seen in non-Western societies. In fact, the symptoms of PTSD are generally fairly consistent across the few cultures that have been studied systematically.[27] Psychosomatic symptoms are probably just as common in

Western as in non-Western societies although they are less often assessed.[28] The questions raised by the Skeptics are important, but at
present there seems no compelling reason to reject the idea that PTSD
reflects one kind of universal trauma response, albeit one that does not
capture everything of interest.

A Separate Disorder?

A number of Skeptics reject the idea that PTSD is a new disorder, regarding it as a fraudulent and artificial redescription of problems that
are already covered well in the diagnostic manuals. Field, for example,
commented: "Clearly PTSD is nothing more than a collection of the
psychological reactions that may occur after exposure to an emotionally traumatic event. One might well question why it is deserving of
special terminology. Well-established diagnoses such as anxiety, phobia, and depression give a clear and specific indication of the subject's
condition and the omnibus term post-traumatic stress disorder has
nothing to recommend it."[29]

   He also rejected as "clinical nonsense" the idea that the same patient could be in a state of high arousal while simultaneously exhibiting
symptoms of emotional numbing, since these responses were contradictory. Along the same lines, Summerfield complained: "The diagnosis is claimed to represent a distinct category of psychopathology, but it
is largely grounded in phenomena that are common to many other
psychiatric diagnoses, such as mood, anxiety, sleep patterns, etc. Above
all, the diagnosis of post-traumatic stress disorder lacks specificity: it is
imprecise in distinguishing between the physiology of normal distress
and the physiology of pathological distress."[30]

Symptom Overlap

To back up this skeptical point of view, we need only consider classic
British research on bereavement. In John Bowlby's highly influential
attachment theory, the typical response to loss of an attachment figure
is a phase of protest and anger that, if it does not succeed in restoring
the loss, is followed by a phase of despair.[31] During this period there is
an oscillation between conscious preoccupation with the loss, often ac-

companied by intrusive images of the person who has died, and defensive exclusion of related thoughts and reminders. In addition to the repeated descriptions of intrusive thoughts, avoidance, and numbness, bereavement researchers have consistently found symptoms indicative of heightened arousal, such as muscle tension, panic, and insomnia. General theories of people's response to severe life events have many similarities to the theories of bereavement outlined above, most of them explicitly recognizing that such events are typically followed by intrusive thoughts and memories and by intrapsychic defenses such as denial and avoidance that help to mitigate the intensity of distress.

It could be objected at this point that although the *individual* symptoms of PTSD are not unique, the particular *constellation* of symptoms is special to the disorder. Some evidence on this point was collected by Dean Kilpatrick and colleagues, who conducted a large survey to evaluate the diagnostic changes proposed for the DSM-IV.[32] Among the issues that the DSM-IV Field Trial investigated was whether PTSD was uniquely associated with high-magnitude traumatic events or whether the same symptom pattern could occur after relatively low-magnitude events that would not fulfill Criterion A (Table 1.1). The sample consisted mainly of people seeking treatment after a variety of traumas but also included a cross section of people from the community. Kilpatrick found that almost all PTSD followed high-magnitude events, and that relaxing the nature of the event required led to very little change in the rate of diagnosable PTSD. This suggested that in the main, PTSD was specifically associated with traumatic events. However, it would be interesting to study in more detail how many people suffering a nontraumatic bereavement would qualify for the diagnosis.

Looking at the symptoms of PTSD outlined in Table 1.1, one can see that the overlap with other disorders, even those described in the DSM itself, is clear: emotional and physiological arousal and avoidance are found in phobic disorders; detachment, loss of interest, and hopelessness about the future are found in depression; sleeplessness, irritability, and concentration problems are found both in depression and in generalized anxiety disorder, which is also typified by hypervigilance and exaggerated startle.

Of all the symptoms of PTSD, reexperiencing the traumatic

event has the greatest claim to distinguishing the diagnosis from other conditions.[33] Although these symptoms are not specifically mentioned as being part of any other DSM diagnosis,[34] the Skeptics are surely correct that they are not unique to PTSD. It is now well-established that a high proportion of depressed patients without PTSD also report involuntary intrusive memories of stressful events. These memories are also distressing, occur at a similar frequency, are accompanied by physical sensations, and involve some sense of reliving the original event. The events that figure in these memories overlap a lot, although depressed people are somewhat more likely to hark back to interpersonal problems such as serious disagreements and breakups, whereas PTSD patients recall proportionately more incidents of personal injury and assault.[35] Despite this, there are indications that full-blown flashbacks to traumatic events, as opposed to more ordinary intrusive memories, are extremely rare in conditions other than PTSD.[36]

More research on the similarities and differences between intrusions in conditions such as PTSD, agoraphobia, hypochondriasis, social phobia, and schizophrenia might be illuminating. Adrian Wells and Ann Hackmann reported that a number of patients with worries about their physical health experienced repeated intrusive images that could be clearly linked to frightening events in childhood.[37] For example, one patient had images of being dead but trapped in a barrel that did not allow him to move or escape. Relevant memories included being locked in dark cupboards and feeling smothered. He also reported seeing people being buried in a nearby cemetery and thinking that they were being buried alive as a punishment. In social phobia, too, persistent images linked to early embarrassing or humiliating experiences are common, although patients have usually lost sight of the link between the upsetting image and the original event.[38]

Coherence of the Syndrome

One response to these criticisms would be to show that PTSD is a coherent diagnosis, in other words, that the symptoms described in the DSM tend to occur together. This would go some way toward answering the objection that the symptoms are simply taken from other, better-established diagnoses and have no inherent unity. The least stringent approach is to show that each symptom correlates highly with the overall PTSD diagnosis, and this is relatively easily demonstrated.[39] Somewhat better is to show that symptom patterns are similar even though the nature of the trauma varies. For example, similar patterns of symptoms have been reported in trauma survivors who had experienced either threat to life, loss of a loved one, or exposure to grotesque death.[40]

Another approach is to examine the structure of PTSD symptoms to see whether they form three groups or clusters corresponding to reexperiencing, avoidance, and arousal. This assumes that the symptoms in each cluster are all produced by their own distinct mechanism, whether psychological or biological. The usual way of doing this is to employ factor analysis, a statistical technique that attempts to identify underlying factors that can explain the interrelationships among a set of variables. Applying these methods to a group of female assault victims three months after their assault, Edna Foa and colleagues found three major factors.[41] The first factor included three reexperiencing symptoms, two symptoms related to deliberate avoidance and two arousal symptoms; the second factor included three numbing symptoms from the avoidance cluster and two arousal symptoms; and the third factor included three reexperiencing symptoms and one arousal symptom. The symptoms of foreshortened future and memory loss were unrelated to any of these factors. In the DSM-IV Field Trial, PTSD symptoms clustered into two groups, one made up of reexperiencing, arousal, and avoidance symptoms and one made up of numbing symptoms.[42] Memory loss was again unrelated to the other symptoms.

The most sophisticated factor analytic study of this kind was undertaken by Daniel and Lynda King and colleagues, using a large sample of male, treatment-seeking Vietnam veterans who were being assessed many years after the war.[43] The authors used a slightly different statistical technique in which they specified how the data should be clustered according to the DSM-IV and then measured how well the results actually fitted this pattern. They reported that the data were consistent with the expected symptom clusters, with two exceptions that had also been reported by Foa and Kilpatrick. One was that the memory loss item was unrelated to the remaining symptoms, and the other was that deliberate avoidance and emotional numbing symptoms were independent. Interestingly, though, the four factors that King and colleagues found (reexperiencing, avoidance, numbing, and arousal) were unrelated to any higher order factor corresponding to an overall PTSD diagnosis. Nor were the reexperiencing and avoidance factors, or the numbing and arousal factors, interrelated. This would be expected if there was a reciprocal relationship between them, with avoidance being a response to excessive reexperiencing or numbing a response to excessive arousal. In a direct refutation of Field's claim that emotional numbing and arousal symptoms are contradictory responses, however, these two factors were strongly positively correlated.

These studies suggest a number of interesting things. First, it is almost certainly misleading to include deliberate avoidance and numbing in the same symptom cluster, as they do not tend to occur together and are probably explained by different mechanisms. Thus, four rather than three symptom clusters are warranted. Second, after a recent trauma, symptoms do not fall into neat clusters corresponding to the DSM-IV categories. This may be because people's reactions show high levels of day-to-day fluctuation. The relations between specific aspects of reexperiencing, avoidance, numbing, and arousal are probably variable and reflect individual differences in appraisal, emotional reactivity, and coping strategies. Third, the four symptom clusters, corresponding to different underlying mechanisms, may be appropriate when PTSD is long-established. These four clusters are not strongly related to one another, however, suggesting that chronic PTSD reflects a variety of more specific psychological or biological processes rather than being a single coherent syndrome.

Comorbidity

All the above findings leave open the question of whether other symptoms not at present thought to be part of the syndrome would correlate equally highly with the diagnosis, were they to be measured. One of the complications in responding to this comes from the fact that PTSD rarely occurs in isolation, often occurring together (being comorbid) with other diagnoses. The evidence on this has recently been reviewed by Patricia Resick, who concluded that the vast majority of people with PTSD also have at least one other diagnosable disorder.[44] The most common of these is depression, and in some groups, such as Vietnam veterans, substance abuse is also common. Data from the U.S. National Comorbidity Survey suggest that both depression and substance abuse are more likely to be consequences of having developed PTSD, whereas comorbid anxiety disorders are more likely to be independent of the trauma and of PTSD.[45]

Resick noted that several studies have found PTSD to be associated with more enduring and widespread problems of experience and behavior, usually referred to as *personality disorders.* These include antisocial personality, characterized by such features as impulsivity, irritability, aggression, and disregard for self and others, and paranoid personality, as shown in high levels of secretiveness, mistrust, and suspicion of others' motives. Again, there are problems of reconciling the traditional view of these personality problems with the symptoms of PTSD and with distinguishing the effects of coping with these symptoms for long periods. Judith Herman suggested that much of what is traditionally called personality disorder is the product of exposure to repeated trauma, particularly in childhood and particularly involving emotional, physical, and sexual abuse.[46] These experiences can produce massive distortions in expectations of other people that cause severe relationship problems, hostility and a sense of pervasive threat, extreme negative emotions that are difficult to regulate, and self-destructive and impulsive behavior. Many trauma experts have concurred with Herman in the opinion that it may be productive to view these more pervasive symptoms as a form of complex PTSD.

The high degree of comorbidity shown by PTSD means that in practice it will be difficult to prove which symptoms belong in the syndrome and which do not. PTSD appears to reflect just one of a number of reasonably common reactions to extreme trauma. Which other reactions are present will depend on numerous factors, such as the presence and extent of any childhood trauma, the duration of symptoms, cultural beliefs and opportunities regarding how to cope with symptoms, and so on. These will vary greatly among samples of combat veterans, assault victims, motor vehicle accident victims, and so on. With time, however, it should be possible to demonstrate that there is a core set of symptoms that are routinely observed, whatever the sample.

What Is Different?

Perhaps surprisingly, in view of the high levels of symptom overlap and comorbidity, there is increasing evidence that PTSD is a distinct disorder biologically. For example, evidence shows that baseline levels of urinary norepinephrine (noradrenaline) are higher in combat veterans with PTSD than in combat veterans with other disorders or in nonpsychiatric control subjects. Blocking receptor sites with the drug yohimbine and thereby increasing circulating levels of norepinephrine produced panic attacks and flashbacks in a substantial proportion of PTSD patients, an effect that has been found in panic disorder but not in other psychiatric conditions, such as depression or generalized anxiety disorder.

In the normal stress response familiar from disorders such as depression, there is increased activity of the hypothalamic-pituitary-adrenal (HPA) system, resulting in an increased production of glucocorticoids such as cortisol from the adrenal glands. These glucocorticoids then cause the suppression of defensive immune, metabolic, and neural reactions to stress that would be harmful if they persisted for too long. They also regulate the further production of stress hormones via a negative feedback loop. Whereas in disorders such as depression there is typically evidence for an increase in HPA axis activity, and in levels of cortisol, the opposite is often true in PTSD. In a series of studies, Rachel Yehuda and colleagues have shown that under normal conditions the HPA axis is suppressed in PTSD, such that levels of urinary cortisol secretion were lower than in nonpsychiatric control subjects and lower than in several other psychiatric groups studied.[47] These reductions in cortisol have been linked to an increase in lymphocyte glucocorticoid receptors to which circulating cortisol is bound. The numbers of these receptors are greater in PTSD than in other psychiatric conditions such as depression and panic disorder.

Yehuda maintains that these results do not mean that PTSD patients are insensitive to stress but rather the opposite. Patients do show a short-term hormonal response to stress, but at the same time there is a much greater sensitivity of the negative feedback loop whereby levels of cortisol are reduced by HPA axis activity. To demonstrate this, she and her colleagues assessed the response to the steroid dexamethasone. Compared with nonpsychiatric control subjects and combat veterans without PTSD, the PTSD group showed an enhanced suppression of cortisol, consistent with the idea of a sensitized negative feedback loop.[48]

There is good reason to think that these biological differences may be important. Heidi Resnick and colleagues measured cortisol levels in women who had shortly beforehand been raped and were attending a hospital emergency room.[49] Three months later they were followed up and assessed for the presence of PTSD. The researchers found that rape victims who had a prior history of childhood sexual abuse were at greater risk of developing PTSD and that while in the emergency room this same group of women had had lower levels of cortisol. Once again, this is consistent with increased negative feedback regulation of the HPA axis being one of the effects of trauma.

Conclusions

The historical and scientific data offer a helpful guide through the welter of accusation and counteraccusation that surrounds this most controversial of diagnoses. It is clear that a psychological reaction to extreme horror or fright, variously called nervous shock or shell shock but with marked similarities to PTSD, has been regularly observed since the middle of the nineteenth century. Interestingly, many of the problems that doctors of that period experienced in distinguishing clear-cut diagnostic categories are still with us today because, with the possible exception of flashbacks, none of its symptoms are unique to PTSD. Rather, as Young suggested, it is largely the existence of the credible traumatic event that transforms a set of nonspecific symptoms into tokens of PTSD.[50] Ironically, the overlap with other disorders is probably greater than had been appreciated, as interest in PTSD has led to new discoveries about the importance of intrusive images and memories in other disorders. In addition to this overlap with other psychiatric conditions, many of the so-called symptoms of PTSD form part of a recognizable nonpathological response to stress. Recent statis-

tical studies confirm that PTSD is not a qualitatively distinct response
to extreme stress but reflects the upper end of a stress–response contin-
uum.[51]

It is equally clear that the condition does not simply pathologize
normal reactions. Rather, what start as ordinary responses to stress become entrenched, causing significant distress and interference with
many aspects of the sufferer's work and social life. It is not the symptoms themselves, but rather their frequency, their persistence, their intensity, and their failure to become more benign with time that define
the disorder. In this respect PTSD is not dissimilar to other psychiatric
diagnoses. For example, hallucinations and delusions are remarkably
common phenomena, experienced by many people from time to time
without undue distress. In schizophrenia, however, these symptoms
show the same characteristics of being frequent, persistent, intense,
distressing, and hard to control.[52]

It is also clear that the Skeptics are wrong to suggest that on a
physiological level PTSD is indistinguishable from everyday responses
to stress. At least some cases of PTSD do show a distinctive biological
profile that differentiates the disorder from other responses to stress
such as major depression and generalized anxiety disorder. In particular, a person with PTSD may have chronically high levels of norepinephrine and a greatly sensitized HPA axis that lead to intense but
short-lived biological responses to stress. The existence of a different
biological profile does not imply that PTSD necessarily involves some
underlying physical deficit or pathology, but could equally well mean
that the event has exceeded the capacity of the body to adapt to the demands that events have made on it. There are also persistent indications that PTSD varies considerably among patients and that not all of
them will share exactly the same biological characteristics.

Studies on the coherence of the syndrome are few but already
suggest several conclusions. If the loss of memory item is omitted, and
a distinction is made between deliberate avoidance and emotional
numbing, there is evidence (for male combat veterans at least) that the
symptom clusters are indeed coherent. Nor is there any inherent contradiction, as Skeptics have charged, between reporting numbing and
arousal symptoms at the same time. However, there is as yet no specific
support for an overall PTSD diagnosis that is defined exclusively in

terms of these symptom clusters. To use a nautical analogy, it remains possible that PTSD is more in the nature of a flag of convenience that draws attention to the oftentimes coexistent parts of the ship below, rather than a mainmast that links individual parts of the ship together in a structural sense.

Despite such criticisms of the PTSD diagnosis, enough evidence has been gathered to justify its survival in some form or other, for the time being at least. A state or states have been identified that are definitely pathological, and these can sometimes be shown to differ from other states. Another big challenge remains, however, that goes to the core of the debate about whether PTSD is primarily a medical or a social entity. Is the disorder really a normal result of overwhelming stress, as clinicians working with Vietnam veterans and battered women originally argued, or is it more like a true psychiatric illness in being the product of a biological or psychological vulnerability that is revealed by failure to adapt to stressful life circumstances? This question is much more complex than it appears on the surface and will be addressed in the next chapter.

3

Is Posttraumatic Stress
Disorder Caused by Trauma?

If PTSD must be understood as a pathological symptom, then it is not so much a symptom of the unconscious, as it is a symptom of history. The traumatized, we might say, carry an impossible history within them, or they become themselves the symptom of a history that they cannot entirely possess.

—Cathy Caruth, *Explorations in Memory*[1]

At first glance, the title of this chapter may appear to pose a question whose answer is obvious. But in fact the question is one of the most hotly debated of all. When PTSD was first introduced in 1980, many people took the DSM-III to be claiming that there was a subset of events so overwhelming in their intensity that they provided in themselves a sufficient explanation for the disorder. The above quotation by Caruth aptly illustrates this view that the traumatic experience is a literal reflection of reality and not the kind of distortion or exaggeration that is typically associated with psychiatric disorder. This was in many ways a radical departure from previous practice. Historically, psychiatric symptoms were often attributed to hereditary weakness, with even very psychologically sophisticated clinicians frequently commenting on the preexisting vulnerabilities of some of their patients.

In modern times it is also commonly believed that people with a mental disorder are likely to have some kind of biological or psychological vulnerability. New studies show that whereas 50 to 75 percent of women and 60 to 80 percent of men experience a high-magnitude traumatic event at some point in their lives, only a minority of these develop PTSD.[2] The clear implication is that the occurrence of the trauma is not on its own a sufficient explanation. Numerous critics of the diagnosis have additionally questioned whether there is any evidence that traumatic stressors form a unique class with their own distinctive effects, and whether their impact is so strong as to override personal vulnerability factors and other environmental effects.[3] Even very recently the question of the causal role played by trauma itself has been raised within the PTSD community by two leading researchers, Rachel Yehuda and Alexander McFarlane, drawing on fifteen years of research into the new diagnosis.[4] We are now in a position to evaluate these persistent observations in the light of modern scientific knowledge.

Measuring Trauma

To begin with, it is instructive to ask the apparently simple question of whether more intense stressors lead to more severe psychological reactions. But what is a "more intense stressor"? For people involved in a motor vehicle accident, for instance, can the stressor be objectively quantified and, if so, is it the amount of damage caused to their own vehicle, the damage caused to all vehicles involved, the pain and injury they personally suffered, the injury or death of others involved, or the length of time they had to wait before being rescued? Or should the stressor be measured subjectively, in terms of the victims' fear of injury or death, of the scenes they witnessed, or of what might have (but didn't) happen? In the case of war veterans we could similarly distinguish between objective measures—such as the length of their tour of duty, the number of days on which they saw action, the loss of close comrades, the number of enemy soldiers they personally injured or killed, or their involvement in the deaths of prisoners or civilians— and subjective measures—such as fear of annihilation, anger at being let down by officers, or guilt over regretted actions. Every trauma raises similar issues, and the individuals involved may experience the same event objectively and subjectively in totally different ways.

In an attempt to overcome the limitations of interpreting individual studies, Bernice Andrews, John Valentine, and I recently reported a meta-analytic review of seventy-seven studies involving people exposed to some kind of trauma.[5] A meta-analysis is a method for assessing the results of numerous studies using a common standard of measurement and then aggregating them, giving much more reliable estimates of the effects of individual factors than can be achieved by a single study. Each of the studies in our review included at least one risk factor for PTSD, such as age, gender, or trauma severity, and one measure of posttraumatic symptoms. We were able to examine the effects of trauma severity in forty-nine studies, involving a total of 13,653 affected people. Compared with a variety of other risk factors, trauma severity was one of the strongest predictors of how many symptoms were reported (Figure 3.1).

This analysis included subjective measures of trauma severity and is open to the important objection that the assessment of severity and outcome are hopelessly confounded because the same person typically makes both judgments. In other words, having PTSD may lead someone to describe the trauma as more severe, rather than a more severe trauma increasing the risk of PTSD. There are at least two main counters to this argument. One is to focus on studies that have used an objective index that does not rely on the affected person's own judgment of severity. For example, studies of events such as the nuclear reactor leak at Three Mile Island and a school shooting showed that the closer an individual was to the trauma scene, the greater the risk of disorder.[6] Being physically injured also consistently increases the risk of PTSD[7] unless, as in World War I, it enables one to escape the dangers of the battlefield.

The second counter is to compare retrospective studies in which trauma severity is judged after symptoms have developed with prospective studies in which trauma severity is measured first. If the symptoms are totally determining the assessment of the stressor, so that having PTSD leads a person to classify his or her trauma as more serious, trauma severity should be very poor at predicting later symptoms in prospective studies. Our review indicated that trauma severity was still a highly significant predictor of later symptoms, but the effect was less strong than in the retrospective studies. This result need not mean, of course, that reports of trauma by people who had developed PTSD were artificially inflated in the retrospective studies. Another explanation is that this group were better at realizing the real impact of the event, whereas people who did not develop PTSD might be minimizing its severity. Whatever the reason why symptoms influence retro-

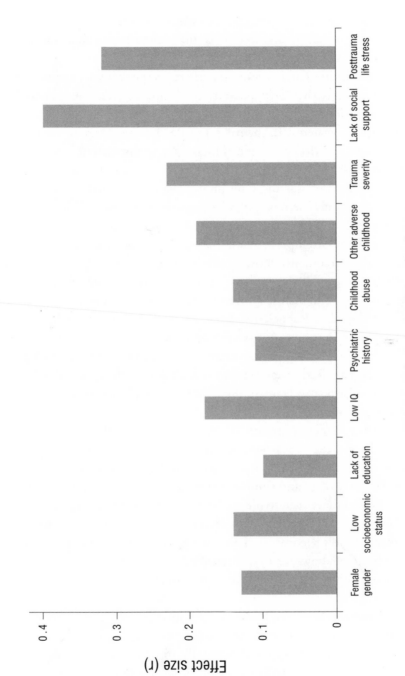

Figure 3.1. Risk Factors for Posttraumatic Stress Syndrome.

spective estimates of how stressful an experience was, the implication
of our review is that trauma severity is still an important risk factor for
later disorder, as implied by the DSM.

These findings do not prove that there is a special class of extreme
stressors that have their own qualitatively distinct effects. A number of
studies have found that events of supposedly lesser magnitude are
sometimes associated with the full set of PTSD symptoms, including
nontraumatic deaths and serious illnesses,[8] a spouse's affair,[9] and repeated episodes of bullying, intimidation, or uncontrollable stress at
work.[10] Victims of stalking typically receive repeated harassing telephone calls, E-mails, letters, and other material; are constantly watched
and followed; and have their homes broken into and their property
damaged. These attempts at manipulating their feelings of threat result
in their not infrequently showing all the symptoms of PTSD even if
they have not actually been physically threatened or assaulted.[11] This
is reminiscent of Wiltshire's observation that some soldiers in World
War I developed shell shock through gradual psychic exhaustion rather
than because of a sudden overwhelming stressor.[12]

In general, however, these examples of PTSD symptoms arising
from lesser magnitude events involving high levels of fear and helplessness seem to be relatively uncommon. When studies have looked to see
how many new cases of PTSD would be diagnosed if the strict rules
about what qualifies as a traumatic event were relaxed, the number has
increased very little.[13] It would be fair to say that events involving the
greatest immediate threat to life or to physical integrity, such as physical and sexual assault and combat, are associated with the highest rates
of PTSD, and that threat to life consistently emerges as a powerful predictor in studies of populations as diverse as combat veterans, political
prisoners, assault victims, and motor vehicle accident victims.[14] It
should be noted, however, that the subjective perception of threat is often a more influential predictor of distress than more "objective" indicators.[15]

As we have seen, the DSM-IV attempts to define these stressors
in terms of both the nature of the event and the quality of the individual's immediate reaction to it. Realistically, in some cases it is impossible to divorce completely the nature of the event from the individual's
interpretation. This is because the complexity of many traumas means

that there will inevitably be wide variety in the nature of individuals' exposure to the same event. A flood, a fire, an accident, or a shooting can produce numerous quite different types of experiences depending on the precise location and expectation of each person involved. And the requirement that the event involve a "threat to life or of physical injury" will in some cases be a matter of judgment. With a street mugging, for example, whether the mugger is armed and dangerous may be ambiguous.

A few studies have begun to look at the question of whether experiencing intense fear, helplessness, or horror at the time of a trauma is associated with later PTSD, as the DSM-IV suggests. For example, Bernice Andrews, Suzanna Rose, and I recently showed a strong relationship between each of these specific reactions in victims of violent crime and the risk of PTSD six months later.[16] Of those victims who did not go on to develop PTSD, 44 percent reported at least one of these emotions at an intense level, compared with 89 percent of those who did develop PTSD. Both in our study and in other studies, however, a small number of those who developed PTSD did not report experiencing any of these emotions intensely. It is likely that some events are over too quickly, or that some victims are too numb at the time to feel intense emotions. This criterion is a very useful marker for an event that confers a high risk of PTSD, but it would appear too restrictive to demand that these reactions are essential if the diagnosis is to be given.

A Skeptic might rightly claim that more intense stressors centered on experiencing or witnessing threats of death or injury could equally well increase the risk of other disorders and that there is nothing unique about their relation to PTSD. Indeed, this might be inferred from the high levels of comorbidity reported in the previous chapter. Very few studies have actually examined this question, but one of them was conducted by Naomi Breslau and Glenn Davis on a sample of Vietnam veterans who were psychiatric inpatients at a Veterans Administration hospital.[17] They found that two risk factors, participation in atrocities and cumulative exposure to combat stressors, conferred a specific risk for PTSD but were unrelated to the onset of panic, major depression, or mania. On the other hand, Richard Mayou and colleagues recently found that after a motor vehicle accident, phobic travel anxiety, general anxiety, and PTSD were all equally common and often occurred together.[18] The three types of disorder all tended to be predicted by the same risk factors, but phobia was more strongly related to the type of accident, having previous lower confidence as a passenger, having previous emotional problems, and finding the accident frightening, whereas PTSD and general anxiety were more strongly related to high levels of rumination and negative interpretations of intrusive recollections. More studies of this kind are needed to support the claim of a specific link between extreme stress and PTSD.

At Risk Before a Trauma

As physicians have believed since the nineteenth century, there is compelling evidence that some people are already at greater risk for PTSD before a trauma has even happened. These risk factors are shown in Figure 3.1. As is the case for other disorders such as depression, greater risk is attached to being female[19] and coming from a socially less advantageous background. There are also a number of interrelated risk factors involving having experienced previous trauma, abuse in childhood, or other childhood adversity; having had a previous psychiatric history; and coming from a family with psychiatric problems. At present, there are numerous explanations for these findings and uncertainty about whether they should be interpreted as showing the effects of a vulnerability that is psychological or biological or both. For example, it could be the case that there is a genetically based family risk of psychiatric disorder.[20] Disorder in parents could be associated both with a greater likelihood of their children experiencing social adversity and with a greater genetic risk of disorder in their children. Alternatively, parental disorder could be responsible for a greater risk of social adversity in children, which in turn makes them more sensitive (either biologically or psychologically) to the effects of further traumas in adulthood.

One intriguing and controversial risk factor shown in Figure 3.1 is low intelligence. To date, the only studies to have examined this factor are military studies conducted in the United States, in some of which soldiers' intelligence was assessed before they were sent to Vietnam.[21] The fact that these precombat intelligence scores predicted later PTSD rules out the possibility that they were simply a consequence of a soldier developing the disorder. Intelligence is influenced by many of the factors previously discussed, such as childhood adversity and social disadvantage, so it is far from clear that intelligence is a risk factor in its own right, or whether some specific aspect of intelligence is important.

Recently, researchers have found evidence that one particular aspect of intelligence in which people differ, working memory capacity, may be involved in suppressing unwanted items in memory that otherwise intrude into consciousness. Working memory capacity has been defined as an ability to sustain, divide, and switch attention among different tasks, and one way of measuring it is to find out how long a series of words people can remember while at the same time solving simple math problems. Rosen and Engle proposed that working memory capacity also reflects people's capacity to maintain attention in the face of interference or distraction.[22] In their experiments they had participants learn a series of lists of paired associates (pairs of words such as "apple–river") and found that people with a higher working memory capacity had fewer unwanted intrusions of irrelevant words that had been present in previous lists.

Reading this research, I was curious whether higher working memory capacity might also help people to suppress unwanted thoughts in general, a finding that would have interesting implications for PTSD. Daniel Wegner, a cognitive psychologist now at Harvard University, has shown that it is hard to deliberately suppress a specific, fairly meaningless thought (he often uses the example of a white bear). Not only is it difficult to deliberately not think of a white bear, but once suppression is relaxed, thoughts of white bears tend to return more strongly.[23] Anne Beaton and I used one of Wegner's experimental designs, including measures of working memory capacity, fluid intelligence (the ability to problem-solve with unfamiliar material), and crystallized intelligence (a measure reflecting prior knowledge, such as the breadth of a person's vocabulary).[24] As predicted, the results indicated that more effective suppression of thoughts about white bears was independently related to higher working memory capacity and greater fluid intelligence but was unrelated to crystallized intelligence. People with greater working memory capacity seem to be better at suppressing their own obsessional thoughts as well.[25] Although it is too early to make any definitive conclusions, these preliminary studies suggest some reasons why certain aspects of intelligence could be advantageous in protecting people against PTSD.

The results of the meta-analysis also showed that, at least for civilians, a person's age and whether he or she belongs to a minority ethnic or racial group is largely irrelevant to the risk of PTSD. This does not appear to be true in combat and war situations, in which younger age and minority status are risk factors. The vast majority of the relevant studies, however, have been based on Vietnam veterans. In Vietnam, minority soldiers had a greater exposure to combat, and it is striking that once the degree of combat exposure is allowed for, all the ethnic differences disappear. Controlling for trauma exposure also abolishes ethnic differences in risk for PTSD in the few civilian studies in which this has been observed.[26] It is not impossible that the risk associated with younger age in the Vietnam studies could also be the result of factors specific to this conflict.

In sum, numerous risk factors influence the chance of a person developing PTSD before that person has encountered a trauma. However, the magnitude of the effects of each of the factors listed in Figure 3.1 is small. If all these risk factors are interrelated, and have overlapping effects, then the extent of any overall pretrauma risk will also be small. If, on the other hand, the effects of all the risk factors are separate and additive, quite a substantial proportion of the risk of PTSD may be accounted for by aspects of the person who meets with the trauma. This would be contrary to the way in which many mental health professionals have interpreted the spirit of the DSM diagnosis.

At Risk During a Trauma

One of the most important but most mysterious and little understood reactions to trauma is known as *dissociation*. This term refers to any kind of temporary breakdown in what we think of as the relatively continuous, interrelated processes of perceiving the world around us, remembering the past, or having a single identity that links our past with our future.[27] It occurs as a part of "normal" as well as "pathological" experience, for example, daydreaming, losing track of time, or performing an activity such as driving a vehicle while one's attention is else-where. In his diary detailing his experiences treating soldiers in World War I, Charles Myers recognized how frequently dissociation oc-curred: "Typically the immediate result of the 'trauma' is a certain loss of consciousness. But this may vary from a slight, momentary, almost imperceptible dizziness or 'clouding' to profound and lasting uncon-sciousness."[28]

Dissociative experiences such as *derealization* (feeling that things around you look unreal or staged, as in a play) and *depersonalization* (feeling that you yourself are in a daze, numb, unreal, or different from your normal self) are not uncommon, particularly when people are anxious. "Out-of-body" experiences, in which one feels one is floating and looking down on one's own body and what is going on around it may accompany life-threatening illness or injury. Other less common dissociative experiences include repeatedly realizing one is wearing clothes one cannot remember having put on, or finding oneself in a place one cannot remember having traveled to. Rarely, people behave as if they possess more than one complete identity, one of which may be unaware of the actions of the other.

Dissociation is frequently considered as a defensive response that protects a helpless person from overwhelming stress, with more ex-treme dissociative reactions such as the development of separate per-sonalities reflecting repeated threats to a person's integrity, particularly during childhood.[29] Less extreme reactions are commonly reported as occurring during the course of a single stressful or traumatic event. For example, 96 percent of soldiers undergoing survival training reported dissociative symptoms.[30] When these symptoms occur in the course of a traumatic experience, they are referred to as *peritraumatic dissocia-tion*. Table 3.1 shows some of the reactions described in one widely used instrument, the Peritraumatic Dissociative Experiences Scale.[31] The idea that these reactions are protective comes from victims' frequent reports that while they are experiencing derealization or depersonaliza-tion, they cease to feel intense fear or pain. Additionally, whereas heart rate normally increases when a person is threatened, dissociation is linked to a decrease in heart rate.[32]

Although dissociation is thought to be a form of protection while the trauma is ongoing and is related to the severity of the trauma, fear

Table 3.1. Illustrative Items from the Peritraumatic Dissociative
Experiences Scale

- I had moments of losing track of what was going on—I "blanked out" or
  "spaced out" or in some way felt that I was not a part of what was going on.
- My sense of time changed—things seemed to be happening in slow motion.
- What was happening seemed unreal to me, like I was in a dream or watching
  a movie or play.
- There were moments when my sense of my own body seemed distorted or
  changed. I felt disconnected from my own body, or that it was unusually large
  or small.
- I felt disoriented; that is, there were moments when I felt uncertain about
  where I was or what time it was.

Source: Marmar et al., 1997

of death, and feelings of helplessness,[33] it has also been argued that it
increases people's vulnerability to later developing PTSD. The reasons
for this will be discussed in more detail in Chapter 8. For now, it is
enough to note that at least five prospective studies have assessed peritraumatic dissociation shortly after a trauma and found it to be a good
predictor of later PTSD.[34] In addition, Holman and Silver found that
people who reported dissociative reactions during a firestorm were
months later more distressed, "stuck in the past," and unable to make
plans for the future. During the fire, survivors with high levels of dissociation were more likely to rescue personal memorabilia such as
photo albums rather than practical items, which the authors suggested
was because the potential loss of their home from the fire posed a
greater threat to their identity.[35]

There is now a new diagnosis in the DSM-IV, *acute stress disorder,*
which depends heavily on the presence of such distinctive dissociative
symptoms occurring after rather than during a trauma. This new diagnosis was partly introduced because experts were concerned that in the
first month after a traumatic incident the ordinary PTSD symptoms
might simply reflect normal, nonpathological responses to extreme
stress. Acute stress disorder requires a traumatic event similar to that
for PTSD, can be diagnosed only during the first month after the

trauma, and is also complex to assess; but, as was hoped, the new diagnosis does successfully predict the onset of later PTSD.[36] In practice, however, it looks as though there is a very high degree of overlap between those people who qualify for a diagnosis of acute stress disorder and those who would receive a diagnosis of PTSD if this were permitted during the first month.[37] In other words, it is not yet clear whether acute stress disorder is a distinct condition or is simply early PTSD under another name.

Closely related to helplessness is the idea of *mental defeat,* defined by Anke Ehlers as "the perceived loss of all autonomy, a state of giving up in one's own mind all efforts to retain one's identity as a human being with a will of one's own."[38] Ehlers and colleagues made an important distinction between mental defeat and the actions of defeat, such as signing a confession or agreeing to go along with the demands of an attacker, and they noted that the actions of defeat may be accompanied by continuing resistance, mental planning, and an unbroken spirit. In contrast, trauma victims who experience mental defeat may describe themselves as being like an object or as being destroyed, or as ceasing to care whether they live or die. Mental defeat, then, goes beyond mere helplessness in attacking the person's very identity.

Ehlers studied former political prisoners in East Germany, arguing that mental defeat should be particularly relevant to this group because one of the aims of torture is to break the prisoner's will. Even allowing for the degree of torture experienced, former prisoners who still had PTSD years after their imprisonment were characterized by having believed at the time that their life was in danger, having reacted with mental defeat, and believing that imprisonment had brought about a negative and permanent change in their personality or life goals.[39] This research is consistent with other important work on torture victims which indicates that political activists are not as traumatized by the experience as are nonactivists, even though they may be more severely tortured.[40] Activists are likely to expect torture and to be better prepared for it, and are less likely to react with mental defeat.

It is also of interest to note that torture victims may use dissociative reactions to protect themselves against fear and pain, underscoring the close connections between dissociation, helplessness, and mental defeat. In the only prospective study to have investigated both dissociative reactions and mental defeat, the researchers found that the on-set and maintenance of PTSD in victims of physical and sexual assault were predicted by both confusion and mental defeat at the time of the assault.[41] The long-term impact of mental defeat is additionally brought home by the finding that it predicts a poor response to expo-sure treatment for PTSD.[42]

As we saw in the last chapter, there is also intriguing evidence that biological reactions during a trauma may also be risk factors. Although these inevitably have been measured after the trauma is over and the person is receiving hospital treatment, they are measured soon enough to be regarded legitimately as an aspect of the trauma response rather than as a later development. At least two studies have found that trauma survivors who will later develop PTSD have a higher resting heart rate,[43] which may indicate the release of particularly high levels of epinephrine (adrenaline) during the incident. Other studies, as noted above, have linked low levels of cortisol immediately after a trauma to a higher risk of later PTSD.[44]

At Risk After a Trauma

What happens after a trauma has been shown consistently to have the biggest impact on whether a person develops PTSD. Two of these fac-tors are shown in Figure 3.1. The first is subsequent life stress, which will tend to increase levels of arousal and generally exacerbate PTSD symptoms; the second is social support from others, which is linked to fewer symptoms. Because most of the studies of life stress have been retrospective, they are open to the familiar objection that greater symptoms may bias people's reports of the amount of other stress they have encountered. Fortunately, prospective studies have shown effects similar to those of retrospective studies.[45]

Social support is a major factor in determining the outcome of a wide range of psychiatric disorders, and PTSD is no exception. Here again, it could be argued that in retrospective studies patients who are recovering least conclude that the support they have received must have been inadequate. Moreover, symptoms of PTSD such as emo-tional numbing, loss of interest, and irritability are likely to make life difficult for friends and relatives, who are unable to understand why the traumatized person is moody, socially withdrawn, and not recovering more quickly. These symptoms could themselves be a potent reason why social support has not been forthcoming, the more so the longer symptoms continue unabated. Again, prospective studies come to the rescue and show that levels of social support soon after a trauma predict the way symptoms develop over the next few months.[46]

There is another convincing reason to believe that social support affects levels of symptoms rather than the reverse. If symptoms were influencing judgments about support, they should equally affect reports of "negative social support," such as coldness, lack of sympathy, and criticism, and "positive social support," such as warmth and encouragement (but in opposite directions, of course). In fact, the most recent research has consistently come up with the surprising finding that only the presence of negative social support counts, and that positive social support appears relatively unimportant.[47] Among people who have been assaulted, women report more negative social reactions than men, and these negative reactions are more likely to exacerbate their symptoms.[48] Negative reactions from family members seem to stand in the way of recovery when trauma victims are treated for PTSD with psychological therapy.[49]

Negative social responses to traumatized people are part of a well-recognized tendency to blame the victim. Even if victims cannot be blamed for causing the event itself, they can be blamed for being in the wrong place at the wrong time, reacting the wrong way, and failing to put the event behind them quickly enough. Psychologists have suggested that onlookers feel uneasy when they observe a severe event befalling someone else for no reason, as it contradicts common assumptions of personal invulnerability. The only way to preserve intact the belief in invulnerability is to find some way to blame the victim. Whatever the reason, critical and hostile responses from family members are related to a much poorer outcome, not just in PTSD but in a wide range of psychiatric disorders.[50]

What accounts for the undoubted power of these negative social reactions? Previous research with battered women on the receiving end of these reactions has shown that they are strongly related to the women criticizing themselves. Self-criticism, and the associated emotions of guilt and shame, are important risk factors for depression. Our research with victims of violent crime has also found that shame is a powerful predictor of how symptoms develop over time. Shame may be due to a feeling of not having taken effective action to prevent the crime. In our study one man said he felt ashamed "because basically I feel a bit like I can't handle it. Physically I can't defend myself."[51] Another woman expressed shame at looking bad to others: "I feel shame that people didn't help me . . . all those people know me that was outside, makes you feel very embarrassed."[52] Other people felt ashamed of their emotional reactions or of the fact that they had been humiliated in public.

The shame findings are particularly important because they provide the first evidence of a mechanism that can link a pretrauma vulnerability factor, childhood abuse, with a failure to recover from adult traumas. In our study, victims who had been abused as children and victims who felt more shame after being assaulted as adults both tended to recover more slowly. In addition, being abused as a child made victims more likely to report shame. Our data showed that the effect of childhood abuse on recovery was almost wholly conveyed by the experience of shame. This means two things: that in the absence of shame, childhood abuse was no longer a risk factor; and that if shame was present, recovery was worse whether or not childhood abuse had occurred. The findings represent a first step in discovering how a person's background could possibly be related to reactions to a traumatic event occurring many years later.

Another important emotion is anger. For the trauma victim, having to put up with unconcerned perpetrators, insensitive friends and relatives, and interminable legal and compensation procedures is intensely frustrating. Feeling disregarded, blamed, let down, or unfairly treated leads to anger that is sometimes uncontrollable and can burst forth in public places in response to relatively minor degrees of provocation. Afterward, the trauma victim may feel intense shame once again at his or her inability to control the anger. Longitudinal studies show that high levels of anger,[53] and more specifically anger with others,[54] predict a slower recovery from PTSD.

Closely connected to observations about the role of emotions such as shame and anger are observations about the role of beliefs, particularly beliefs about the future and beliefs about symptoms and reactions to the trauma more generally. Some trauma victims may believe that their lives have been irremediably ruined and that they will never have anything to look forward to again. Anke Ehlers and David Clark have described a variety of common negative thoughts about post-trauma symptoms: for example, people may interpret irritability to mean that their personality has changed for the worse, interpret emotional numbing to mean that they will never be able to relate to others again, or interpret flashbacks to mean that they are going mad.[55] A series of studies has found that negative interpretations of the event itself, of subsequent symptoms, and of the future are more frequent in people who react to an assault or a motor vehicle accident by developing PTSD, and particularly in those whose symptoms persist.[56] Prospective studies have shown that people who early on report negative interpretations of symptoms are slower to recover from PTSD.[57]

The final posttrauma factor to be considered is how people choose to cope with their symptoms. Extensive evidence now shows that attempts to suppress unwanted thoughts are usually doomed to failure,[58] and it has been suggested that the deliberate avoidance of intrusive thoughts and memories will similarly be unhelpful for the majority of trauma victims. At this point psychological theory clearly departs from the commonsense view that avoiding thoughts about a trauma is a good thing and will be associated with a better, not a worse, outcome. The theoretical link between greater avoidance and higher symptom levels has in fact been confirmed in a number of retrospective studies of victims of assault and motor vehicle accidents,[59] and prospective studies have shown that avoidance and thought suppression are related to a slower recovery from PTSD.[60]

There is a danger of our losing sight of the traumatic event among this welter of risk factors before, during, and after a trauma. Fortunately, all is not as confusing as it seems. Patterns are emerging that suggest many of these factors are related and may form consistent pathways ending in PTSD. For example, one important pretrauma factor is previous exposure to other extreme stresses. There are now good reasons to think that prolonged early stresses that exceed a child's coping abilities and are associated with early psychiatric problems produce alterations of biological stress systems and a reduced brain volume.[61] Effects on the developing brain may lead to relatively permanent changes in the biological systems involved in responding to stress, including sensitization of the HPA axis.[62] This may produce an adult whose responses to new traumas are more extreme, are possibly more alarming in their own right, and may take longer to extinguish themselves.

In addition, early stress appears to increase the risk of dissociation and the failure of the body to produce adequate levels of cortisol in response to trauma.[63] There is good evidence that early stress also affects many posttrauma risk factors and increases the likelihood of additional upsetting events, negative social support, negative emotions such as shame, and negative beliefs about the self.[64] In turn, these factors are associated with a greater use of avoidance and thought suppression.

Conclusions

The scientific studies of PTSD have led to a number of challenging and unexpected conclusions. Whatever the intention of the original DSM-III diagnosis, there is support for both of two opposing positions. On one hand there is clear evidence that the intensity of a trauma, and the presence of specific event qualities such as threat to life or physical integrity, is related to the likelihood of a person developing the disorder, supporting the idea that PTSD is a response to the intense fear, helplessness, or horror that overwhelming trauma can produce. This must be qualified by noting a minority of instances in which the repetition of harassment and intimidation appears to have led to equally powerful experiences of intense fear and helplessness, and to virtually identical symptoms. On the other hand there is equally clear evidence for the impact of numerous risk factors operating before, during, and after a trauma, supporting the idea that individual characteristics and reactions also influence the likelihood of a person developing PTSD.

A strong possibility, therefore, is that both pretrauma risk factors and the intensity of the traumatic event itself operate through common pathways to increase the risk of later PTSD. There may be several alternative peritraumatic pathways involving dissociation, mental defeat, or increased heart rate. But we do not have to subscribe to nineteenth-century notions of vulnerability as a hereditary or constitutional weakness. Experiencing trauma intensely *may* arise because of innate biological or psychological vulnerabilities, but also because of sensitivities that are a natural result of exposure to excessive previous stress or because of characteristics of the event itself. We might also wonder whether sometimes a different kind of sensitivity results from excessive shielding from more minor stress. Perhaps these different pathways will help to account for the heterogeneous presentation of PTSD noted in the previous chapter. It is plausible that PTSD arising from a single overwhelming event in a person with no previous risk factors will look different to PTSD arising from a relatively minor event in a person who has previously been exposed in a different context to multiple or overwhelming stress events.

The evidence we have reviewed also demonstrates that this debate is in any case too narrow. The existence of potent posttrauma risk factors suggests that some people will develop PTSD in the absence of either preexisting vulnerability or a particularly intense trauma. In this case the presence of negative social support, negative emotions or beliefs about the self, or ineffective coping strategies will block normal recovery. Again, PTSD arising through this pathway may present in a different way. These conclusions do not resolve the question "Is PTSD caused by trauma?" but they suggest that the question be reframed (much less elegantly) as "Will PTSD occur without trauma (defined as present or past experience of intense fear and helplessness)?" To this, we can answer an unequivocal "Most of the time, no."

Our review of risk factors has not yet identified the core psychological process that underpins the disorder, explains the symptoms, and is modified by successful therapy, although it has provided many clues. In fact, there seem to be two such processes, or sets of processes, and below in this book I will argue that recognizing their distinctiveness is critical to clarifying how we think about PTSD. One set of processes is concerned with the traumatic moments themselves, with the element of horror or fright, and with how extreme stress affects the way these events are encoded into memory, stored, and later retrieved. Related to the operation of these processes are arguments about the remembering and forgetting of trauma, which, as we have already noted, have provided fuel for some of the major psychological controversies of the century. The other set of processes involves the impact of a trauma on individuals' lives and highlights the massive readjustments that people often need to make to integrate the traumatic experience into their preexisting views of the world. Essentially, this process is concerned with meaning and identity, and, by considering the wider effect of the trauma and its consequences, it addresses other reactions, such as anger, guilt, and shame, which often accompany PTSD.

4

A Crisis of Identity

My thoughts were frequently occupied by the loss of my humanity. What had I become? What had I descended to as I sat here in my corner? I walked the floor day after day, losing all sense of the man I had been, in half-trances recognizing nothing of myself.

—Brian Keenan, *An Evil Cradling*[1]

A convincing riposte to Skeptics who are suspicious of the PTSD diagnosis must contain some account of why a minority of people do not simply adjust naturally to a trauma and learn to overcome their shock and horror, and why similar traumas can leave one person psychologically weakened while another person appears unaffected. From what we have already discussed, it has become clear that the severity of any traumatic incident is almost impossible to weigh without considering a person's subjective response to it. We also have learned that what happens after the trauma, in the form of negative thoughts, emotions, coping strategies, and changes in the sense of self, has as much, if not more, to do with whether the victim develops PTSD as with what happened during the event itself. In other words, the meaning and impact of the event extends beyond a simple perception of danger or helplessness to a more complex reflection on its wider consequences, on its attendant humiliations, and on what victims' reactions both at the time and afterward say about the kind of person they are. This wider effect of the traumatic event distinguishes PTSD from more circumscribed anxiety disorders such as phobia, where in most cases fear is acquired without an abrupt challenge to more fundamental assumptions and beliefs. In this respect PTSD is more like depression, where the experience of loss, humiliation, entrapment, or betrayal produces intensive rumination on self-identity, relationships, responsibility, blame, and chains of causation.[2] In the same way, traumas tend to lead to intense questioning about "Why me?" with a person continually replaying events and trying to identify whose actions were responsible and why people acted in the way they did.

We have already encountered this focus on the wider meaning of trauma in the context of the Vietnam war, where some people argued that psychiatric casualties would be particularly heavy, not because of the dangers of jungle warfare but because of the fundamentally immoral nature of the conflict. One of the things critics of the war had in mind were the damaging psychological consequences of being involved in any accidental or deliberate mistreatment of civilians. Thus, an implicit distinction was drawn between the *mortal* danger and the *moral* danger in which soldiers might find themselves. As other commentators have noted, Freud also drew attention to soldiers' conflict between their wish to do their duty and their wish to avoid demands that were either *dangerous* or *outrageous to their feelings*.[3]

The same distinction was evident in World War I. British clinicians Myers and Wiltshire, treating servicemen close to the front line in France and trying to avoid their having to be repatriated, tended to focus their treatment on recall of the details of the traumatic moments themselves. Although they were clearly aware of the possible relevance of past events in their patients' lives, they were by necessity limited in what they could hope to achieve. In contrast, other doctors, such as Rivers, whose patients came for extended stays in military hospitals in Britain, had more time to consider the effects of combat on the person as a whole. As Rows commented: "The prolongation of the illness is not always due to dreams and memories of incidents connected with the war. Of equal, or perhaps greater, importance in the longer cases are the memories of experiences in their earlier life with which a strong emotional tone was connected."[4]

Why do such commonplace mental events as self-critical thoughts and painful emotions increase the risk of more permanent disorder after a traumatic event, rather than simply dissipating of their own accord? Why are they often suppressed rather than reflected upon and assessed realistically? Is this connected with the often repeated observations that some people are more psychologically vulnerable to traumatic events because of earlier life experiences? As we have seen, one way of thinking about these questions is in terms of traumatic circumstances shattering deeply held beliefs and assumptions that previously guided a person's actions. According to the psychiatrist Mardi Horowitz, people are motivated to resolve discrepancies between these old beliefs and the new contradictory evidence provided by the trauma, discrepancies that lead to thoughts about the trauma constantly intruding.[5] If the discrepancies are too great to be resolved, the only alternative is deliberate avoidance of the thoughts or emotional numbing, in which the person finds that he or she has become emotionally distant and uninvolved with loved ones.

This influential and intuitively appealing approach has a number of implications that do not seem to be wholly supported by the evidence available. For example, one implication is that people with PTSD will not become truly symptom-free until the discrepancies have been resolved. Although they may cease to be bothered by intrusions, the theory predicts that they will show evidence of avoidance or emotional numbing. It would not be unreasonable to expect that there would be signs of emotional arousal as well, such as problems with sleep or concentration. On the other hand, once resolution is attained, the PTSD symptoms should disappear for good. In fact, the evidence suggests that in some people PTSD is a recurrent disorder, disappearing and then reappearing when a person experiences major life changes or meets powerful reminders of the trauma, or occurring for the first time long after the trauma.[6] No studies have yet looked at whether avoidance, numbing, and arousal symptoms are always present in the intervals when people have been successful at putting an unresolved trauma out of their minds.

Another implication is that people with the most positive experiences in life, who should therefore hold the most positive assumptions, would be the ones most affected by traumatic events. In fact the opposite is the case, with experience of previous trauma (particularly childhood trauma) being a major risk factor for a person developing PTSD. This is puzzling, because we would expect people who have already been traumatized to have lost at least some of their protective illusions about the world. In discussing this point, Ronnie Janoff-Bulman suggested two possible resolutions.[7] The first was that people with the most positive assumptions have the greatest initial distress but recover more easily. This has never been investigated and would be surprising, if true. In general, people who experience most distress at one point in time are also likely to experience more distress later. Her other suggestion was that previous trauma would be a risk factor to the extent that the victim had not reestablished a stable and secure inner world. This is plausible but introduces a quite new idea, namely, that trauma does not have to shatter illusions when they have been shattered already. If this is the case, how are we to conceive of this inner world that harbors psychological vulnerability?

The traditional view of therapists who treat PTSD with cognitive therapy is that this inner world consists of conditional beliefs and assumptions that have been created by past experience and about which a person may be more or less aware. For example, a truck driver who was often ill as a child may believe that he is weak if he does not shake off his posttraumatic symptoms after his truck crashes and return to work immediately. A police officer who was brought up to have excessively high standards may believe that it must have been her fault if she injured a suspect during an arrest, even when she believed she was in physical danger.

Despite the success of the cognitive approach, the psychiatrist Patrick Bracken has criticized it as being excessively individualistic.[8] According to Bracken, it places too much emphasis on meaning as something produced solely by an individual's own mind, and as involving distortions to be corrected by one-to-one therapy. He suggests that in reality, responses to trauma are heavily influenced by social and cultural expectations, dynamics, and customs, and he gives the example that rates of mental disorders and suicide are rarely elevated when one country is at war with another. This suggests that the effects of even extreme stress can sometimes be modulated by a societal context emphasizing the need for people to make sacrifices to defeat a common enemy. In addition to this social and cultural perspective, we have seen that the interpersonal context, particularly in the form of negative social support, has a powerful effect on both the development of and recovery from PTSD.

Although negative thoughts and beliefs are much in evidence after trauma, it is possible that they are often a reflection of some deeper, underlying process. As the quotation from Brian Keenan that opens this chapter illustrates, experiences such as mental defeat, with its obliteration of a sense of personal agency, seem to describe a more fundamental assault on what it is to *be* a person, rather than just on what that person is made to think. It is also striking that survivors of trauma frequently experience a sense of disconnection and alienation from their families and friends, lose their trust in other people and institutions, comment that they will never be the same person again, and report dramatic shifts in their fundamental values and reasons for living.[9] These observations offer an important clue that trauma does not just affect beliefs but also identity. In contrast to the sometimes more individual focus of beliefs, identity involves locating a person's place in his or her social world.

Self and Identity

Cognitive therapists treating severe and long-lasting psychological problems have come to think that cognitive vulnerability is more than just a set of conditional negative assumptions and involves more complex structures in memory, produced by repeated negative experiences, that help to shape the interpretation of ongoing events. Several leading therapists have called these mental structures *schemas*. When schemas are activated, people automatically attend to information that is consistent with the schema and tend to ignore what is inconsistent or unexpected. Although the schema concept is of considerable practical value, and makes sense to many therapists and their clients, the term does not tend to be used precisely or consistently. For example, it may refer both to an underlying cognitive structure in memory and to specific kinds of content, such as "I'm worthless."[10] Christine Padesky described schemas as core beliefs that were rigid, held to be absolutely true, and associated with strong emotion.[11] She emphasized the importance in therapy of identifying positive schemas that could be strengthened at the same time that maladaptive schemas were weakened. For Padesky, however, positive schemas seem to be different in kind as well as in content, as she proposes that they are generally not rigid and held with such absolute conviction.

Another influential cognitive therapist, Jeffrey Young, described sixteen "early maladaptive schemas," including emotional deprivation, abandonment/loss, mistrust, social isolation, incompetence, shame/embarrassment, and unrelenting standards, and explicitly located the source of these schemas in patterns of social interaction, especially with caregivers.[12] These experiences are thought to produce learned patterns of thinking about and relating to others, patterns that may be more or less accessible to conscious awareness. Like negative thoughts, these constellations of feelings and actions tend to become prominent when someone encounters a situation that is similar to the one that originally helped to form the schema.

As Young noted, the schema concept represents a convenient clinical shorthand rather than being a properly defined and measurable construct. His list of schemas is highly heterogeneous, some of them being defined in terms of beliefs, others in terms of behavior patterns, and still others in terms of emotions such as fear and shame. There is controversy over whether the content of schemas can necessarily be put into words or whether they consist of more complex emotional responses and action tendencies that are only approximately described by verbal labels such as "abandonment" and "deprivation."[13] Little evidence that schemas do correspond to an organized body of knowledge in long-term memory has been offered,[14] and there is uncertainty about whether schemas can be directly modified or whether therapists should regard negative and positive schemas as fixed and instead aim to alter the balance between them. Finally, there has been little discussion about how schemas are related to a person's overall identity and whether schemas can develop through repeated observation or imagination or whether they are invariably based on direct experience.

An alternative approach that has many similarities with the notion of schemas but is more strongly rooted in basic social psychological research is explicitly concerned with identity. Many influential psychologists now think that a person's identity does not consist of a single unitary "self" but rather of a collection of multiple "selves" that are experienced at different times and in different contexts.[15] These overlapping ways in which we experience our own identity correspond to a set of related structures in long-term memory that contain some constant features of the self but also contain information relating to the self at specific ages and in the performance of specific roles. So there might be selves in memory corresponding to how we felt looking after a baby brother, being disobedient, pleasing and disappointing our parents, playing netball or soccer, and so on.

Other selves that have been suggested include "ought" or "ideal" selves that reflect how we have been socialized to take on moral standards and aspirations, and a "feared" or "undesired" self that reflects characteristics we have been socialized to avoid.[16] Strauman and Higgins presented evidence that emotions are reflected in discrepancies between self-representations.[17] For example, anxiety is related to the existence of large discrepancies between the person we think we actually are (selfish, perhaps) and the person we think we ought to be (self-sacrificing), whereas depression is related to discrepancies between the person we think we actually are (looked down on, perhaps) and the person we think we would ideally be (admired). Strauman showed that presenting subjects with words corresponding to their individual self-discrepancies produced negative emotional states, affected immunological functioning, and aided the retrieval of specific negative childhood memories.[18] Looking at the discrepancy from the opposite perspective, other researchers suggest that both anxiety and depression are strongly related to feeling too close to a feared or undesired self and striving to avoid experiencing it.[19]

In this way of looking at the self, past experiences create both positive selves in which there are feelings such as security, pleasure, relatedness to others, and positive achievement, and negative selves in which there are feelings such as fear, abandonment, anger, helplessness, guilt, and shame. Importantly, these selves do not have to have been directly experienced but may be brought about by observation and learning. For example, ideal selves may be created by a person's wish to emulate people who appear to be exceptionally heroic, successful, self-sacrificing, or morally uplifting role models. Likewise, undesired selves may be created by a person's wish to avoid becoming like people who are observed to be exceptionally miserable, unsuccessful, selfish, or destructive. Not infrequently, parents provide the models for these ideal or feared selves.

Generally, people are motivated to inhabit positive selves and to avoid negative selves. Depending on upbringing, some of these selves will be more strongly established, and linked to much more powerful and persistent emotions, than others. Being brought up by parents who encouraged independence while providing a secure emotional base, for example, might strengthen a "competent" or "optimistic" self, whereas parents who lived up to their own high moral standards might help to create a correspondingly inspiring ideal self. In contrast, rejecting parents might strengthen an "abandoned" self, whereas feckless parents who failed to provide for their family might help to create an undesired self to be avoided at all costs. In one of the few studies to have tested these ideas, being the victim of physical violence at home was shown to relate to young adults seeing large discrepancies between the kind of person they believed themselves to be and the kind they thought they ought to be.[20]

The advantage of the notion of multiple selves over a unitary self is that it can cope better with the sheer complexity of experience, whether lived, witnessed, or learned about. No childhood is wholly good or bad, and nobody grows up without some unpleasant experiences. Even in a generally loving and supportive family, a child may experience areas of inappropriate criticism, demands for achievement or emotional support that are beyond the child's capacity, or repeated instances in which parents' behavior fails to live up to the standards they insist on for their children. Equally, within families where parenting is consistently overcontrolling, harsh, or insensitive, a child is likely to have positive experiences to look back on. Even children who have been severely abused may grow up to have happy and fulfilled lives as adults, given the right circumstances. These facts of life make it more likely that everybody has both positive and negative selves that reflect the often contradictory nature of experience. What is perhaps unique about the self is the potential for inconsistency among alternative selves. This is particularly likely when a person's experience has been inconsistent and he or she has had no opportunity to make sense of it. One of the most common legacies of a "difficult" childhood is that bad feelings and bad experiences are not deliberately reflected upon and put into a more general perspective but rather tend to be suppressed and ignored.

According to this approach, the self that we as adults experience at any moment depends on a number of factors. Perhaps the most important is context, which may include where we are, who we are with, and what we are doing. Some selves will be more accessible because they are in more common use. Other selves may be experienced less often, triggered by illness, mood changes, and events that are unexpected, delightful, or unwanted. As we have seen, even single words can trigger marked mental and physical changes. For example, the word *brave* might produce a strong reaction in a person with a self experienced as cowardly and shameful.

The implication is that traumatic events may have a number of quite unexpected consequences. In some people they may contradict positive, optimistic selves by the confrontation with death or disaster. In others they may trigger an unexpected "competent self" that rises to the occasion. In still others they may trigger an undesired or feared self in which the person feels overwhelmingly weak, inadequate, or alone. We therefore can think of trauma as having the potential to unleash two related processes, the threatening of positive selves (similar to the shattering of assumptions) and the unexpected endorsement of unwanted selves. Positive selves may include highly valued roles as a sporting hero, a loved partner, a devoted parent, a high achiever, a desirable lover, a moral person. Injury, disfigurement, the destruction of property, or the death of others may be seen as destroying these roles and the possibility of ever inhabiting again these desired selves. Vulnerability will arise from two main sources: the investment of identity in a single positive self whose apparent removal leaves the victim bereft of his or her major source of personal meaning and gratification, and the existence of unwanted or feared selves for which the traumatic event may appear to provide compelling evidence.

As in depression, the protracted rumination that often follows trauma can be seen as being associated with these two related consequences for identity. First, have positive selves been lost forever, or can they be revived and what will be necessary to revive them? Loss of a positive self leads to the question of who is responsible for the enormous pain involved and who will make restitution? This may be accompanied by a form of "positive" rumination about life before the trauma, involving mentally undoing mistakes, obtaining justice, and punishing wrongdoers. The implicit aim of this positive rumination is the construction of a more neutral, less painful version of the event in which some awkward facts or unwanted emotions are excluded, and which will enable a person to reinhabit a familiar positive self. Second, does the trauma provide evidence for unwanted or feared selves? In this case trauma victims may have already made up their minds that they are in some important sense responsible even if this seems unreasonable to the outside world. "Negative" rumination driven by the conviction that they themselves are to blame because of something about their person is extremely unpleasant and will likely motivate avoidance and thought suppression.

These responses may be related to two common forms of posttrauma distortion, which Patricia Resick and Monica Schnicke have called *overassimilation* and *overaccommodation*.[21] Overassimilation refers to some victims' attempts to distort what happened so that the event does not contradict prior beliefs, for example, a woman raped by a male friend or work colleague who tells herself that it isn't really a rape but some sort of mistake or misunderstanding. One way of conceiving this denial or minimization of the event would be in terms of her preserving a positive identity in which she could rely both on her judgment of other people and on people who know her not to betray her. Overaccommodation, an opposite response, refers to a person abandoning preexisting beliefs and basing predictions about the future on the new information the trauma provides. For example, an assault victim may conclude that everyone on the street is a potential mugger and that he is constantly in danger. This may reflect the existence of a previous negative identity in which he felt powerless and at the mercy of others hostile to him.

Placing the focus on identity and emphasizing the creative, constructive processes involved in overcoming trauma deals well with some of the objections that were raised earlier to the theory of shattered assumptions. Rather than a series of single states in which these assumptions first existed, then were shattered, and finally had to be rebuilt, we can see people as inhabiting a variety of possibly contradictory selves at different times. Because these selves are responsive to context, mood, and so forth, many trauma victims will be able to influence their current felt identity. By changing their habits, where they work and live, whom they see, how they travel, and, most importantly, what aspects of the trauma they choose to think about, they can exercise considerable control over which selves they experience, even without any explicit attempt to repair damaged positive selves or to challenge the reality of negative selves. Therefore, it is not unexpected that symptoms of PTSD will come and go over time as circumstances change and trauma reminders are met or avoided. More obviously, the focus on identity offers a persuasive explanation for why previous trauma is a risk factor for PTSD despite the likelihood that positive illusions have already been shattered.

Vulnerable Identities

Mick Power and I recently proposed that psychological distress is usually related to a set of seven core themes, which occur alone or more often in combination: the Self as powerless, the Self as inferior, the Self as nonexistent, the Self as futureless, the Other as abandoning, the Other as betraying, and the Other as hostile.[22] Although this is far from being an exhaustive list, these themes repeatedly emerge from everyday events and interactions that are universally experienced to some degree or other. Everyone has felt powerless and been betrayed, sometimes in minor ways that have made little mark but at other times in major ways that have permanently affected identity in the form of recognizable feared or undesired selves that are accompanied by persistent negative thoughts and upsetting emotions. In contrast to the more individualistic focus implied by placing negative thoughts at the core of people's difficulties, the themes emphasize that as social beings our identity depends closely on relationships with others. Traumatic events have the power not just to make us have negative thoughts but to threaten our very sense of self, a more profound response that is frequently encountered not only in PTSD but in other disorders such as depression that occur in response to adversity.

The Self as Powerless

The most predictable description given by a person with PTSD is that he or she felt helpless or powerless (see the sidebar for some typical examples related to each core theme). Frequently, this is expressed as the conviction that death is unavoidable. Helplessness is reported both by PTSD sufferers who are themselves direct victims and by those who

Examples of Core Themes Given by People with PTSD

Experiencing the Self as Powerless

- I was paralyzed with fright.
- I could see the car coming toward me on the wrong side of the road, and I knew there was nothing I could do.
- I felt like I was an observer watching what was happening to me.
- Time seemed to stand still as I waited for him to stab me.
- I felt crushed by his weight so that I was small and insignificant.
- I just stood there and watched as he died in front of my eyes.

Experiencing the Self as Inferior

- If only I wasn't such a careless person, this would never have happened.
- I must be stupid not to have recognized that those men were following me and to have gotten out of the car.
- It's my own fault for being gullible; I should never have agreed to go to his house.
- It's been months since the attack, and I'm still not over it—what's wrong with me?
- I'm just the kind of person other people feel they can take advantage of.

Experiencing the Self as Nonexistent or Futureless

- It's as though the crash destroyed my personality as well as my body.
- During the attack I felt that I had ceased to exist as a person.
- Now that I've lost the use of my legs, there is no reason to carry on.

- Now I just live from day to day.
- My life is ruined for good.

Experiencing the Other as Abandoning

- I just felt all alone.
- I was surrounded by people, but none of them cared what would happen to me.
- I couldn't bear the thought that I would never see my family again.
- After he raped me, he just left me to die.

Experiencing the Other as Hostile and Betraying

- I just felt he hated me and wanted me to suffer.
- She won't be satisfied until she's destroyed my career and turned everyone against me.
- He was the one person I always thought I could rely on.
- She was supposed to look after me but instead she just used me.
- The hospital has done everything it could to cover up the mistake and pretend nothing went wrong.

Experiencing the Self More Positively

- Having lived through this has actually made me feel stronger as a person.
- I enjoy spending time with my family in a way I never used to do.
- Every day I wake up feeling grateful I'm alive.
- Compared with before, I try to make more of a contribution and to do more things I regard as really important.
- For the first time in my life I appreciate my good fortune.

only witness trauma happening to others. In some cases there are physical causes. One of the most potentially terrifying diseases is the neurological condition Guillain-Barré syndrome, in which patients may rapidly become paralyzed and unable to communicate or even breathe without assistance. During this time, any belief that they might die is exacerbated by their complete inability to take action, communicate their concern, or obtain reassurance. But even healthy people experience helplessness as involuntary, a paralysis that involves the will as well as the muscles.

Among other things, powerlessness undermines a positive identity of being competent to act to protect oneself and others. The common illusion of being in control of events, to which most people are susceptible, for once cannot be sustained and may prove hard for a trauma victim to regain, particularly when the trauma is prolonged. Abduction and imprisonment may be accompanied by numerous acts that are not only brutal and degrading but deliberately emphasize the complete inability of captives to influence their situation. It can be an awesome and sometimes impossible challenge for a person to rebuild a positive identity after prolonged traumas involving physical, and particularly sexual, torture that the person wants above all to forget.[23]

In addition, powerlessness may reevoke an undesired helpless self who, for example, was previously unable to prevent illness, violence, or intimidation. Not uncommonly, a helpless self develops because of a person's inability to protect himself or herself from abuse or to protect a mother or siblings from a violent father. In a recent study comparing people with PTSD and depression, Martina Reynolds and I found significantly more helplessness and a significantly greater history of childhood physical abuse in the group with PTSD.[24]

The Self as Inferior

Powerlessness is often linked to two forms of experienced inferiority associated with the emotions guilt and shame. Powerlessness and guilt occur with the omission of acts that trauma survivors believe they ought to have performed and that may have prevented harm coming to others. Accident victims, for example, may feel guilty for not having made greater attempts to anticipate what was going to happen, to issue a warning, or to rescue others after the event. They may reproach themselves for "freezing" and being temporarily unable to act, even though this is often part of what we think of as being "in shock." Even in shipping disasters, passengers who attribute the bad things that happened during the sinking to themselves and their actions have more symptoms of PTSD.[25] In the same way, Freud's identification of soldiers' conflict between following orders and carrying out acts outrageous to their feelings may also reflect the coming together of powerlessness and guilt.

Guilt unmixed with powerlessness may result from causing death or injury by a needless assault, dangerous driving, giving the wrong drugs, botching a surgical procedure, or a hundred other ways. Whether or not guilt is mixed with powerlessness, it is an emotion that reflects the undermining of a previous positive self. Having acted in a way that has harmed others may fatally damage people's ability to see themselves as caring, responsible members of society. The need to rebuild this positive self may lead to an urgent desire to be punished and to make restitution to the person who has been harmed. In some countries, the making of financial compensation to victims and their families is recognized in the penal code and taken into account when perpetrators are sentenced.

Survivor guilt may reflect a determined but futile search on the part of trauma survivors for reasons why they lived when others died. Faced with a catastrophe that demands an answer, and failing to come up with any adequate explanation, survivors may conclude that they should have died and are now living because of some kind of mistake. The more a dead person was valued, the less justification survivors feel for their continued existence and the more likely they are to believe that they have in some way let down or betrayed that person by not taking his or her place. This reaction will probably be exacerbated by any preexisting feelings of inferiority or unworthiness, which will cast events in an even more unjust light. The psychiatrist Jonathan Shay has given a moving account of survivor guilt in combat veterans. Combat, he notes, calls forth a passion of care among men who fight beside each other that is comparable to the earliest and most deeply felt family relationships.[26]

A traumatic event sometimes leads to intense shame. In contrast to guilt, which comes about when harm has been caused or might have been caused to others, shame reflects undesired *thoughts, impulses, actions,* or *characteristics* that are experienced as inferior or unworthy and that must be concealed in order to forestall rejection by others.[27] Observers may be puzzled by victims' degree of self-reproach for actions that seem only too reasonable and for their difficulty in taking the extremity of the circumstances into account. Often, a preexisting tendency to overly high standards and an unrelenting self-criticism function in order to help people avoid the discomfort of inhabiting an inferior self. This strategy may previously have worked reasonably well, and even led to high levels of achievement, but it is insufficiently flexible to be adjusted to the reality of the trauma. The trauma is experienced as a personal failure and acts as a prompt that reinstates the undesired self and causes victims to ruminate on other perceived deficiencies.

Other clues to the existence of an undesired inferior self are often encountered in how people react to the occurrence of posttraumatic symptoms. As we have seen in previous chapters, Rows drew attention to soldiers' fear of their symptoms, and Ehlers and Clark developed a more systematic model that described numerous ways in which normal reactions both during and after a trauma may be interpreted in a negative way.[28] From the identity perspective, these negative interpretations may reflect either the undermining of a positive, competent self by unexpected physical and mental reactions that are not understood, or the threat of an earlier undesired self being reinstated that is experienced as inferior because it is seen as being "weak."

At risk sometimes are the very people who have spent their lives avoiding an undesired "weak" self by taking responsibility for others and shrugging off more minor adversities in the belief that stress can easily be overcome with sufficient determination and courage. Ironically, their past resilience may have created similar expectations in others who have come to rely on them and are unwilling to accept that they in their turn may need support and looking after. Typically, this group will return to work as quickly as possible after a traumatic event and make few allowances for their own reactions. They may even take on additional responsibilities, for example, by caring for or negotiating on behalf of others who were affected by the traumatic event. Eventually, they become exhausted and are unable to suppress their symptoms any longer.

For this group their symptoms are a source of shame because they evoke an undesired self that is felt to be inadequate. As we saw in the last chapter, this inadequate self may also be reexperienced because of actions taken during the trauma or because of perceived powerlessness to defend themselves or their loved ones. Shame produces particular problems because people have a natural urge to conceal what has happened not only from themselves (through avoidance) but from therapists who are trying to help.[29] Deborah Lee and colleagues described the treatment of a woman who had been followed and harassed for two years before her stalker tried to murder her. Before the attack she had been well-adjusted and successful:

> Rose was very reluctant to talk about what had happened to her. . . . She suffered from intense feelings of shame when she thought about the attack, and these feelings pervaded throughout her everyday existence. . . . Assessment of Rose's childhood revealed that her mother had been very critical of her behavior and appearance. . . . Consequently, as a result of these childhood experiences, Rose developed core beliefs about herself as inadequate, unlovable, ugly and vulnerable to being picked on because of these attributes. . . . Every time she thought about the attack, she saw it as confirming evidence that she was deeply unlovable, ugly and had traits that others wanted to attack.[30]

The Self as Nonexistent or Futureless

This loss of identity may be thought of as a fatal undermining of a previous positive self that provided a sense of meaning and purpose. Shay noted that a common utterance of the combat veterans he treated was "I died in Vietnam" and that most viewed themselves as already dead at some point in their combat service, often after a close friend was killed.[31] Loss of identity is also sometimes described after a robbery, rape, or abduction in which the attacker treated victims as though they, or their survival, were of no consequence. It may be part of the state of mental defeat encountered in the last chapter—a condition that goes beyond powerlessness to encompass a total surrender of one-self and one's rights and expectations as a human being. To experience such a loss of identity is likely to enter an intensely disturbing state for which most people are entirely unprepared.

Describing his captivity by fundamentalist militia in Lebanon, Brian Keenan wrote: "I am full with nothing. . . . I have been lifted up and emptied out. I am a bag of flesh and scrape, a heap of offal tossed unwanted in the corner of this filthy room. Even the filth here has more life, more significance, than I have."[32] Yet something remains, even in extremis: "Many times I think of death, pray for it, look for it, chase after its rapturous kiss. But I have come to the point of such nothingness that even death cannot be. I have no more weeping. All the host of emotions that make a man are no longer part of me. They have gone from me. But something moves in this empty place. A pro-found sense of longing, not loneliness, simply longing."[33]

Being unable to see any personal future, a symptom of PTSD, may arise when events appear to invalidate positive identities. Trau-matic injuries, burns, or debilitating disease can lay waste cherished dreams of sporting success, love, or family life. Traumatic bereave-ments destroy loving and intimate relationships into which a person may have invested many years and that may have been the repository of most future hopes and plans. As we saw in the last chapter, apprais-ing the trauma as having caused permanent damage is strongly associ-ated with long-lasting PTSD symptoms.

The response to such catastrophic losses takes us to the limits of human understanding. Many who have been affected neither expect nor want to "get over" them and would feel insulted by the suggestion that their feelings might or should diminish with time. Arguably, it is not for mental health professionals to make glib judgments about the pain of bereavement. In some cases patients will admit to not wanting their intrusive memories of loved ones to go away in case it signified that the loved ones were no longer important.

Where professionals are perhaps on stronger ground is when re-actions to loss fail to abate after many months and continue, in the suf-ferers' own judgments, to interfere with their lives. The person who has single-mindedly invested the most time and effort in the dead person, lost activity, or abandoned dream may be the one who is least able to adapt to the loss by taking on or even imagining an alternative positive identity. Whether or not he or she should do so will never be anything but a very personal decision, and one that is likely to have a big impact on whether PTSD symptoms are resolved. Professionals can assist, if they are allowed to, by pointing out the danger of becoming locked in a ruminative cycle of anger with others, however justified the anger may be. The evidence is clear that anger with others is likely to retard, not expedite, recovery. Professionals can also help in identifying conflicting feelings about a dead person that are hindering even a slow and gentle disengagement from intense, painful absorption with his or her memory.

The Other as Abandoning

The state of feeling abandoned and unloved by someone else is usually associated with depression, yet little research has explicitly addressed abandonment in the context of PTSD. Abandonment is, however, frequently accompanied by anger and, as we have seen, this *is* known to be a prominent feature of PTSD. Inquiry into what was experienced at the moments when trauma survivors faced death sometimes reveals that thoughts of being alone or abandoned by God are prominent. They are times when people may have poignant thoughts of loved ones from whom they are estranged and with whom death will forever prevent them from being reconciled. Likewise, these moments may bring thoughts of the trauma victim abandoning others, just as he or she was abandoned earlier in life.

These feelings of estrangement and isolation may extend to the immediate posttrauma period when the person who has caused the injury has run off without thought for the survivor's welfare, when survivors are injured and waiting for help to arrive, when they are surrounded by people who cannot rescue them because they are trapped inside a vehicle or building, or when they are in a hospital waiting to be treated. Another common complaint is that survivors feel alone because nobody understands their symptoms or why they are taking so long to recover, and because they are faced with impossible bureaucratic hurdles in order to obtain justice or compensation. The lack of what they may regard as the support that is their right reinforces feelings of being abandoned, not just when the event happened but in its aftermath as well. Perhaps the sense of abandonment is related to the longing Brian Keenan described in his cell in Beirut.

The Other as Hostile and Betraying

PTSD often occurs after traumatic events that involve the actions of other people, whether these are related to war, accidents, assaults, or disasters that have a human origin. In part this is because such events challenge those aspects of our identity that depend on relationships with others, and on our right to be valued and treated with consideration. Encountering evidence that we are not valued, even by strangers, is unsettling, as minor everyday incidents of discourtesy in the supermarket or the parking lot readily demonstrate. This is another source of the anger that so commonly accompanies PTSD.

Direct hostile intent is only too evident in assaults and robberies, and even more so in cases of persistent harassment, intimidation, bullying, and stalking. These experiences do not bring with them just fear about possible injury but raise more profound questions for victims about why they were selected. Even confident people with no prominent undesired selves corresponding to the status of "weakling" or "outsider" may come to feel that they are somehow "marked" as potential victims or that other people can identify something about them deserving of scorn and attack.

In contrast, indirect hostile intent arises in motor vehicle accidents, medical blunders, or disasters of human origin where rules may have been broken, safety procedures ignored, and negligence or carelessness displayed. These events also have the potential to be highly disturbing as they undermine basic trust in other people and institutions. Basic trust is necessary to our belief that we can safely cross the street, drive through a set of green lights, buy food, eat in a restaurant, and any of hundreds of everyday activities. Once this trust is disturbed and we question the benevolence of those on whom we rely to be safe, our relationship with others becomes a perpetual source of danger.

The degree of betrayal depends on the extent of any relationship of trust or obligation. Arguably, individual drivers have some duty of care to other road users even though they do not know them personally, and a failure to obey the rules of the road, for example, by drinking and driving, will be experienced with anger as a betrayal of sorts. But betrayal is most acute when there is a personal relationship or an institutional obligation to provide care. The most obvious case is that of incest, which often has serious psychological consequences.[34] A lesser degree of betrayal, being let down in a crisis by a partner, leads to increased risk of depression,[35] and as discussed in the last chapter, PTSD is made worse when someone looks for support from people who criticize instead of comfort. Being betrayed by an institution that has a duty to safeguard ordinary citizens, such as a hospital, motor vehicle manufacturer, or railway company, typically produces intense anger and determination to identify who is responsible. In the context of a relationship of trust and obligation, trauma due to direct hostility or negligence intensifies victims' perceptions that they are disregarded and therefore of little value. Only too often this experience of being disregarded is compounded by frustrating encounters with legal representatives, courts, insurance companies, and others to whom victims turn in the aftermath of a trauma.

Jonathan Shay commented on the extent to which modern warfare involves a high dependence on others to provide intelligence, effective weapons, and logistical and artillery support, as well as to issue orders and to follow procedures that will reduce the risk of unnecessary casualties. This produces multiple opportunities for soldiers to feel betrayed by their own side, whether because of being issued weapons that failed, being hit with "friendly fire," being sent on ill-advised or morally repugnant missions, or being exposed to levels of risk that are disproportionate when compared with other unit members. Incompetence, negligence, or favoritism can make the difference between life and death. Shay concluded from his work with Vietnam veterans that "moral injury" involving betrayal of "what's right" was a critical aspect of long-lasting combat trauma, resulting in rage, a paranoid attitude to the world, and a comprehensive destruction of social trust.

Rebuilding a Positive Identity

Many trauma survivors would be insulted by the suggestion that anything good had come from their experiences and would see this as an attempt to belittle their suffering. It is therefore a source of constant surprise how many survivors are willing to talk about what they have gained and even on occasion to admit that they are glad the event happened to them. As we have seen, traumas may undermine long-established identities and provide opportunities for survivors to radically reappraise their lives. In some cases, previous negative identities will be contradicted by positive information about how the survivor dealt with the unexpected challenge, exceeding his or her own and others' expectations. This may result in an incompetent self being supplanted by a competent one. The compulsory abandonment of cherished plans for the future also brings with it the chance for the survivor to examine those plans more dispassionately at the same time as mourning the loss. In the end, alternative plans and goals may come to be seen as having been more worthwhile all along. Of course, positive change and growth through trauma are quite possible even if the victim started off with a positive self-image.

Identity reconstruction is most often found in three areas.[36] One is an increased importance to survivors of their relationships with friends and family. Survivors may look back to a pretrauma life in which they had less time for relationships and valued them less. The trauma may have brought with it not only an enforced end to a crowded or workaholic lifestyle but a renewed appreciation for the unique role family plays during a crisis. Survivors may rediscover intense pleasure in ordinary relationships and find their lives richer and more fulfilling. The personal experience of severe suffering may bring them closer emotionally to others, for whom they may now feel an empathy that was formerly lacking.

Survivors may also devote themselves to campaigning or charitable causes. Some set up telephone help lines to provide support to other victims who have endured similar experiences. In Britain in 1986 Diana Lamplugh responded to the abduction and presumed murder of her daughter Suzy by creating the Suzy Lamplugh Trust, which aims to enable people to live safer lives by providing practical personal safety advice. Faced with such developments as an increase in violent street crime and assaults on teachers, nurses, and public servants in the workplace, the trust has developed into a large national organization and has achieved international recognition for campaigning, publishing literature on safety, and organizing practical training.

The third area is an increased involvement with religious and spiritual issues. Confronted with a collapse in existing beliefs about human justice and fairness, trauma victims may seek reassurance about underlying order and meaning through organizations such as established churches. They may come to welcome the opportunity to adapt their priorities and give more time and thought to their purpose in life, their involvement with the community, and their relationship with God. Alternatively, a previous faith in God may come to be fatally undermined by a victim's experiences.

The possibility of positive change is summed up well in Judith Herman's *Trauma and Recovery,* one of the most insightful books on severe traumatization, particularly through child abuse: "The survivor who has accomplished her recovery faces life with few illusions but often with gratitude. Her view of life may be tragic, but for that very reason she has learned to cherish laughter. . . . Having encountered evil, she knows how to cling to what is good. Having encountered the fear of death, she knows how to celebrate life."[37]

Conclusions

In this chapter we have seen that in some cases traumatic events prompt an intense questioning that leads to a dramatic shift in beliefs about oneself and one's relationship to other people. This process is not specific to PTSD but is also typical of depression, another disorder that may follow severe misfortune and that often accompanies PTSD. Although this questioning will occasionally lead to positive change, when the trauma is followed by depression or PTSD, it probably will have led to distressing conclusions that are accompanied by negative thoughts and emotions. The response to the Skeptics' argument that negative thoughts and emotions are perfectly normal after trauma is that they are problematic when they do not resolve of their own accord and are the focus of protracted rumination. Why they persist is not yet fully clear, but there are numerous important clues that what is happening is not just at the level of thoughts and emotions, although these are often what is most accessible, but involves wider notions of identity and a person's sense of belonging in a social world.

In PTSD, thoughts and emotions do not simply resolve themselves, I have suggested, when they interact in one of two ways with individual identity. The undermining of positive selves by feelings of powerlessness, guilt, or emptiness is not corrected either because of the sheer extent of the assault on the person's identity through prolonged maltreatment or because of an absence of alternative positive selves that can eventually take their place. Likewise, the experience of abandonment, weakness, and shame is not corrected because it is supported by existing negative selves that appear to provide confirmation for this way of seeing the event and its aftermath. Seven overlapping core themes express the most common aspects of identity that traumatic events call into question.

This approach to identity rejects the simple idea of a monolithic structure that is flattened by trauma and has to be rebuilt. Identity may instead be thought of as more akin to an area of sand dunes that stands in the path of a tornado. When the tornado has passed, the configuration of the dunes will be different, with some being larger and others smaller than they were before. The contours of the ground below will help to determine which dunes have withstood the blast and which have shifted. The changes may be subtle, and it will take some time to assess all the ways in which the area has changed. While it will never be possible to restore the dunes exactly to the way they were before, there are opportunities to rebuild dunes that have been moved or destroyed and to level sand that has accumulated in unwanted places.

Are we saying that in explaining psychological disorder the impact of meaning or identity is as important as that of physical factors such as the degree of injury and of biological factors such as posttrauma heart rate and cortisol levels? Is it possible that subjective interpretation can have a causal influence on the development of disorder and, if so, how does it bring this about? Derek Bolton and Jonathan Hill have pointed out in their book *Mind, Meaning, and Mental Disorder* that human beings are genetically and culturally programmed to pursue basic goals such as satisfying the desire for food, shelter and sex; creating intimate, nurturing, and cooperative relationships; and minimizing threat.[38] A person's belief that events threaten to frustrate the achievement of these goals, or have destroyed any hope of their being achieved, will be sufficient to activate a range of biological reactions that are innate responses to physical and social threat, and to loss.

This underscores the point that the biological changes associated with all psychiatric disorders should not necessarily be taken to mean that there is some specific underlying pathology. These changes may instead reflect how essentially intact systems are responding to seemingly insuperable obstacles that are impeding them in the present or have impeded them in the past from attaining their goals. For example, some of the psychological and biological changes that we associate with depression could arise from someone's perception that because a person he or she loved had died in a car crash, he or she would never again have an intimate, trusting relationship.

We noted in the last chapter, however, that the biological changes we associate with PTSD are not the same as those in depression. As well as considering the impact of changes to identity, we need to consider other ways in which the event was perceived at the time and how the person appraised the possibility of severe injury or death. We also need to explain why the person with PTSD is likely to vividly reexperience the event in the present when confronted with reminders of it and remains constantly in a state of vigilance and high arousal even though the event is long past. Issues of identity are unhelpful in accounting for these seemingly automatic, uncontrollable responses that have little to do with deliberation and meaning-making. Instead, we need to examine what is known about the immediate experience of fear, helplessness, and horror, and what effect such situations have on our memories.

5

The Puzzle of Emotional Memory

Horrible experience creates permanent mental pictures. Vivid ones. Moving pictures. At Chowchilla the kids talked of their memories with such remarkable detail that they sounded "painterly" at times. The memory of trauma is shot with higher intensity light than is ordinary memory. And the film doesn't seem to disintegrate with the half-life of ordinary film. Only the best lenses are used, lenses that will pick up every last detail, every line, every wrinkle, every fleck. There is more detail picked up during traumatic events than one would expect from the naked eye under ordinary circumstances.

—Lenore Terr, *Too Scared to Cry*[1]

We remember events that have an impact on us. Even something as inconsequential as encountering unexpected rudeness on a shopping expedition, for instance, may often result in a repeated memory coming to mind for several hours afterward, as we replay what was said, why it was said, and how we responded and muse on how we would have liked to respond, whether with the ferocity of a Hulk Hogan or the graceful wit of an Oscar Wilde. Everybody knows that momentous events are preserved in memory, often in great detail, and often for years. Is this myth or scientific fact?

Somewhat surprisingly, the scientific answer is that the arousal of emotion, particularly extreme emotion, has dramatically contradictory effects on the functioning of memory. Numerous studies have found that emotion makes memory worse, while just as many studies have found exactly the opposite. Understanding the relation between emotion and memory is one of the major challenges presently facing the scientific community. It is also of considerable practical importance. One domain where this question is of more than academic interest is in the evaluation of eyewitness testimony given in court. Not uncommonly, the guilt or innocence of a defendant is decided by the memory of what a single witness saw for a few fleeting moments when in a state of fear or shock. If justice is to be done, it may be critical to understand whether that witness's memory is likely to be more or less accurate, or whether the reliability of his or her report is unaffected by emotional state.

Emotion Makes Memory Better

Studies of *flashbulb memory* have provided some of the most striking evidence for the role of emotion in the formation of vivid and persistent memories. In the first and most famous systematic investigation of this phenomenon, participants were asked what they remembered about the circumstances in which they first learned of the death of President John F. Kennedy and of other well-known historical figures. James Kulik, one of the investigators, described his own memory: "I was seated in a sixth-grade music class, and over the intercom I was told that the president had been shot. At first, everyone just looked at each other. Then the class started yelling, and the music teacher tried to calm everyone down. About ten minutes later I heard over the intercom that Kennedy had died and that everyone should return to their homeroom. I remember that when I got to my homeroom my teacher was crying and everyone was standing in a state of shock. They told us to go home."[2]

Information that tended to be recalled included where participants were, what they were doing, who the informant was, their own and the informant's emotional reaction, and the aftermath. Brown and Kulik named these "flashbulb memories" on the basis that they possessed "a primary, 'live' quality that is almost perceptual. Indeed, it is very like a photograph that indiscriminately preserves the scene in which each of us found himself when the flashbulb was fired."[3] At the same time, Brown and Kulik were clear that this was an imperfect analogy because flashbulb memories did not record all details indiscriminately and were usually far from complete.

What kinds of events might lead to the formation of a flashbulb memory? Brown and Kulik originally suggested that the three main (and interrelated) characteristics were surprise, level of emotion, and "consequentiality," by which they meant that the event had a lot of direct or indirect consequences for the person, or, put in another way, it had to be personally important. In support of this, they found that more black than white North Americans had flashbulb memories for the assassination of Dr. Martin Luther King. Few subsequent tests of these ideas have assessed all three of Brown and Kulik's characteristics, or have ensured that the public event had sufficient impact to generate a large number of flashbulb memories. One exception was a study by David Pillemer, who found that the majority of his participants had flashbulb memories for the attempted assassination of President Ronald Reagan and that these memories tended to be highly stable over time.[4] Ratings of consequentiality or impact were low in the sample, but participants did report moderate levels of emotion and surprise, and both of these factors were related to flashbulb memory formation.

Investigations of other public events, such as the assassination of Swedish Prime Minister Olof Palme, the nuclear accident at Chernobyl, and the loss of the space shuttle *Challenger*, have confirmed that memory for the circumstances in which someone learned about important, emotion-arousing events tends to be persistent and associated with vivid visual images.[5] But one of the limitations of these studies is that investigators are totally dependent on their respondents' accounts and have no means of confirming what people say they remember. By collecting memories of the *Challenger* explosion shortly after the event and then following respondents up to check on their recall a year or two later, Neisser and Harsch showed that a minority of apparent flashbulb memories, even ones in which respondents had high confidence, turned out to be inconsistent.[6] Neisser also suggested that memories for these public events might be long-lasting because participants had often talked about them with others (that is, rehearsed them) rather than because of the way they were encoded at the time of the event.[7]

Discussing these criticisms, Brewer argued that most of the errors found by Neisser and Harsch were probably not complete fabrications but had more to do with a confusion between the first exposure and subsequent exposures to the news.[8] Rather than recalling the first time they heard about an event, respondents might be reporting a genuine flashbulb memory for a second or third hearing. This explanation does not seem very convincing if *surprise* is the key factor in flashbulb formation because only the first reception of the news would meet this criterion. It seems much more plausible, however, if *importance* or *emotion* is the key factor, since these reactions are likely to last longer and thus could result in the formation of several flashbulb memories. Is it the case that these events are memorable only because people talk about them more? To date, studies have found little evidence to support Neisser's rehearsal hypothesis.[9]

In one of the most detailed studies of its type, Martin Conway and colleagues investigated the formation of flashbulb memories after the resignation of British Prime Minister Margaret Thatcher in 1990.[10] More than 85 percent of a U.K. sample reported flashbulb memories compared with 28 percent of a non-U.K. (largely North American) sample. In contrast to the non-flashbulb memories, which tended to decay over time and were prone to reconstructive errors, most of the U.K. participants' descriptions of their flashbulb memories collected eleven months after the event corresponded exactly to their descriptions given two weeks after the resignation. Their reports showed full and accurate recall of the circumstances in which they received the news and often included idiosyncratic details. The researchers noted that the actual words participants used were not the same, suggesting that participants were not recalling their previous description but rather a memory of the actual reception event. Flashbulb memory formation was strongly associated with the level of importance attached to the event and with participants' emotional response to the news.

Brown and Kulik had suggested that their findings could be accounted for by a special type of memory system that was brought into play when a person encountered a surprising, consequential, and emotion-arousing event. Unlike an ordinary memory, which is quickly forgotten, the memory record created by the event remained fixed for a long period of time. They speculated that the memory was not of a verbal or narrative form but might consist of an image. Subsequent research has indicated that people frequently report vivid memories, but these only rarely concern public events and are often lacking in any element of surprise or consequentiality.[11] Vivid memories are much more likely to concern events that are personally important and that are associated with strong emotions. This suggests that flashbulb memories should be regarded as a particular type of emotional memory rather than as a special class of memory in their own right.

David Pillemer described numerous examples of emotional memories in his book *Momentous Events, Vivid Memories.*[12] Many of them were negative, but he also provided many instances of positive events leading to vivid, lasting recollections. Some of them involved a romantic attraction, or the first encounter with a person who would prove to be an important influence, or a flash of insight, or a turning point in a person's life. Sometimes the significance of the event became apparent only later. Pillemer argued that these memories of specific events were almost invariably emotion-laden and personally important, and he drew attention to the frequent descriptions of sensory images that accompanied them. Like Brown and Kulik, he had for some time been convinced of the existence of two separate memory systems, writing that one system "is present from birth and operational throughout life. . . . The memories are expressed through images, behaviors or emotions. [A second memory system] emerges during the preschool years. . . . Event representations entering the higher-order system are actively thought about or mentally processed and thus are encoded in narrative form."[13]

One of Pillemer's most intriguing observations was that people describing frightening experiences often shift spontaneously into the present tense without realizing what they are doing. He gave this example from an interview with Robert Krueger, the U.S. ambassador to Burundi in 1995, telling how he and his security officer, Chris Riley, were ambushed:

> We heard this "Pop, pop, pop, pop, pop, pop, pop, pop, pop." All of a sudden Chris *says,* "Jesus, it's gunfire." And I *look* and I *see* the dirt kicking up all around us, and I *see* the windows shatter, the car in front of me, I *look* around and I *see* Larry Semme, the security officer in the—in the Toyota following me, in a Land Cruiser, with his long frame, and I can *see* the bullets hitting his car and the windows shatter

there, and then I *see* his long frame lean out with a pistol, and he *returns* fire to up above, and meanwhile, Chris has said, "Back up Eddie." He *backs* up. We're so close to the car in front of us that we *have* to back up to get around, and there's so little room to get around that we *side-swipe* all the way down. The car that was close in front of us had two dead and three wounded. The car behind me had ten bullets through it. Ours—ours had only one.[14]

Pillemer suggested that in describing terrifying events like these, people experience an upswell of perceptual imagery, so that they are no longer simply recounting an episode but are effectively reliving some salient aspect of it, causing them to spontaneously fall into the present tense.

Emotion Makes Memory Worse

To other psychologists the idea that emotion would improve memory appeared unlikely. They argued that because emotion leads to a narrowing of attention, it could not lead to more detailed memories.[15] Other theorists have seen emotion as having a disruptive effect on mental processing in general and on memory in particular. Students of eyewitness testimony have addressed this question in several different ways. One of the most common is to present experimental participants with two versions of a film or series of pictures. In one version the pictures contain an emotion-arousing scene (such as someone being hit by a car on a pedestrian crossing) while the other is similar except that this scene is replaced by a neutral scene (such as someone being helped over the crossing). Recall for details of the two series of pictures is then compared. In a study titled "Mental Shock Can Produce Retrograde Amnesia," Loftus and Burns presented their participants with two versions of a film depicting a bank robbery, one of which ended with a fifteen-second sequence in which a young boy was shot in the head.[16] Recall was tested with a series of twenty-five questions and was found to be worse overall in the violent version of the film. In particular, there was significantly worse recall of a critical item about the number on a football jersey of a boy playing in a parking lot.

By the end of the 1980s, impressed with evidence of this kind, more than three-quarters of a sample of sixty-three experts on eyewitness testimony agreed that the evidence favored the idea that very high levels of stress would impair the accuracy of memory.[17] Moreover, 71 percent of the experts agreed that the statement "very high levels of stress impair the accuracy of eyewitness testimony" was sufficiently reliable to offer as evidence in court. The majority were firmly of the opinion that witnesses would have more difficulty remembering violent than nonviolent events. Support for this view has been obtained from studies of actual crime victims. One investigation compared the ability of victims of different types of crime varying in severity to provide descriptions to the police. Robbery victims were able to provide more detailed accounts than rape and assault victims, and uninjured victims provided more details than injured victims, whatever the crime.[18]

In studying real life, researchers are faced with two difficult problems. One is that events are likely to differ enormously, both in the details of what happened and in the mental state of the victim and the way he or she interprets the event. The other problem is to know what the right point of comparison is for the memory of the emotional event. Mary Koss and colleagues addressed this by surveying a large sample of women and asking them whether they had ever experienced rape or attempted rape.[19] Those who did not report such an experience were asked to select another intense experience and to classify it as either positive or negative. All participants then rated the quality of their memories for the selected event. Koss found that rape memories, compared with other unpleasant memories, were rated as being less clear and vivid, less likely to occur in a meaningful order, less well-remembered, and less thought and talked about. Although this is one of the best studies in the area, there is some uncertainty about how to interpret the results. For example, we do not know whether the length of time that had elapsed since the rapes was the same as the length of time elapsed since the other unpleasant events. It is also possible that respondents who selected alternative unpleasant events did so on the basis of having very vivid and clear memories of them, which would have biased their responses. The argument is that Koss and colleagues were comparing memories that differed not only in their content but also in whether they had been freely chosen from among a number of experiences. This problem could have been circumvented by comparing rape memories with memories of a second event, such as doing badly at an exam, that had also been specified in advance. Nevertheless, Koss's results are consistent with some of the other findings above in challenging the notion that traumatic events are invariably well-remembered.

Another of the few systematic studies in this area assessed memory in a sample of recent, non-treatment-seeking rape victims.[20] Two weeks after a rape, approximately two-thirds of women had a clear memory of the event while one-third had difficulty remembering at least a few aspects of it. About 10 percent of the sample said that they were unable to recall many or most aspects of the event. Ten weeks later 82 percent reported a clear memory, and none of the original 10 percent with problematic recall were still having problems remembering the event. The researchers noted that the initial amnesia for the event was not due to victims having a greater level of symptoms overall, to their having consumed more alcohol, or to their having general memory problems for events other than the rape. Rather, there appeared to be a specific problem in remembering the rape that improved over time.

Two Complications

Science has made a certain amount of headway in accounting for these seemingly contradictory findings. Investigations of memory for real-life events have repeatedly confirmed that the detailed information directly associated with highly emotional or traumatic events is very well-retained over time. Laboratory studies have indicated that high-arousal and low-arousal events are remembered equally well at short retention intervals but that memory for high-arousal events increases over time and is superior once time has been allowed to pass since the experiment. A persuasive case was made by the Swedish psychologist Sven-Åke Christianson that the effect of increased arousal on eyewitness testimony is to increase the accuracy of recall for the central aspects of the event that has been witnessed, while simultaneously decreasing accuracy for its peripheral aspects.[21] Critical objects such as a gun or knife being used in a robbery tend to attract attention, a phenomenon called *weapon focusing*, so that while they are well-remembered, recall of other aspects of the situation may suffer. In studies where ordinary people are asked to recall their most traumatic event, they typically report remembering more central than peripheral details, with greater emotion being related to better recall of the former.[22]

From this sort of finding we can conclude that the accuracy of recall may be both good and bad, depending on what it is that is to be remembered. High levels of emotion may result in a narrowing of attention so that less detail is encoded into memory in the first place. On the other hand, the details that are encoded seem to be remembered particularly well. At first sight, this makes it rather surprising that people seem to recall so well the circumstances in which they heard of surprising news events, since such details are usually incidental and unlikely to be a central aspect of the event. But the definition of a flashbulb memory does not require people to remember everything about the circumstances, and it is sufficient for a single detail, such as who else was present in the room, to be recalled clearly. Even these memories, as Brown and Kulik noted, are typically incomplete.

Most of these studies also assume that the effects of stress are consistent and simply differ in degree, so that the more potent the stressor, the better (or worse) the memory. But for most of the twentieth century, psychologists have been aware of the fact that the relation between arousal and performance on a task often takes the form of an inverted U, so that performance tends to be best at moderate levels of arousal and worse at very high and very low levels of arousal. This is called the Yerkes-Dodson law.[23] Stress and arousal are concepts that overlap to a considerable degree, and contemporary psychologists have also noted that the relation between stress and memory performance may take the form of the inverted U.[24] Essentially, the study of stress requires an understanding of the biological processes that may affect memory functioning and how these change as levels of stress increase. This will be discussed in more detail in the next chapter; for now, it is enough to bear in mind that the effects of moderate stress may be opposite to the effects of extreme stress.

One of the difficulties in studying emotion and memory, it is clear, is to know how much stress a person has experienced and therefore what effects to anticipate. It is difficult to quantify the effect on people of learning about a traumatic event (such as an assassination) that has happened to someone else whom they did not know personally. However, it is likely that most studies with nonclinical samples (other than the rape studies) have only been concerned with the effects of moderate levels of stress. Only a minority of participants who describe "their most traumatic event" actually describe an experience that would meet the DSM-IV criterion for a traumatic stressor.[25] It would be dangerous to assume, therefore, that these studies can tell us much about PTSD. People with PTSD, on the other hand, provide a valuable benchmark by virtue of the high-magnitude events they have usually suffered in person and the continuing high levels of emotional impact. More than that, people with PTSD sometimes demonstrate memory phenomena that are very rarely seen in the laboratory. In this respect, PTSD may hold the key to our understanding of emotion and memory.

Memory and PTSD

The puzzling contradictions that have been encountered in the nonclinical studies are equally present in the literature on PTSD. If anything, the contrast between two opposing processes, one working to make memory better and one to make it worse, is even more evident.

For example, the DSM-IV describes PTSD as characterized by high-frequency, distressing, intrusive memories that individuals are unable to forget and make great efforts to prevent coming to mind. Child psychiatrist Lenore Terr has written movingly about the children she interviewed and treated after the Chowchilla bus kidnapping in 1976, and it is her description of their memories that opens this chapter. Trauma experts such as Bessel van der Kolk have noted that some aspects of traumatic events seem to become fixed in the mind, unaltered by the passage of time. In their survey of traumatized patients, he and Rita Fisler described traumatic memories as containing prominent perceptual features such as visual images, sounds, smells, and bodily sensations. They were typically fragmented, with the fragments being exceptionally clear and vivid and accompanied by intense waves of feeling.[26] Another leading researcher, Roger Pitman, has theorized that stress hormones released in response to a trauma lead to an over-consolidation of memory for the experience, demonstrated in the form of strong conditioned fear reactions as well as intrusive recollections and reexperiencing symptoms.[27]

But another of the DSM-IV criteria for PTSD is amnesia for the details of the event. Patients typically remember that the traumatic event happened but describe blanks or periods during which their memory for the details of the event is vague and unclear. Writers on trauma such as Terr, Herman, and van der Kolk all acknowledge that confusion and forgetting are as typical of trauma memories as is the vivid, lasting recall. More systematic studies of patients' memories of personally experienced traumatic events confirm that the memories do not invariably remain unaltered over the passage of time[28] and that they tend to be disorganized and contain gaps.[29] During psychotherapy it is common for patients to say that these details are returning to them and that they now recall numerous aspects of the event that they had forgotten. The most dramatic examples of memory loss occur when patients describe complete amnesia for the fact that the event occurred in the first place, followed by recovery of memory. These experiences, which are usually explained in Freudian terms (as a result of repression) or through disturbances to ordinary consciousness (for example, dissociation), are discussed in detail in Chapter 7.

How should we make sense of these contradictory findings? The first step is to distinguish clearly between two different types of memory, which have variously been called ordinary or narrative memories on one hand and traumatic memories, reliving experiences, or flashbacks on the other. As we have seen in Chapter 2, this distinction was made by Janet at the beginning of the twentieth century and has since been revisited by several contemporary trauma researchers.[30] To avoid confusion, we will continue to use the term *traumatic memory* to refer to *any* memory that relates to a traumatic event, rather than in this narrower sense, and will contrast ordinary or narrative memories with *reliving experiences* or *flashbacks*.

Unless they have been rendered unconscious during a traumatic incident, people with PTSD have ordinary autobiographical memories about the event, just as they do about all the other episodes involving school life, growing up, friendships, and so on, that make up their personal history. These memories reflect what a person can consciously recall about the event and contain those details that they attended to sufficiently to store in long-term memory. They are the basis for thinking, planning, and communicating. The trauma will usually be followed by intense, prolonged thinking as the victim replays and tries to establish the exact sequence of events, imagines alternative outcomes, evaluates people's actions, and assigns blame. At some point, planning will be required to deal with the short-term or long-term consequences of the trauma, which may range from the trivial to the overwhelming. Communication will almost always be necessary, with the level of detail varied according to the demands of the situation. Thus the amount of detail will tend to be low when a person is informing casual acquaintances, higher when giving information for a police or legal report, and higher still when talking to family and close friends, depending on the need to disclose and the willingness of other people to listen.

All of these activities depend on the availability of conscious memories of the trauma that can be called up as required and related to preexisting beliefs, plans, and aspirations. They may be deliberately brought into awareness or may be brought into awareness involuntarily ("triggered") by external reminders of the trauma, or by words, thoughts, and images related to the trauma. Like other autobiographical memories, they do not remain static over time. One reason is that each time they are recalled, people automatically create a new memory for that act of remembering to add to the original memory. If during each act of remembering certain parts of the memory receive a lot of attention and other parts are ignored, the ignored parts will become harder and harder to retrieve and the contents of the available memories will gradually change. For example, a young man who is assaulted in a bar may selectively focus on his attacker's aggression and the fact that he was hit first while ignoring his own contribution in words and actions to inciting the conflict. The repetition of an edited, "cleaned-up" version for his family and friends, or for the police, may gradually lead to his being unable to gain access to the original memory and becoming totally convinced of the truth of the new, sanitized version.

As we noted in Chapter 1, the characteristic symptoms of PTSD include the experience of *reliving* the traumatic event. Flashbacks are a kind of memory experience that most ordinary people, and most psychologists, rarely, if ever, come across. They differ in numerous ways from what we think of as normal memory. For example, reliving is usually packed with sensory detail, such as vivid visual images, and may include sounds and other sensations; however, these images and sensations are typically disjointed and fragmentary. During flashbacks individuals may reexperience the pain they had from a traumatic injury, even though the injury has long ceased to cause them any discomfort. If, while the trauma occurred, a person was very cold, reliving may be accompanied by changes in temperature so that the person feels subjectively very cold, even when he or she is sitting in a warm room. Steph Hellawell, who has conducted extensive research on flashbacks, has recorded people saying that ordinary memories of the trauma are not as "harsh" or "painful" as flashback memories: "Ordinary memories of the trauma are not so harsh on yourself mentally. During flashbacks you get the horror of the whole feel of the thing. Flashbacks are much more colourful. . . . With flashback memories I actually feel similar pain as experienced at the time of the accident. I actually have the same sense of apprehension and shock which I associated with the accident. Ordinary memories of the accident are not as painful as flashback memories."[31]

Flashbacks also involve reliving the emotion experienced during the most intense moments of the traumatic event, in which people may have been paralyzed with terror, with the conviction that they were going to die or with horror and revulsion at what they were seeing. "Reliving" is reflected in a distortion of the sense of time such that the events seem to be happening in the present rather than (as in the case of ordinary memories) belonging to the past: "In flashbacks, there is the feel of blood running through my fingers and the feeling of dampness on my legs. You actually believe the scenes are in front of you at that time and there is a strong taste in your mouth and the feeling that your adrenaline is pumping faster."[32]

Another way in which reliving episodes differ from ordinary autobiographical memories is that they do not seem to occur as a result of a deliberate search of memory, but are always triggered involuntarily by external or internal cues. Rather than individuals searching deliberately through the contents of their memory to see what they remember, flashbacks are like slides that are suddenly flashed up on a screen by an unpredictable projectionist. When people have flashbacks, they can tell what the memory contains by looking at the screen (or in this case the images in their minds), but this is not the same as laboriously re-constructing a segment of the past, such as their movements between 2 p.m. and 3 p.m. the previous Thursday. Flashbacks are usually trig-gered by specific reminders that relate in some way to the circum-stances of the trauma, such as a hospital series on television, the sound of a police siren, or the smell of smoke. They can also be triggered by particular thoughts or images related to the event. As a result, people with PTSD become skilled at avoiding situations likely to trigger flash-backs and often will have found a way to describe their trauma that makes it unlikely they will experience one. For example, they may avoid using certain words (such as "rape") or thinking about the fright-ening moments of the event.

If patients with PTSD are asked by a lawyer or therapist to pro-vide a detailed account of the trauma, reliving will tend to occur, punc-tuating the narrative at one or more places. These reliving episodes are hard to control and are relatively unresponsive to the demands of the social situation. They give the subjective sense of repeating themselves in exactly the same form over and over again, unlike ordinary memo-ries, which as we have seen alter and mutate a little each time they are retrieved.[33] It has been noted that these fixed and unchanging memo-ries (Judith Herman has called them *frozen memories*[34]) may involve sequences of images or "video clips" as well as stationary images.[35] In-terestingly, the standard view of memory in cognitive psychology is that, whatever else memory is, it is "not like a video recorder" that faithfully stores a copy of a pattern of images captured on the retina. The experience of people with PTSD, however, is that this is exactly what their flashbacks are like: "Flashbacks feel like a number of events rolling on to each other. In flashbacks I can pick out everybody, it seems so vivid—I can see details that I am unable to see during my or-dinary memories. . . . While I am having a flashback I try and get my mind to change certain events but they don't change."[36]

Although clinicians and researchers working with traumatized victims routinely describe flashbacks,[37] relatively little research is avail-able to back up the many informal observations. In one of the first sys-tematic studies of flashbacks in PTSD, Martina Reynolds and I wanted to confirm that they were indeed more characteristic of patient samples than of nonpatients who had also been exposed to very stressful events. We interviewed matched groups of nonpatients and patients suffering from either PTSD or depression and asked them about the images or thoughts related to a stressful event that were currently coming most frequently to mind.[38] Flashbacks, either on their own or in combination with other images and thoughts, were reported as most frequent by 43 percent of the PTSD patients, 9 percent of the depressed patients, and none of the nonpatients. Steph Hellawell and I also have found that people with PTSD readily recognize these descriptions of narrative memory and reliving, and if they are asked to provide a detailed written description of their trauma, they can retrospectively distinguish at which points during the writing they did and did not experience reliving.[39]

Despite being unusual phenomena, flashbacks appear to involve a breakdown in the everyday processes responsible for binding together individual sensory features to form a stable object, episodic memory, or action sequence. Insufficient binding means that objects or memories will be fragmented or incomplete. According to one prominent theory, this binding is brought about by a person focusing attention on an object or scene so that the individual features are integrated by virtue of sharing the same location in space.[40] During traumatic events, attention tends to be restricted and focused on the main source of danger, so that sensory elements from the wider scene will be less effectively bound together. Laboratory research has shown that such unattended patterns or events, providing they are sufficiently novel, produce long-lasting memory traces whose existence can be detected even though they cannot be deliberately retrieved.[41] A distinct possibility is that flashbacks involve the automatic activation of these memory traces of unattended aspects of the trauma scene.

Conclusions

New studies comparing people's memory for traumatic and positive events continue to appear, some finding that traumatic memories are recalled better and others finding that they are recalled worse.[42] The most realistic conclusion appears to be that emotional memories are better *and* worse remembered. As events begin to increase in emotional intensity, central details are retained for longer, often in the form of a visual image, and peripheral details are worse recalled. But there seems to be a point at which the intensity of the emotion interferes with the clarity of recall, with the result that memories become fragmented and disorganized. These observations are an important part of the puzzle, but they do not really explain how memories for the same extreme trauma can both be exceptionally clear and have important gaps in the same individual. Similarly, trauma researchers have wondered how a memory may at some times be consciously represented and experienced with little feeling, whereas at other times the same memory may evoke pangs of searing emotion.[43] The reader may have guessed that the answer lies in the distinction between ordinary memories and flashbacks. In the next chapter I will discuss how different theories explain these two types of memory and examine the biological processes associated with extreme stress that will begin to provide the answers we are seeking.

6

Trauma, Memory, and the Brain

Every street lamp that I pass
Beats like a fatalistic drum,
And through the spaces of the dark
Midnight shakes the memory
As a madman shakes a dead geranium.
—T. S. Eliot, "Rhapsody on a Windy Night"[1]

Several attempts have been made at constructing a plausible theory to explain the puzzling features of memory in PTSD. In this chapter we will look at two broad types of theory, one suggesting that information about trauma is coded in a special way in the ordinary memory system and the other suggesting that the information is coded in two different memory systems. Both types of theory do a good job of accounting for some aspects of the disorder, and it is difficult to discriminate between them purely on the basis of clinical observations. Increasingly, scientists interested in memory are trying to develop better theories by understanding what is happening at a neurobiological level in the brain. We will therefore look at some recent advances in the neurobiology of fear and memory that may help us in understanding PTSD.

One Memory or Two?

Single Representation Theories

An influential approach to memory suggests that it can be thought of as a network involving many thousands of nodes with a dense set of interconnections between them. Each node represents a person, an object, a feature such as color or shape, a concept, or an emotion. As the network learns that certain things represented by the nodes tend to go together (such as ham and eggs), the connections between those nodes are strengthened, so that if someone says the word "ham" to a person, the word "eggs" is likely to come to mind. The network can also learn about individual events (such as successfully finding a taxi after a night at the theater). In this case there might be created a structure or representation in memory with interconnections between the nodes representing "theater," "taxi," "darkness," "pouring rain," and "relief." In this theory, the representation consists of the pattern of interconnections between the nodes.

Peter Lang was the first person to apply this notion of an associative network to fear.[2] In trying to explain why people with phobias have such a persistent terror of, for instance, heights or spiders, Lang proposed that a previous frightening experience had created a fear structure in memory consisting of stimulus information about the traumatic event (such as the view of the street from the roof of a skyscraper), response information about emotional and physiological reactions (such as a lurching feeling in the pit of the stomach), and meaning information (such as the sense of being in danger of falling). Meaning information was important in Lang's theory to distinguish situations in which people voluntarily risked danger by climbing a cliff or bungee-jumping and might have similar sensations but without the same degree of threat. He proposed that when someone encountered a situation with matching features or cues (for example, walking across a high bridge with a view similar to that from the top of the skyscraper), the original fear memory would be automatically activated. The structure of the memory would result in the person having the same physiological response and interpreting being on the bridge as threatening.

Several influential theories have been based on a network model of memory.[3] Edna Foa and Barbara Rothbaum have proposed an emotional processing theory and suggested several ways in which a traumatic event leads to a memory structure that is different from one created by an everyday experience. One way involves particularly large numbers of potent stimulus-danger interconnections being formed between the relevant nodes, so that their connections to each other became much stronger than their connections to non-trauma-related nodes. For example, someone who was attacked in an alley would form an association between the "alley" node and the "danger" node that was much stronger than the connections between the "alley" node and nodes associated with other emotions formed when the person had previously walked down alleys in neutral or positive mood states. Now having to walk down an alley would selectively activate the danger structure in memory, causing the person to become afraid (the arousal symptoms of PTSD), to have information in the network enter consciousness (the intrusion symptoms of PTSD), and to attempt to avoid and suppress the intrusions (the avoidance symptoms of PTSD). Foa and Rothbaum also proposed that the memory structure would contain large numbers of response elements, which might be associated with negative evaluations of the self (such as seeing oneself as weak or vulnerable). Another suggestion was based on the observation that the severity of the event frequently disrupts the cognitive processes of attention and memory at the time of the trauma and produces dissociative states such as out-of-body experiences (described in more detail in Chapter 8). They argued that this disruption leads to the formation of a disjointed and fragmented fear structure in memory.

According to Foa and Rothbaum successful resolution of the trauma occurs by integrating the information in the fear network with the person's already existing memory structures, a process that is made difficult by the high levels of both emotion and fragmentation. Rather than being in an alley activating only the fear structure, the strength of the interconnections would have to be reduced so that other non-threatening representations of being an alley could also be activated and no one representation would dominate. Such integration requires, first, the activation of the fear network so that it becomes accessible for modification. This is brought about by techniques that reevoke the fear, such as having the person vividly imagine the event or visit the scene of the trauma. Second, information that is incompatible with the fear network must be incorporated into it so that the overall memory structure is modified. This information basically involves associating the traumatic scene, either in imagination or in reality, with low levels of fear. How this is achieved in therapy is discussed in Chapter 9. Finally,

Foa and Rothbaum proposed that if the fragmented trauma memory were to become fully integrated, it would have to be streamlined and reorganized through repeated retelling.

Some evidence in support of these ideas has come from analyses of trauma narratives produced by rape victims at the beginning and end of psychotherapy for their PTSD.[4] The percentage of thoughts and feelings increased over the period of therapy, particularly thoughts reflecting attempts to organize the trauma memory. Although in the sample as a whole the degree of fragmentation in the narrative did not change over this period, where there were reductions in fragmentation these were associated with better treatment outcome. More recently, evidence has been collected supporting the prediction that higher levels of fragmentation in the trauma narrative are related to the occurrence of dissociative responses at the time the event occurred.[5]

Some of the main objections to the associative network approach to emotional disorders are theoretical ones and have been discussed by depression researchers John Teasdale and Phil Barnard.[6] They pointed out that in the original form of the network model, there was only one node for each emotion, so that simply talking about fear, say, would necessarily have the effect of arousing fearful feelings to some degree. The single level of representation also prevents the model from distinguishing between remembering an event in an emotion-laden, "hot" way and remembering it on another occasion in a more detached, "cool" fashion. Nor can it easily explain why some therapy clients completely agree intellectually with their therapist's argument that they are a good person but continue to have a gut feeling that they are a bad person.

A more general problem with the network approach is that it cannot represent knowledge at levels of meaning beyond that of the word or sentence, whereas there is every reason for thinking that the meaning of emotional events tends to be complex, multilayered, and often impossible to capture in words. Other objections to the network approach are more specific to PTSD. It is unclear how network models would explain the special characteristics of flashbacks, such as the exclusively automatic retrieval and the distortion in the sense of time. Even more puzzling, how is it that the same person's trauma memories can at one moment be vague and confused and at other times clear and vivid?

Dual Representation Theories

As we saw in the last chapter, cognitive psychologists have proposed that there are both verbal and perceptual memory systems and that experiencing events with high levels of emotion or importance results in long-lasting, vivid traces being stored in the perceptual memory system.[7] The idea that there is a fundamentally distinct type of memory for traumatic events dates back at least as far as Pierre Janet, the French neurologist who distinguished traumatic memory from ordinary or narrative memory.[8] Janet proposed that extremely frightening experiences might be unable to be assimilated into a person's ordinary beliefs, assumptions, and meaning structures, in which case they would be stored in a different form, "dissociated" from conscious awareness and voluntary control. Traumatic memory was inflexible and fixed, in contrast to narrative memory, which was adaptable to current circumstances; traumatic memory involved a constellation of feelings and bodily reactions, whereas narrative memory consisted of independent elements that did not invariably coexist; traumatic memory was evoked automatically by reminders of the traumatic situation, whereas narrative memory occurred in response to conscious attempts at recollection.

Janet's ideas have been reintroduced to trauma therapists and researchers by Onno van der Hart and Bessel van der Kolk.[9] Lenore Terr came to similar conclusions based on her observations of traumatized children: "Traumatic memory, however, functions differently from the more ordinary kinds of childhood memory . . . traumatic remembrance is far clearer, more detailed, and more long-lasting than is ordinary memory. As with matters of perception, it appears that overwhelming excitation creates a different state of thinking—in the case of memory, a clearer, more detailed picture with little chance of gradual wipeout."[10]

These writers and researchers have identified a different kind of trauma memory system, but on the whole they have not explored how flashbacks and ordinary memories coexist. As we saw in the last chap-

Dual representation model

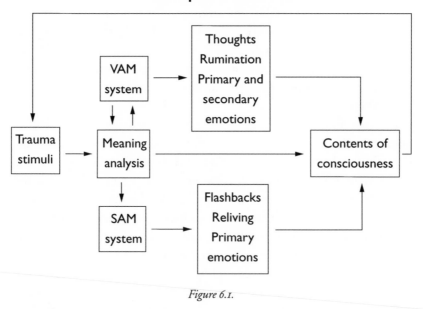

Figure 6.1.

ter, it does not seem to be the case that narrative memory simply stops when the trauma starts and does not resume until it is over. Rather, both the narrative memory system and the special trauma memory system continue to operate alongside each other, but from time to time one may take precedence over the other. The most recent version of a dual representation approach to PTSD attempted to capture this dynamic relationship between the two memory systems and was put forward by Tim Dalgleish, Stephen Joseph, and me in 1996.[11] Our model is shown in diagrammatic form in Figure 6.1. We suggested that narrative memory of a trauma reflects the operation of a *verbally accessible memory* system (or VAM), so called to reflect the fact that the trauma memory is integrated with other autobiographical memories and the fact that it can be deliberately retrieved as and when required. VAM memories of trauma are therefore represented within a complete personal context comprising past, present, and future. They contain information that the individual has attended to before, during, and after the traumatic event and that received sufficient conscious processing to be transferred to a long-term memory store in a form that later can be deliberately retrieved. These memories are available for verbal communication with others, but the amount of information they contain is restricted because they record only what has been consciously attended to. Diversion of attention to the immediate source of threat and the effects of high levels of arousal greatly restrict the volume of information that can be registered during the event itself.

VAM memories are used to evaluate the trauma both at the time it is happening and afterward, as the person considers the consequences and implications of the event and asks himself or herself how it could have been prevented. Thus the emotions that accompany VAM memories are mainly directed at the past (regret about missed opportunities, anger about careless risks taken) or at the future (sadness at the loss of cherished plans, hopelessness at the thought of finding fulfillment). They also include emotions generated by a person retrospectively evaluating what happened at the time. This might involve guilt or shame over a perceived failure to fight back against an attacker or to help other people who were injured. We called these *secondary emotions* because they were not experienced at the time of the trauma itself.

In contrast, we proposed that reliving reflects the operation of a *situationally accessible memory* system (or SAM), so called to reflect the fact that flashbacks are only ever triggered involuntarily by situational reminders of the trauma (encountered either in the external environment or in the internal environment of a person's thoughts). The SAM system contains information that has been obtained from more extensive, lower-level perceptual processing of the traumatic scene, such as sights and sounds that were too briefly apprehended to receive much conscious attention and hence did not become recorded in the VAM system. The SAM system also stores information about the person's bodily response to the trauma, such as changes in heart rate and temperature, flushing, and pain. This results in flashbacks being more detailed and emotion-laden than ordinary memories.

Because the SAM system does not use a verbal code, these memories are difficult to communicate to others and they do not necessarily interact with and get updated by other autobiographical knowledge. For example, a man could have a flashback of being beaten up in a street fight and experience that as happening in the present while knowing that the person beating him up was at that moment sitting in jail. SAM memories can be difficult to control because people cannot always regulate their exposure to sights, sounds, smells, and other cues that act as reminders of the trauma. The emotions that accompany SAM memories are restricted to those that were experienced during the trauma or subsequent moments of intense arousal (what we called *primary emotions*). They mainly consist of fear, helplessness, and horror but may less often include other emotions such as shame.[12] The longer the trauma is drawn out, the more opportunity there is for the person to experience a range of emotions and for these to be coded into a SAM memory.

As shown in Figure 6.1, the different kinds of thoughts and memories all have the potential to become available to consciousness, at which point people can choose whether or not to attend to them. If they do choose to attend to them, the feedback loop at the top of the diagram indicates that they will then become part of the input to the system. This will allow flashbacks generated by the SAM system to be processed by the VAM system, an important mechanism that appears to underlie psychological treatment for flashbacks and is discussed in more detail in Chapter 9.

Essentially, the associative network theories imply that there is a single type of trauma memory that gradually changes over time, either in therapy or as the person makes a normal recovery. In contrast, the dual representation theories predict that two types of trauma memory can be detected in the same individual at the same time. What evidence supports this? Mack and Rock, working with healthy participants, have argued persuasively that only those objects to which attention is voluntarily directed or that capture attention are consciously perceived.[13] Under even ordinary conditions of attentional diversion, people frequently fail to see highly visible but unexpected objects before their eyes, a phenomenon known as *inattentional blindness*. Mack and Rock suggest that these effects are produced both by the conscious diversion of attention elsewhere and by the inhibition of attention to parts of the visual field that are irrelevant to the immediate task. They have shown the equivalent phenomenon in other senses, for example, auditory deafness and tactile insensitivity, and suggest that their results are related to some people's reports of not feeling any pain after a serious injury. Critically, Mack and Rock have also found that the unattended objects or items that are not consciously seen in their experiments are nevertheless encoded and analyzed in considerable detail and can unconsciously affect participants' responses on tests of indirect memory.

These surprising laboratory findings appear to be very relevant to trauma victims, who may report that they simply failed to hear words that were shouted or shots that were fired in close proximity to them. Just like the participants in Mack and Rock's studies, their attention is captured by the immediate source of threat, so that they fail to notice other salient aspects of the trauma scene. The findings are also consistent with the experiments reviewed in the last chapter showing that unattended objects or events can leave long-lasting unconscious memory traces. New evidence suggests that the perceptual features of these unattended objects are recorded in a set of memory stores. Each individual feature, such as color or location, is encoded in parallel in its own limited-capacity store. Information about how features are bound together into a whole is dependent on attention and is recorded in a separate memory system.[14] These results support the idea that information can be encoded in considerable detail even though not consciously perceived at the time, with the result that there can be alternative representations in memory of the same experience that differ significantly in what they contain.

Other experiments address the issue of the kind of information that might make up these alternative representations in memory. It has long been thought that our memory for what we see exists in two forms, one in a perceptual (imagery) code and one in a verbal code.[15] Recent studies are consistent with this view and additionally suggest that the two types of memory can compete or interfere with each other. Jonathan Schooler and colleagues have carried out a number of studies showing that having to verbalize the appearance of a previously seen object or picture makes it harder for a person to distinguish it from similar objects or pictures in a recognition test.[16] More generally, in tasks requiring knowledge that is hard to put into words, having participants verbalize information seems to interfere with their ability to use their perceptual memory of the event, an effect called *verbal overshadowing*.

Steph Hellawell and I have conducted the first study to test the single and dual representation theories specifically with people suffering from PTSD.[17] We decided to begin by seeing whether we could demonstrate that flashbacks and ordinary memories of trauma had different characteristics predicted by the theory. Comparing the two types of memory is not easy to arrange because flashbacks are hard to control and both types of memory may occur close together in time. We therefore decided to describe the difference between the two types of memory to people with PTSD and then have them write a detailed narrative of their traumatic event. At the completion of the narrative we asked them to retrospectively identify periods during which they experienced the two types of memory. There were two reasons to think that this procedure would be effective. First, the writing of a trauma narrative is a recognized part of several types of therapy for PTSD and has been found to elicit detailed memories. Second, ordinary people writing about traumatic events may have episodes during which they appear to spontaneously relive the event.[18] We predicted that flashbacks and ordinary memories identified using these methods would differ in several ways predicted by the theory.

In one part of the study we focused on differences in the words people would use during the two types of memory. We expected that during parts of the narrative involving the experience of reliving they would use more words describing seeing, hearing, smelling, tasting, and other bodily sensations, as well as more verbs and references to motion, reflecting the operation of the perceptually based SAM system. We also expected that the emotions people reported would differ, with more fear, helplessness, horror, and thoughts of death described during the reliving sections and more secondary emotions such as sadness reported during the narrative memory sections.

We found that people had little difficulty discriminating reliving and ordinary memory sections in their narratives. On average, participants wrote for forty minutes, producing around five hundred words during periods of reliving and around three hundred words during periods of ordinary memory. Some had only one reliving section, but it might be very long or very short. Others had numerous reliving sections. There seemed to be no consistency in the number of reliving sections or in where these occurred in the narrative. With the exception of words to do with taste (which occurred too rarely), all the predictions came out as the theory suggested.

We were also curious to see whether reliving and ordinary memory episodes would differ in the extent to which they were associated with physiological changes and spontaneous movements. It has long been thought that vividly imagining something can cause someone to make the movements that would be appropriate if that person were in a real (rather than imaginary) situation. In this case, reliving episodes should be linked to behaviors such as crying out, trembling, clenching fists, freezing, gasping, flushing, and so on. Observations of all of these behaviors were therefore made throughout the narrative task, with the observer being unaware at the time of whether the participant would later classify that period as involving reliving or ordinary memory. Again, as predicted, we found that reliving sections of the narrative were accompanied by significantly more frequent bodily movements, breathing changes, vocalizations, and facial changes such as flushing.

The final part of the study involved the most stringent test of the theory. We reasoned that if reliving experiences are based on a perceptual memory system, then they should interfere with performance on other tasks that also made demands on this system, but not interfere with unrelated tasks. As far as we could tell, no other theory would have any reason to make this prediction. So while participants were writing their narratives, we stopped them on two occasions, once when they were in a reliving phase and once when they were in an ordinary memory phase, and had them carry out two tasks. One task, trail-making, involved using a pencil to connect consecutive letters (a, b, c, etc.) and numbers (1, 2, 3, etc.) that were scattered randomly on a sheet of paper. This task requires visual searching for numbers and letters in a variety of spatial arrangements, and we predicted that it should be particularly badly affected by reliving. The other task involved counting backward in threes, and we did not expect this task to be affected. Needless to say, the participants had absolutely no idea why they were being asked to do these tasks or what kinds of results were expected.

The results showed that trail-making performance was much worse when participants had been halted during a reliving phase of their narrative than when they had been halted during an ordinary memory phase. One possible explanation is that they were more upset during the reliving phases, which would negatively affect all test performance. Our results did not show this, however. Counting backward in threes was adversely affected to an equal extent when participants were halted in the reliving and ordinary memory phases.

In summary, our study offers preliminary evidence that two types of trauma memory exist simultaneously. As predicted by dual representation theory, they differ in the information they contain, in the emotions that are associated with them, in the spontaneous movements and facial changes that accompany them, and in their effect on the performance of related tasks. All this evidence is indirect and in need of confirmation by alternative methods of investigation. At some point, techniques for detecting activity in different brain regions, such as functional magnetic resonance imaging, will almost certainly help to confirm or refute the theory. At this stage, however, it will be very helpful to review what is known about the neurobiology of fear and memory to see whether dual representation theory is plausible, not only psychologically, but anatomically as well. The study of how the brain carries out psychological processes is part of the field called *cognitive neuroscience*.

Cognitive Neuroscience and Fear

Much of our understanding of the brain mechanisms involved in the response to trauma comes from studies of classical conditioning in which animals have been made to fear an initially neutral stimulus such as a green triangle by pairing it with a noxious experience such as an electric shock. This procedure produces conditioned fear reactions to the green triangle that can then be eliminated or extinguished by re-presenting it numerous times without the animal experiencing another shock. In recent years we have come to realize that there was a major error in the way these experiments were interpreted. Initially, scientists thought that extinction was a form of unlearning, in which the strong associations created between the green triangle and shock were systematically weakened. But just as clinicians have frequently noted the return of fear in their patients even after therapy appeared to have successfully eliminated it,[19] it has been found that conditioned fear reactions in animals can be reinstated easily after successful extinction.

One way of reinstating fear is simply to place animals into a different context from the one in which extinction was carried out and to re-present them with the green triangle.[20] The implication scientists have drawn is that during extinction the original associations between the green triangle and shock are not being unlearned. Rather, overcoming fear involves acquiring new learning that can under certain conditions take precedence over the original memories. The animal learns that in the new context the green triangle no longer signals shock, without forgetting that in the original context it did.

What will happen in a completely new context when a green triangle is presented? It will depend on whether this context elicits the original fear memory, in which the green triangle signaled shock, or the more recent memory, in which it was nonthreatening. This in turn is likely to depend on two factors. One is the accessibility of the memories, which is influenced by how often and how recently the memory has been elicited. The second factor is the number of features the new context has in common with the two memories or, to put it another way, whether the new context reminds the person or animal more of one experience than the other. For example, a man who has been repeatedly humiliated in childhood and finds it difficult to stand up for himself as an adult may be systematically trained to be assertive in a variety of social situations. This new learning is likely to remain highly accessible as long as he continues to practice being assertive after therapy has ended and does not encounter situations or people who remind him too strongly of his original humiliations. Unexpected encounters with such people, who might have a similar facial expression or tone of voice or use similar phrases, are likely to lead to the spontaneous return of fear.

Studies of the neuroanatomy of brain systems controlling fear are very illuminating. A key part of the brain is the amygdala, a small area in the temporal lobe adjacent to the hippocampus. The amygdala is responsible for initiating a variety of biologically hard-wired responses to threat, including release of stress hormones, activation of the sympathetic nervous system, and behaviors such as fighting, fleeing, and freezing.[21] Information about threat is conveyed from the sense organs to the amygdala via a number of separate pathways. Studies of rats learning to associate sounds with fearful consequences suggest that there are rapid subcortical pathways involving parts of the brain that are older in evolutionary terms and that involve very few synapses. Relevant information about the sounds signaling threat can reach the amygdala and activate defensive responses extremely quickly. Brain imaging studies with human participants learning to associate pictures of faces with an unpleasant loud noise have similarly suggested that there is a subcortical pathway to the amygdala that processes visual fear-relevant information and can activate defensive responses even when participants are consciously unaware of what is triggering their fear.[22] These subcortical pathways mainly process information at the level of individual perceptual features such as color, shape, or direction of movement.

Studies with rats show that in addition to the subcortical pathways, there are other pathways involving a series of cortical structures, including unimodal sensory cortex, association cortex, and the hippocampus, all of which project independently to the amygdala. These areas of the cortex allow increasingly complex information processing to occur, not just at the level of individual perceptual features but at the level of whole objects or scenes, with integration of information from other senses and the provision of a context in space and time. In evolutionary terms, these parts of the brain are more recent. The pathways involve more synapses and are slower, but they permit a much more complex analysis of what it is in the environment that is most closely associated with the fearful event.

A strong case has been made that the hippocampus is involved in learning about the context in which fear was conditioned. It is not required for the animal to learn the association between the green triangle and shock but is involved in the recording of less central details such as the appearance of the cage, the amount of light, and the position of the animal. This has been demonstrated by examining what animals are able to learn after the hippocampus has been lesioned. The operation appears to disrupt learning about context but leaves intact the simple acquisition of conditioned fear to a stimulus such as a green triangle. In contrast, the hippocampus appears to have an important role in the extinction of conditioned fear.[23] It is likely that this is because the hippocampus is necessary for discrimination between the original context (in which the green triangle signaled shock) and the new context (in which the green triangle is no longer associated with shock).

How does context discrimination prevent the mobilization of fear responses in the presence of a green triangle? It has been proposed that the hippocampus is able to exercise inhibitory control over the amygdala. Encountering a green triangle will now activate both the original learned association between the triangle and shock (for which the hippocampus was not required) and the new (hippocampally dependent) memories that the triangle no longer signals shock. Provided the new learning has been thorough enough, these new memories will take precedence and prevent the amygdala from activating fear responses.

These inhibitory messages may be conveyed either through the direct connections between the hippocampus and amygdala or, more likely, via the projection of the hippocampus to the prefrontal cortex, a large area at the front of the brain variously thought to be the site of executive control, a current sense of self, or the capacity to be aware of one's protracted existence across subjective time.[24] Lesion studies with rats have demonstrated that the nerve fibers connecting the prefrontal cortex to the amygdala are needed for the extinction of fear to occur, and brain imaging studies with human volunteers also confirm that these pathways could allow emotions to be regulated by higher cognitive processes such as reasoning and labeling.[25] Via this route new information, depending on its content, can both decrease and increase amygdala activity, reducing fear when the context has changed and the danger is past, or increasing it when there is reason to think that the situation has become more dangerous. The psychologist Graham Davey has made a particular study of this process, known as *stimulus revaluation*. He gives the example of a woman who is making a good recovery after being mugged in the street when she learns that her attacker has subsequently stabbed and killed another victim. This new information leads to a dramatic upward revaluation of the threat and a consequent increase in fear.[26]

These neuroanatomic findings suggest mechanisms that could explain the durability of fear conditioning and the return of fear. Fear is acquired through both subcortical pathways and a variety of higher-level cortical pathways that project to the amygdala. Extinction, on the other hand, is based on projections from the cortex to the amygdala, with the central involvement of the hippocampus. These projections have the capacity to inhibit the activation of the amygdala when the person or animal is in a context associated with safety, but in unfamiliar contexts where there are no safety cues or in contexts associated with threat, no inhibition occurs and the original fear response is reinstated. Moreover, the return of fear may occur in response to unexpected encounters with low-level perceptual features of the original learning situation that received little cortical processing, such as movement of an object at a particular speed and in a particular direction.

Cognitive Neuroscience and Memory
Declarative Memory

For our purposes the distinction between declarative and nondeclarative, or explicit and implicit, forms of memory is important to bear in mind even though it does not map exactly onto clinical observations of different kinds of memory in PTSD. Declarative memory involves representations of facts and events that are subject to conscious recollection, verbal reflection, and explicit expression.[27] Declarative memory is supported by a complex of brain structures involving the medial temporal lobe and hippocampus. During encoding and retrieval, these structures interact with the prefrontal cortex, which as noted above is considered to be a major site of executive control. As applied to memory, one function of executive control is to inhibit the entry of unwanted or irrelevant material into consciousness. As we will discuss in more detail in Chapter 8, such inhibitory processes are typically regarded as an essential element in efficient mental functioning.

Within the declarative memory system the hippocampus appears to be specialized for the learning of context (including temporal context)[28] and the learning of relational properties among stimuli. It is thought to be crucial in binding together the separate features or elements of an episode to make a coherent and integrated ensemble. The hippocampus may encode separate stimulus elements and the relations among them such that the representations can be utilized flexibly and accessed in a variety of ways.[29] It has also been suggested that the hippocampus is the structure particularly associated with memories of conscious experience.[30]

One prominent view is that the hippocampus is not a permanent repository for declarative memories, since damage to this region interferes with new learning but leaves memory for events in the remote past intact. Instead, long-lasting memories are stored elsewhere in the cortex.[31] James McClelland and colleagues proposed that the hippocampus is a rapid learning system that can respond to momentarily changing circumstances, distinct from a neocortical memory system that provides for longer-term storage and learns slowly about the underlying structure present in ensembles of similar experiences.[32] The representation of an experience in the neocortical system depends on a widely distributed pattern of neural activity. The repeated reinstatement of hippocampally based memories, for example, through being brought to mind and rehearsed over and over, permits the neocortex to learn by making a series of small adjustments to the connections between neurons.

In accounting for the existence of these different types of memory systems, McClelland pointed out that the neocortical system, although efficient at gradually extracting underlying rules and consistencies, is unable to respond rapidly to new information that contradicts what has already been learned. Such information tends to produce *catastrophic interference,* with the system being unable to integrate the new data and responding by ignoring relevant past experiences.[33] As an example of this problem, McClelland describes trying to teach a computer simulation of this neocortical memory system about the properties of birds. The system performs well when it is given lots of examples of birds and is told that all of them can fly. When it is presented with a penguin, however, a bird that cannot fly, the system experiences catastrophic interference and responds either by classifying the penguin as a nonbird or by concluding that birds cannot fly after all.

The existence of a hippocampal system, however, may permit the rapid formation of representations of the new information (the penguin) in a way that avoids interference with the knowledge already available in the neocortical system (all birds can fly). McClelland proposes that the most efficient way of allowing the neocortical system to integrate the new information is via a process he calls *interleaved learning,* in which the system is gradually exposed to the new information interleaved with old examples from the same domain. In the case of the penguin, this would involve presenting the memory system with examples of birds that can fly interleaved with examples of birds that cannot fly (like the ostrich). This process enables the system to be slowly reorganized so that eventually it can successfully classify both eagles and ostriches as birds.

What has all this got to do with trauma? The computer modelers' description of catastrophic interference is eerily reminiscent of clinical accounts of how trauma overturns long-held assumptions and is hard to integrate with previous knowledge. In the overassimilation we identified in Chapter 4, some traumatized people deny the reality of the event and classify it as a nontrauma, equivalent to classifying the penguin as a nonbird. In overaccommodation they let the fact of the trauma overturn everything they previously assumed to be true, equivalent to concluding that no bird is able to fly. Equally strikingly, high-frequency intrusive memories could be seen as the brain's way of inputting important information repeatedly into the memory system. The procedures that therapists have traditionally used to help people adjust to trauma and other shocking experiences (sometimes called *working through* or *emotional processing*) tend to involve the repeated appraisal and reappraisal of the event alongside preexisting expectations, plans, and goals. Interleaved learning is an interesting way of conceptualizing this.

Nondeclarative Memory

Nondeclarative memory is thought to be expressed in a wide variety of types of learning, including the acquisition of motor skills such as playing the trumpet and cognitive skills such as reading, as well as the acquisition of conditioned responses. Nondeclarative memories cannot be deliberately, consciously recalled. We cannot say how we play the trumpet or why we suddenly feel afraid in the same way that we can say what we had for dinner last night. Instead, nondeclarative memories seem to be automatically elicited in a rather inflexible way under conditions that bear a strong similarity to the conditions of the original learning. Nondeclarative memory tends to be expressed through indirect measures, such as an increase in speed after repeated practice, or a change in skin conductance after presentation of a green triangle that has been paired previously with shock. None of these expressions of memory is thought to be primarily mediated by the hippocampus, and there is some evidence for a complete separation between memory systems underlying declarative and nondeclarative memory.[34]

Tulving and Schacter proposed that some nondeclarative memory phenomena reflected the operation of a separate "perceptual representation system."[35] This system, they suggested, is concerned with the identification of perceptual objects and does not depend on brain regions supporting episodic and semantic memory. It develops early and is differentially preserved later in life. For Tulving and Schacter, the products of the perceptual representation system do not provide a basis for conscious awareness of previous experience. As we saw in the last chapter, however, other theorists have proposed memory systems that have qualities similar to those of the perceptual representation system but that could support some degree of conscious awareness.[36] The relation of these ideas about image-based memory to the declarative–nondeclarative distinction has so far received little attention.

The Effects of Fear on Memory

Given the studies reviewed in the last two sections, it appears that the hippocampal processing of information about fear-evoking situations results in the laying down of integrated, coherent representations of conscious experience, located in the appropriate temporal and spatial context. These representations are available for deliberate recall. It is possible, however, for information to reach the amygdala via a number of different routes, independently of the hippocampus. For example, the visual areas of the inferior temporal cortex, which are involved in the late stages of sensory processing, project strongly to the amygdala. The pathway from the thalamus to the amygdala has a less sophisticated processing capacity and would be capable of transmitting lower-level sensory features of frightening situations. Memories formed in these ways would not be open to deliberate recall but could be accessed automatically by reminders, particularly perceptual features, similar to those recorded in the fear memory.

Recent research indicates that stress has very different effects on the hippocampus and amygdala. The physiology of the hippocampus under acute stress mirrors the Yerkes-Dodson inverted U–shaped function for cognitive performance that we encountered in the last chapter. Declarative memory is initially enhanced by release of the adrenal hormones adrenaline and corticosterone, and the sympathetic nervous system, together with the amygdaloid complex, constitutes a powerful mechanism for ensuring that emotional events are preferentially retained in memory.[37] Equally, there is evidence that prolonged, intense stress associated with high levels of corticosterone (cortisol in humans) tends to impair the functioning of the hippocampus. This then tends to reverse the improvement in declarative memory,[38] so that there is less binding of individual features into a coherent whole or of location in a temporal and spatial context. Even in the absence of stress, administration of cortisol over a four-day period at concentrations appropriate to a highly stressful event produces a reversible worsening of verbal memory.[39] In contrast, the functioning of the amygdala appears generally to be enhanced as stress increases, consistent with the formation of overly strong conditioned responses.[40]

These memory systems, and the effects of stress upon them, provide a plausible neural basis for the VAM and SAM memories proposed above and for the symptoms of PTSD. A person can deliberately recall VAM memories and use them to consciously evaluate a trauma, to relate it to past and present, and to communicate about it with others. These flexible, declarative memories, subject to modification and change but often vague, disorganized, and full of gaps, strongly suggest a form of representation that depends on the hippocampus.

Equally, there are many similarities between the notions of SAM memory and nondeclarative memory although, of course, flashback memories are not nondeclarative in the usual sense of this term. As noted earlier, flashbacks are a highly perceptual form of memory that are elicited automatically and are under only limited conscious control. They have been claimed to be relatively stereotyped and unchanging even after multiple recall episodes, whereas ordinary memories are altered by repeated recall. They are also reexperienced in the present;

that is, they do not possess an associated temporal context. All these features are suggestive of an image-based, non-hippocampally dependent form of memory that is unable to encode information about past versus present. From a neuroanatomic perspective, it is interesting that the amygdala projects strongly to almost all regions of the brain involved in visual processing. The function of these projections is poorly understood, but one possibility is that they could support the experience of flashbacks. Given the highly visual nature of most reexperiencing in PTSD, it is also interesting that the amygdala has many more anatomic connections with visual than with auditory areas of the brain.[41]

Recently, scientists have wondered whether the effects of stress on the hippocampus may be long-lasting, particularly in people who have been exposed to extreme trauma over some considerable period of time. Douglas Bremner and colleagues, among others, have found evidence for smaller hippocampal volumes in patients with PTSD arising from both combat and abuse in childhood.[42] This is consistent with the finding from animal studies that the release of corticosteroids during prolonged stress produces hippocampal damage[43] and with the repeated demonstration that PTSD patients tend to do worse than comparison groups on standard memory tests. Not all studies of PTSD patients have found evidence for reduced hippocampal volume, however, and in addition, levels of cortisol tend be lower than normal, not higher, in PTSD.[44] Not enough is yet known about the nature of the damage sustained by the hippocampus during stress nor about how cortisol, in conjunction with a variety of neurotransmitters, may bring this about. For the present, Bremner's theory that trauma damages the brain remains intriguing but controversial.

Even if the association between PTSD and a smaller hippocampus turns out to be reliable, other interpretations are possible.[45] For example, a smaller hippocampus may reflect a preexisting genetic or environmentally produced vulnerability factor making it more likely that PTSD will develop after a trauma. Recent evidence of a dramatic nature has strengthened this argument. This comes from a study of monozygotic twins, selected because one served in Vietnam while the other did not.[46] Monozygotic twins are genetically identical, allowing researchers to examine the effect of combat exposure and genetic vulnerability separately. The results showed that although there was a strong correlation between PTSD symptoms and smaller hippocampal volumes in the combat-exposed veterans, there was an equally strong correlation between the veterans' symptoms and the hippocampal volumes of their twins who had never been to Vietnam. This strongly suggests that smaller hippocampal volume may sometimes be a risk factor for PTSD rather than always being a result of exposure to trauma.

Conclusions

The study of trauma reveals many complex processes that are poorly understood. One of the most fascinating concerns the paradoxical nature of trauma memories, which may be vague or vivid, intrusive or quiescent, under or out of control, and experienced in the present or the past. Some of these puzzling observations are beginning to fall into place. Once we accept the idea that there are two memory systems rather than one, and that high levels of stress affect them in different ways, the pattern of results we reviewed in the last chapter ceases to look so contradictory. There are good reasons to think that the declarative memories typically studied in the laboratory and in nonclinical samples will be more vivid and durable under conditions of moderate stress, although there is likely to be a narrowing of attention onto the most salient features of the event. When the events are more severe (as in the case of the rape memories studied by Mary Koss and Mindy Mechanic), declarative memories will start to become more vague and confused.

At the same time as they prevent the laying down of detailed, organized declarative memories, high levels of stress will promote the storage of permanent, non-hippocampally dependent representations that are reexperienced in the form of flashbacks. The findings reported by Steph Hellawell and me support the idea that VAM and SAM memories coexist but differ greatly in their characteristics. The two memory systems help to explain the odd fact that the PTSD patient still feels threatened despite being well aware that the trauma is over. As Ehlers and Clark insightfully put it, for the PTSD patient the threat *is* still present.[47] My proposal is that this current threat is contained within the memory system that records images rather than conscious perceptions and that has no way of distinguishing the present from the past.

To the extent that clinical studies with PTSD patients do not specify which type of memory they are measuring, their results are likely to be inconsistent. A good example is provided by the issue of the stability of memory for trauma over time. As we discussed, it has been argued that trauma memories are "frozen" in time and are experienced over and over in the same form.[48] Yet studies of memories for trauma at two points in time have found that the memories do not always remain the same.[49] An obvious resolution (although this has yet to be tested) is that the content of flashbacks remains stable and the content of declarative memories undergoes modification and change.

Do dual representation theories explain the available evidence better than the single representation approach? Certainly the associative network model seems inadequate to explain the complex results found in the laboratory and in real life. A more recent version of the single representation approach has been put forward by Martin Conway and Christopher Pleydell-Pearce.[50] These cognitive psychologists argued that memories for autobiographical events consist of a hierarchy of information, ranging from the very general (for example, how the event relates to life periods and life themes) to the very specific (for example, perceptual details of how things look or feel, which they referred to as event-specific knowledge or ESK). Like Foa and Rothbaum, they argued that under extreme stress the representations would be fragmented and that ESK would be poorly integrated with the rest of the trauma memory. These conditions might make it easier for specific reminders that matched the ESK in the trauma memory to automatically activate the representation in the form of a flashback. At other times, more general information about the event could be utilized to produce a narrative account for family and friends.

This approach meets many of the deficiencies of network theories but suggests that there is an important distinction in memory between higher-level information about traumas and the largely perceptual ESK. The current debate centers on whether both types of knowledge are processed by a single memory system or whether each is processed by its own memory system. It is likely that advances in neuroimaging techniques will eventually enable us to answer this question. Meanwhile, the distinction between types of memory put forward in this chapter will be enormously helpful in answering some of the other pressing questions surrounding trauma. In particular, the distinction is central to the question of how therapy for PTSD works and also helps to illuminate the most contentious and heated debate in the field, the vexatious question of whether the memory of trauma can be forgotten and then recovered.

7

Myths, Memory Wars, and Witch-hunts

While the histories of the 142 patients reveal that horrible sights formed a
definite causative factor in 51 cases, and a probable factor in 13 more, it is
certain that these figures are far below the true mark, owing to the remarkable repression of memory which takes place in connexion with sights. In
some instances sights are completely obliterated from conscious memory,
and in others this obliteration is partial, the patient striving to keep the
sight memories from re-entering his own consciousness.

—Harold Wiltshire, "A Contribution to the Etiology of Shell Shock"[1]

Amnesia for the traumatic event, usually ascribed to repression, was a
common feature of the shell shock cases described by physicians such
as Harold Wiltshire and Charles Myers during World War I, even in
the absence of head injuries and proximity to explosions. This association between amnesia and trauma was uncontroversial until the false
memory furor exploded onto the scene in the early 1990s. Most psychologists had little experience of hostile public campaigns and divi-
sions that split the academic community, apart from periodic demon-
strations over animal experimentation, accompanied by occasional
attacks launched at buildings and individuals involved in animal research. Going way beyond the public visibility of the animal rights
campaigns, this controversy produced enormous personal bitterness,
public accusations, lawsuits, interference with the right of free speech,
harassment, and physical attacks—all accompanied by intense media
scrutiny. For those involved in the public debate, it was an extremely
stressful time, during which principles of professional practice and
reputations were being repeatedly challenged. It also revealed the
extraordinary rapidity with which psychologists, psychiatrists, and

other scientifically trained professionals were willing to abandon their habits of logical thinking and support extreme positions in the absence of even minimal empirical evidence. And it was all to do with memory for trauma.

Thus, supposedly scientific contributions on both sides of this debate questioned the motives and integrity of people with whom they disagreed and attempted to disparage opponents' professional abilities. Some of these contributors made exclusive claims for the scientific legitimacy of their own perspectives, subjecting opposing data to fierce examination while being relatively uncritical of studies that supported their points of view. Much of what was written was obfuscatory and confusing. Logical errors abounded, for example, in the conclusion that because a memory was recovered in therapy, the practitioner must have been using "recovered memory therapy."

In trying to account for this collective failure of rationality, it is essential to provide some background to the controversy and to mention the considerable roles played by the media and by individuals with no scientific or professional qualifications to speak about memory, trauma, and childhood. I therefore make no apology for describing the development of the false memory movement and the factors that increased its visibility and impact, as well as the consequences for the practice of therapy today. Ironically, the scientific questions underlying the debate are extremely interesting and topical, and as the politics gradually subside, clinicians and scientists are actually starting to make some real progress in understanding the nature of memory and forgetting. This will be the subject of the next chapter.

False Memories and the Misdirection of Therapy

The gradual revelation during the 1980s of the widespread sexual and physical abuse of children, and the realization that for years this abuse had been ignored or simply overlooked, led to an unprecedented development in clinical services for abuse survivors, offered both by clinics and hospitals and by private psychotherapists. As these therapists started working with survivors of prolonged trauma, they began to encounter clinical phenomena for which they had received little if any training and with which they were often poorly equipped to deal. In addition to the flashbacks that we have already discussed, therapists came across patients who described recalling episodes of abuse that they had completely forgotten. These apparent recovered memories were often vivid and detailed and were initially recalled with high levels of surprise and emotion. In some cases patients behaved as though they had multiple personalities, some of whom not only acted in strange and unpredictable ways but said they remembered terrible events in childhood that the host personality was not aware of.

Some examples of multiple personality, now referred to as *dissociative identity*, are presented by psychoanalyst Phil Mollon in his book *Remembering Trauma*.[2] He described a middle-aged patient, Joaney, who would for hours at a time enter a state of mind in which she believed herself to be a fifteen-year-old girl. During these periods Joaney expected the world to be similar to the way it was when she was really fifteen and was unable to understand why cars looked different and why there was a much later date on the newspaper. Another patient, Alicia, had a second personality who was temporarily in control and would leave notes for Alicia to keep her informed of important events.

During this period enormous numbers of books on sexual abuse were published, aimed at therapists and at the general public. Perhaps because it was what they genuinely believed, or perhaps because they were trying to make their books more sensational and sell in greater numbers, some Saviors made claims about the frequency of sexual abuse in the population or about its effects that were not supported by evidence. Rather than acknowledge openly the difficulties of defining and measuring sexual abuse, others were content to repeat terrifyingly high figures that obscured real and important differences in the nature of the experiences. Of course, sexual abuse was much more common than had been thought. But before long, some Saviors seemed prone to believe that sexual abuse was everywhere.

A common assumption was that these early traumatic experiences were the cause of the person's later psychological problems, that therapists needed to understand the links between the past and the present, and that the person's experience eventually had to be accepted and validated instead of being dismissed and ignored as had so often happened in the past. In particular, therapists felt it was essential for patients to overcome inappropriate feelings of guilt and responsibility for abuse that was in reality the responsibility of the adults concerned. These assumptions were readily generalized by some Saviors to cases in which the trauma had apparently been partially or wholly forgotten, or in which the memory seemed to be vested in a subpersonality. In line with Freud's original seduction theory, the thinking was that trauma memories had been repressed and if patients were to recover, their experiences had to be brought fully into consciousness.

For the first time in history, these developments, along with recognition of the extent of relationship violence, started to give a voice to male and female abuse survivors; to reveal the exploitative and often terrifying reality of life in many families, children's homes, and other institutions; and to expose the sexual crimes of adults in positions of responsibility, trust, and power. At the same time, there was widespread coverage of these issues in all broadcast and print media, and it became much more common for patients in therapy to spontaneously bring up and want to discuss their experiences of abuse, and in some cases to take legal action against their abusers. This crusading zeal and wish on the part of therapists and mental health professionals to in some small way atone for the omissions of the past were to have a number of unforeseen consequences.

As trauma therapy spread, so the links of reasoning that supported its use gradually became stretched. Initially, therapists felt reasonably confident when they could trace low self-esteem, eating problems, and other difficulties to feelings patients could consciously associate with the abuse they had always remembered. Noting that abuse was sometimes forgotten and appeared to be remembered only later, some therapists began to argue that the very existence of certain symptoms and difficulties indicated that abuse had probably occurred, even if the patient had not recalled it. The (even less) logical extension of this argument was that patients should be helped to recover these memories, and that if they had suspicions, vague feelings, or images relating to abuse, then it was very likely to have occurred. There was little questioning by these Saviors of whether vivid experiences that appeared to be memories were actually always true and whether the uncovering of abuse memories was necessarily in the patient's best interests.

One of the most influential books of the 1980s was *The Courage to Heal.* Its authors, Ellen Bass and Laura Davis, made clear that they were not trained as psychologists and that the book was not based on scientific theory but on extensive personal experiences with abuse and its treatment. It is in many ways a moving and insightful book, full of the authentic voices of abuse survivors and containing many positive and helpful messages. But the book also demonstrates how instinct and compassion can lead to assumptions that may not be justified and that may have unfortunate consequences. Thus in the first edition of their book the authors wrote: "For many survivors, remembering is the first step in healing. To begin with, you may have to remember that you *were* abused at all."[3] And later: "Yet even if your memories are incomplete, even if your family insists nothing ever happened, you still must believe yourself. Even if what you experienced feels too extreme to be possible or too mild to be abuse, even if you think 'I must have made it up' or 'No one could have done that to a child,' you have to come to terms with the fact that someone did do those things to you."[4]

Other influential trauma therapists, some of whom did have a higher level of professional training, also appeared to fall into the trap of assuming that memory was invariably a reliable guide to what had actually happened and that attempts to recover memories, for example, using hypnotic age regression, were likely to uncover the truth.[5] It is important to emphasize that this constellation of attitudes and techniques, which has sometimes been dubbed *recovered memory therapy*, never achieved the status of an "official" therapy or became part of standard training for therapists. Rather, they inhabited a hinterland of therapy for childhood sexual abuse and were used on an ad-hoc basis by certain therapists and counselors when they seemed to be appropriate within the overall context of treatment. It is unclear how many practitioners could legitimately be called "recovered memory therapists," in the sense that they operated largely or exclusively according to these principles, in the same way as hypnotherapists would routinely use hypnosis as part of their treatment. However, some trauma centers specializing in dissociative identity disorder appeared to adopt these principles and apply them to large numbers of their patients.

Another consequence of the increasing focus on violence and abuse, and on the assumption that the victim should always be believed, was the mobilization of campaigners who were willing to defend some adults accused of abuse and to question the credibility of some of the accusations, whether they were made by children or by adults describing their childhoods. A key figure appearing in the defense of the accused during the 1980s was Ralph Underwager, pastor and director of the Minnesota Institute for Psychological Therapies. Underwager defended some accused on the grounds that the accusations were probably false and based on inappropriate questioning on the part of police and child welfare officers. In 1992 Underwager played a major role in the founding of the False Memory Syndrome Foundation, an organization dedicated to supporting parents whose adult children had made what were regarded as false accusations of abuse against them.

The founders of the FMSF were Pamela and Peter Freyd, the mother and father of cognitive psychologist Professor Jennifer Freyd. The previous year it had come to their attention that Jennifer was recalling some distressing events from childhood at the same time as developing her betrayal trauma theory to explain how instances of sexual abuse could be remembered and forgotten. Jennifer's account of this period is given in her book *Betrayal Trauma,* in which she explains that although she made no attempt to discuss her private life in public, Pamela responded to the news of her daughter's activities by publishing an article giving her own version of the family history, circulating it to Jennifer's colleagues and to the media, and founding the FMSF.[6]

From its outset, the FMSF was extremely successful at attracting (usually quite favorable) publicity, and over the next few years both the FMSF and other false memory societies claimed that there were many thousands of cases known to them in which previously happy families were disrupted by false accusations of abuse triggered when an adult child entered therapy. In addition to encouraging accused parents to call them and tell them of their experiences, one of the first actions of the FMSF was to form a scientific advisory board, mainly consisting of academic psychologists and psychiatrists. Although some of these individuals acted in a purely advisory capacity, others enthusiastically championed the notion of a "false memory syndrome" in the media and in professional journals. One of them, John Kihlstrom, then at Yale University, put forward a definition of the syndrome that has achieved wide currency:

A condition in which a person's identity and interpersonal relationships are centered around a memory of traumatic experience which is objectively false but in which the person strongly believes. Note that the syndrome is not characterised by false memories as such. We all have memories that are inaccurate. Rather, the syndrome may be diagnosed when the memory is so deeply ingrained that it orientates the individual's entire personality and lifestyle, in turn disrupting all sorts of other adaptive behaviors. . . . False Memory Syndrome is especially destructive because the person assiduously avoids confrontation with any evidence that might challenge the memory.[7]

The eminence of the scientific advisors was surprising because at this stage no evidence for the syndrome had been put forward other than the personal experience of a few individuals. One of the first lessons of a professional training in mental health is that to understand a family the therapist needs to consider the (often totally opposing) perspectives of all its members. In the vast majority of cases there was only the parents' testimony that the memory was objectively false, that there had been any personality or lifestyle changes, or that the sufferer was impervious to contrary facts and alternative theories.

One advisory board member who did have good reason to doubt the reliability of memory was Elizabeth Loftus, the foremost American expert in the study of eyewitness testimony. Her article published in 1993 in the *American Psychologist* was a landmark event, establishing the arguments for the false memory position in a high-profile professional journal.[8] Loftus suggested that at least some of the memories of childhood sexual abuse recovered in therapy might not be veridical but might be false memories "implanted" by therapists who had prematurely decided that the patient was an abuse victim and who used inappropriate therapeutic techniques to persuade the patient to recover corresponding "memories." Among her most telling observations questioning the plausibility of recovered memories of abuse were the following:

- These memories were sometimes highly unusual, for example, of satanic rituals with human sacrifices;
- the age at which the events were supposed to have oc-

curred sometimes was so young that it preceded the development of explicit event memory;

- there was typically no independent corroboration of the events;
- therapists sometimes seemed to have fixed ideas about the ubiquitous influence of child abuse; and
- therapists might hold mistaken beliefs about the accuracy of memory and might employ procedures such as hypnosis or guided fantasy that increased the risk of imaginary scenes and images being interpreted as actual events.

Two other cognitive psychologists, Stephen Lindsay and Don Read, also reviewed relevant psychological studies on autobiographical memory, eyewitness testimony, suggestibility, and the fallibility of memory, concluding that the creation of false memories within therapy was a possibility that must be taken seriously.[9] Elizabeth Loftus and Ira Hyman collected experimental evidence to demonstrate that a proportion of people asked to vividly imagine made-up scenes from their childhoods will later come to mistake those scenes for actual events.[10] In one example, Hyman and colleagues conducted three interviews with participants in which they were asked to recall events from their childhoods supplied by their parents.[11] Mixed in with true events were several false events, one of which involved the six-year-old participant knocking over a punchbowl at a wedding and spilling the contents over the bride's parents. The participants generally recalled the true events and remembered more about them over the three interviews. Although none remembered the punchbowl incident at the first interview, by the third interview a quarter of the sample claimed to have a memory for it.

Participants who agree to these false memories tend to report more dissociative experiences (see Chapter 8 for details of these), to be higher in imagery ability, and to be of a more generally suggestible disposition. Kathy Pezdek has demonstrated, however, that there are probably limits to people's willingness to accept such made-up experiences as their own, and that it is difficult to implant false memories about unlikely and unpleasant events.[12]

Just as in these experiments, it has been proposed that patients might also be willing to accept suggestions about childhood abuse made by their therapists. Lindsay and Read noted that the likelihood of suggestive influences leading to memory errors is increased by the perceived authority and trustworthiness of the source of suggestions, by repetition of suggestions, by their plausibility and imageability, and by the adoption of an uncritical attitude toward establishing the truth or falsity of apparent memories.[13] They proposed that such features might characterize a type of therapy that they called *long-term, multi-faceted, suggestive memory work,* involving repeatedly encouraging a patient to imagine or fantasize about what might have happened coupled with an absence of warnings about the unreliability of memory.

Susan Clancy and Richard McNally have conducted some interesting studies comparing the suggestibility of women who think they have been abused but have no memory of it (the "repressed memory" group), women who report recovering memories of abuse (the "recovered memory" group), women who report having always known they were abused (the "continuous memory" group), and women who say they were never abused (the "control" group).[14] In one study, women were asked to rate their confidence that certain nontraumatic events from childhood had happened to them, such as finding a ten-dollar bill in a parking lot. On a later occasion they were required to vividly imagine a subset of these events and rerate their confidence that they had actually occurred. Although this procedure led to a slight increase in the belief that the imagined events had happened, this effect was larger for the control group than for the recovered memory group.

Another study involved showing participants a list of related words (such as "candy," "bitter," "sour," "sugar") and testing whether they would later falsely remember having seen another word (such as "sweet") that was highly associated with all of them but was never actually shown. In this experiment the recovered memory group was more prone than the other groups to agree that they had seen the nonpresented word, but the repressed memory group did not differ from the control group. It is hazardous, however, to draw parallels between this kind of word experiment with its compelling associative cues and the situation of people with recovered memories of incidents of abuse.[15] Studies are not consistent in showing that people claiming repressed or recovered memories are more suggestible than nonabused people.[16]

What ignited the debate about false memory, however, was not these scientifically based concerns but the public pronouncements of a small number of campaigners, journalists, politicians, and academics. Extra fuel was provided by polemical texts such as the book *Making Monsters: False Memories, Psychotherapy, and Sexual Hysteria.* Later, authors of *The Revenge of the Repressed* and *Victims of Memory: Incest Accusations and Shattered Lives* eloquently attacked what they perceived as an overwhelming surge of false accusations of sexual abuse.[17] These stories were so sensational that they were not generally covered by specialist medical and science correspondents but by ordinary news and features reporters who were less able to evaluate or less concerned with the credibility of the claims. One-sided family stories and unsubstantiated claims about accusing children and their therapists were repeated in press releases, newspaper reports, interviews, and broadcast programs, generally with little attempt at balance.

An analysis of the media coverage of this debate in the United Kingdom found that the peak year for false memory stories was 1994. The authors, Kitzinger and Reilly, commented that "the trajectory of the story in the media was influenced by the different access to, and credibility of, the parents versus their offspring. Individual journalists judged the parents to be very ordinary, 'credible,' 'nice,' and 'clearly in great pain.' By contrast, adults alleging abuse were often not interviewed at all. . . . Those alleging abuse, in any case, often have low credibility. As one journalist explained, 'They may have taken drugs, they may have gone into alcohol, they may be slightly unbalanced. So we never quite trust them.'"[18]

Kitzinger and Reilly made a number of other interesting observations. Compared with other issues drawing on scientific knowledge, such as the controversies over human genetic research and food safety, journalists writing about recovered memory felt free to draw on their own experiences in evaluating the claims being made. Even though the topic of memory is complex, stories were often reported without any reference to science. Rather, the early reporting was concerned with case studies and legal hearings. The issue also played into long-standing agendas in some parts of the U.K. media such as supporting family values and denigrating psychotherapy and counseling, a particularly British obsession: "Asked about the editorial reaction to her own article attacking psychotherapeutic malpractice, one journalist commented that it was: 'Total glee! We're going to get the therapists. We're going to get the therapists!' . . . The therapists are kind of weak-minded and they're in the business of feelings, which in journalism is the bloody last thing that you would ever express in the office."[19]

Kitzinger and Reilly also confirmed another experience of scientists and therapists who have talked to the media on the topic—the wish of journalists to have a clear-cut story. They commented that media interest was minimized by the report of the British Psychological Society's (BPS) Working Party on Recovered Memories, of which I was a member, which concluded that these memories could on some occasions be true and on other occasions be false and that there was no reliable evidence of false memory syndrome being a widespread phenomenon in the United Kingdom. Although scientifically this represented the state of affairs at the time, journalists were frustrated. I vividly remember one of them at the press conference asking us what their headline was supposed to be the next day.

Among the most frequently cited claims by the false memory proponents at this time was the existence of a well-defined syndrome of epidemic proportions, based on therapists' slavish adherence to the idea that sexual abuse was the commonest cause of psychological problems and to the scientifically untenable notion of repression. Patients were described as recalling bizarre and impossible events that completely contradicted their happy family backgrounds, memories that were triggered only when they entered therapy. Parallels were frequently drawn with the seventeenth-century Salem witch-hunts. This frightening scenario was supposed to affect a million psychotherapy patients and countless more innocent parents.[20] Could these claims be true? Ironically, for all the appeals to science, their impact depended largely on striking narratives of the kind that false memory supporters found wanting when put forward by people arguing that recovered memories could be genuine.

And Now for Some Evidence

As Kenneth Pope has argued, the evidential base for a widespread false memory syndrome was itself weak.[21] Just like the recovered memory practices being attacked, it depended largely on anecdote and on a number of crucial but untested and unchallenged assumptions. It is time therefore to examine the available evidence. There are two main sources: that obtained from the false memory societies and that obtained from general surveys of the population, of therapists, or of patients in therapy. First, how robust is the claim that the false memory societies have identified thousands of people who all have had the same experience and who all tell the same story? A survey by Gudjonsson of around four hundred British False Memory Society (BFMS) members obtained a 70 percent response rate, with approximately 70 percent of responders agreeing that recovered memories were involved in the accusations, 20 percent not being sure or not answering the question, and 10 percent denying that recovered memories were involved.[22] Thus, clear indications about the possible involvement of recovered memories were obtained from only about half the membership of the BFMS. No comparable analysis of people contacting the American FMSF has been published. These data obviously are uncorroborated in that we do not know whether the accusers would agree that the memories were indeed recovered from prior amnesia.

Second, how robust is the claim that memories of sexual abuse can be forgotten and later recovered? More than twenty longitudinal and retrospective studies have now found that a substantial proportion of people reporting childhood sexual abuse (somewhere between 20 percent and 60 percent) say they have had periods in their lives (often lasting for several years) when they had less memory of the abuse or could not remember that it had occurred.[23] It has sometimes been objected that such questions often don't rule out the possibility that people would have remembered if only they had been asked. But even when more probing questions are asked, such as "Was there ever a period when you would not have remembered this event, even if you were asked about it directly?" similar results are obtained.[24]

Although the rates vary among studies, broadly similar findings about forgetting of trauma have been obtained by clinical psychologists, psychiatrists, and cognitive psychologists, in both clinical and community samples. These data too are open to the objection that the respondents might be mistaken. In the remaining sections we will examine the evidence for some key propositions of the false memory argument: that the content of recovered memories is either stereotypical, conforming to therapists' preconceptions about childhood sexual abuse as a ubiquitous cause of psychological disorder, or highly unusual, for example, of satanic rituals with human sacrifices; (b) that the age at which the events are supposed to have occurred may precede the development of explicit event memory; (c) that there is typically no independent corroboration of the events; (d) that recall generally occurs within therapy among patients who are initially totally amnesic about the abuse; and (e) that therapists may hold inaccurate beliefs about the accuracy of memory and may employ procedures such as hypnosis or guided fantasy that increase the risk of imaginary scenes and images being interpreted as actual events.

Content of Recovered Memories

As we have seen, it frequently has been claimed that the content of recovered memories tends to be bizarre and implausible, for example, involving alien abduction or satanic ritual abuse. Several surveys now have been published that indicate the kinds of conditions surrounding memory recovery and the content of the memories. The BPS Working Party reviewed the frequency with which, according to records kept by the false memory societies, recovered memories involved reports of satanic or ritual abuse.[25] The American data were abstracted from a report produced in the summer of 1993 by the director of the FMSF. This indicated that 11 percent of callers mentioned such abuse when asked an open-ended question and 18 percent when asked a closed question. The British data were derived from inspection of around two hundred records of correspondence and telephone calls received by the BFMS and were made available to the BPS Working Party by its director, Roger Scotford. In this sample, satanic or ritual abuse was explicitly mentioned in 6 percent of the callers' records. In his larger BFMS survey, Gudjonsson reported that 8 percent of respondents agreed that accusations involved satanic or ritual abuse when asked a closed question about it.

For its report the, BPS Working Party sent questionnaires to a wide variety of chartered psychologists in the United Kingdom, many of whom did not see patients in the relevant group, and obtained a response rate of 27 percent.[26] Almost half of the 810 psychologists with relevant caseloads who replied said they had at some time had a patient retrieve a memory from total amnesia while in therapy with them. A subset of this sample was followed up in a telephone survey and asked detailed questions about up to three recent clients who had had recovered memories.[27] Just 5 percent of the memories involved ritual cult abuse, and one memory involved an alien abduction.

The earlier mail survey also inquired about recovery of memories for events *not* involving childhood sexual abuse. More than a quarter of the respondents reported having clients with such memories in the past year. One concern was that these memories might arise only in the course of recovering memories of abuse and might be part of a similar pattern of false recall. This did not appear to be the case, since non-abuse-related recovered memories were just as common when no abuse was reported as when it was. In the follow-up survey therapists were asked about the content of these non-abuse-related memories. The most frequent categories involved other child maltreatment, traumatic medical procedures, and witnessing violence or death. Other studies have similarly reported the existence of recovered memories of events that have nothing to do with sexual abuse.[28]

Before we leave this topic, it is perhaps worth noting that despite the absence of evidence for widespread satanic ritual abuse, there are occasional examples of ritual and child murders that are not in dispute. In Britain in 1994 Frederick and Rosemary West were charged with twelve murders when the bodies of several children and young women were found buried beneath their house. Frederick West later committed suicide in prison, and his wife was convicted of murder. In Belgium Marc Dutroux, who had previously served a prison term for multiple child rape, was at the beginning of 2002 still awaiting a court appearance after being charged with murder and abduction following the discovery of a pedophile ring operating in the southern city of Charleroi. Dutroux led police to a concealed cell in his basement where they found two children, abducted three months earlier. The bodies of several other children were found buried on his properties. In January 2002 it was reported that a couple in Germany had been convicted of a murder in which they hit their victim more than sixty times with a hammer and machete and then drank his blood. The couple had been part of occult groups and had taken part in occult activities while previously living in London.

Age of Memory

Psychologists currently disagree about the earliest age at which people can retain and later bring to mind memories of significant childhood events. Some reports put this as early as the third year of life.[29] What can be stated is that there is little evidence for the later retrieval of narrative memories from the first two years of life and that memories from the third year of life are rare. This phenomenon is known as *infant amnesia*. For our purposes it is important to distinguish between memories for single events falling completely within the period of infant amnesia, which would be highly implausible, and memories for a series of events that were claimed to begin within the period of infant amnesia but continued for several years afterward. The latter could be due to guesses about the age of onset of a well-remembered pattern of events and so would not necessarily challenge what we know about memory.

According to the American FMSF data, 26 percent of allegations involved abuse that had begun when the child was aged zero to two. Only 6 percent of allegations, however, involved abuse that ended before age five, that is, fell completely within the period of infant amnesia.[30] In the British BFMS records reviewed by the BPS Working Party, 4 percent of allegations involved abuse that ended before age five, and in Gudjonsson's survey, 7 percent of allegations involved abuse ending before age five.[31] The BPS Working Party's follow-up telephone survey of British therapists found that 2 percent of the events in their patients' recovered memories were reported to have begun and ended before age three.[32]

Corroboration

In general, memories of childhood appear to be reasonably accurate, and there is no evidence that they are systematically biased by mood states such as depression.[33] Although it is not clear why recovered memories should be less accurate than memories an individual has always been aware of, some commentators have demanded stringent evidence of the authenticity of a memory before they are willing to concede that it has been recovered after a period of amnesia.[34] In fact there is quite a lot of corroborative evidence for recovered memories. This is not always evident from the accounts given of individual cases by Skeptics, who often omit the corroborating facts.[35]

Jonathan Schooler and colleagues described a very interesting series of individual cases in which high-quality corroboration of forgotten trauma was available and other explanations for apparent memory recovery were systematically considered.[36] In one of these cases a forty-one-year-old woman (ND) described recovering a memory after a session of group therapy for child abuse victims, during which the therapist had mentioned that victims often continue to be victimized as adults. ND described this experience as follows: "What she [her therapist] had said popped into my mind, and then all at once I remembered being a victim when I was like in my early twenties, when I was a nurse at a hospital. And it really kind of freaked me out because I remembered that not only had I been a victim but I had to go to court and prosecute the person who had attacked me. And he had been found guilty. And yet I had forgotten all of that. . . . I had to just sit there for a while because it was just this extreme emotion of fear and total disbelief. Disbelief that it happened, disbelief that I could have forgotten something that traumatic."[37]

What is striking about this case, the facts of which were corroborated by her lawyer, is that the events were so protracted in time. This contradicts the argument that while single events can be forgotten, people are unable to forget repeated or protracted events.[38] Other corroborated cases have been documented by Ross Cheit's Recovered Memory Project.[39] This Internet-based resource details upward of eighty corroborated recovered memory accounts drawn from legal, academic, and other sources. Some of these, like that of Ross Cheit himself, who remembered being abused between the ages of ten and thirteen by a camp administrator, or Frank Fitzpatrick, who remembered being abused at age twelve by a priest, also involved repeated instances of victimization.

Another individual case study of considerable interest was reported by Corwin and Olafson.[40] Videotapes were available recording the forensic assessment by David Corwin of a six-year-old girl who was alleging physical and sexual abuse by her mother. Eleven years later the girl requested to see the videotapes because she had forgotten most of the details of the alleged abuse. During a further interview with Corwin, which was also videotaped, the girl spontaneously recovered a memory connected with her allegations of the sexual abuse. Although at this point she recalled other details that had not featured in the original assessment, the gist of her recovered memory conformed well to the events she had described at age six.

Corroborative evidence for recovered memories was also provided in Linda Williams's follow-up study of adult women whose sexual abuse in childhood was documented by hospital records.[41] In her sample, approximately one in six of the women who recalled this abuse at an interview said that there had been a period when they had completely forgotten the abuse. When these current accounts of the abuse and the original records were compared, Williams reported that the accounts of women with recovered memories were just as accurate as those of women who had always remembered the abuse.

Feldman-Summers and Pope asked a sample of psychologists for any corroborative evidence concerning their own recovered memories of abuse. Forty-seven percent reported some corroboration, for example, the abuser acknowledged some or all of the remembered abuse, someone who knew about the abuse told the respondent, or someone else reported abuse by the same perpetrator.[42] Gudjonsson also noted that eight respondents in his survey of BFMS members admitted there was some truth to the allegations.[43] The BPS Working Party asked from the therapists in their survey about corroborative evidence. Overall, in 41 percent of their cases it was reported that the client had found some sort of corroboration, and in 5 percent (eleven cases) the therapist actually saw the evidence.[44] Corroboration rates were lower when the trauma recalled was childhood sexual abuse rather than some other event, but corroboration rates were similar whether or not memory recovery techniques had been employed. Other recent studies have similarly reported evidence for the corroboration of recovered memories.[45]

When and How Are Memories Recalled?

A central issue is whether recall occurs exclusively during therapy sessions, or after the onset of therapy, as opposed to before therapy. Feldman-Summers and Pope found that although more than half of memories were recovered in the context of therapy, 44 percent of their respondents stated that recovery had been triggered exclusively in other contexts.[46] Nearly a third of respondents in the BPS Working Party's initial survey reported that clients had recovered memories before any therapy.[47] Just less than a quarter had clients recovering childhood sexual abuse memories in therapy with them, and around one in five in therapy with someone else. In another community survey, being in therapy was unrelated to whether sexual abuse had been forgotten and then remembered or had been continuously recalled.[48]

Equally important is the way in which memories are recovered. It is sometimes assumed that memories are invariably recovered from total amnesia, thus adding to their implausibility. In fact, this does not seem to be the case. For example, Harvey and Herman described cases illustrating partial amnesia, in which some knowledge of abuse was retained although many salient facts and episodes were forgotten, and total amnesia, in which the fact that abuse had occurred at all was forgotten along with memory of any specific episodes.[49] Numerous therapists and researchers have emphasized the complexity of traumatic memory and described different degrees of forgetting, ranging from total amnesia, through a vague sense or suspicion, to varying amounts of partial forgetting.[50]

Therapists and Their Practices

At least three studies have provided confirmation that some therapists hold beliefs that run contrary to what we know about memory. One survey of around 860 hypnotherapists and family therapists attending conferences and workshops in the United States was mainly concerned with beliefs about hypnosis.[51] The other, by Deborah Poole and colleagues, investigated U.S. and U.K. psychologists' practices and experiences as well as more general beliefs concerning memory recovery of

sexual abuse during childhood.[52] Both surveys also found a high proportion of respondents endorsing the belief that recovered memories
can be false. In Poole's study the British respondents (who were all
chartered clinical psychologists) were less likely than their U.S. counterparts to use memory recovery techniques such as hypnosis and age
regression, although both groups had similarly high rates of respondents reporting memory recovery in at least some clients.

The majority of the respondents in the BPS Working Party's initial mail survey believed that false memories were possible, although
the proportion with this belief (67 percent) was smaller than in the
other two surveys asking this question.[53] Twenty percent of those who
had experienced recovered memories in their own practice thought
they had also encountered examples of false memories. The majority of
respondents also believed that recovered memories were sometimes or
usually accurate (although only a small minority believed they would
always be so)—a question not asked in the other surveys. Use of hypnotic regression was reported by 10 percent of respondents but was
more common in Poole's survey.

One of the problems with asking whether certain therapeutic
techniques have been employed is that they may have been used for
purposes other than memory recovery. For example, hypnosis is often
used simply to relax people, without giving any age regression or memory recovery instructions. In detailed questioning by interview, the
BPS Working Party therefore tried to distinguish between techniques
used specifically to aid recall as opposed to more general therapeutic
purposes.[54] In 21 percent of client cases, techniques to aid recall were
used before the recovery of the first memory. However, use of techniques to aid recall before the first memory recovery was not associated
with faster memory recovery, and these cases were just as likely to be
accompanied by reports of corroborative evidence as cases in which no
techniques were employed.

Questions of Validity

One doesn't need to be a scientist to see the problems with all the data
presented above. The information provided by members of the false

memory societies is mainly uncorroborated, in that we do not know whether the accusers would agree that the memories were indeed recovered from prior amnesia. Breakdown in family communications is also going to limit the accuracy of what families are able to say about the basis for the accusations. Nor in most cases does anyone other than those involved know with any certainty whether the events complained of did in fact occur. Equally, the data from surveys of patients themselves and their therapists are open to the objection that the respondents might be mistaken in thinking these were genuine memories. As we have seen, some corroborative evidence has been provided for some individuals, but while this is supportive it does not prove that even their memories are accurate. In addition to these general problems, two more specific issues have been raised.

The first issue has to do with whether we can rely on someone's account that he or she had completely forgotten a traumatic event and how that person would have arrived at this conclusion. In describing his series of individual cases, Jonathan Schooler noticed that a few respondents who thought they had forgotten the events *had* apparently talked about them in the relatively recent past.[55] This was described by friends and family, although the person who recovered the memory found this hard to believe. Schooler speculated that if the experience of recovering the memory is shocking, people assume that they must previously have completely forgotten it. He suggests that recovered memories may not be telling us just about the operation of the memory system but about how well we monitor the system ("meta-memory"). That is, when we are asked whether we have forgotten something, we have to try to retrieve any occasion when we might have remembered it in the past. If these occasions do not come to mind, we might falsely infer that the event had been forgotten for a long period of time.

The second issue is also concerned with how we answer questions about the operation of our own memories. There is a group of patients who report complete memory gaps lasting for several years, a phenomenon that has again been linked to the existence of early trauma. But how do people judge the adequacy of their childhood memories in the first place? Don Read, Robert Belli, and colleagues argued that people rely partly on the ease or difficulty with which they can bring instances to mind.[56] In one experiment participants were asked to report either four, eight, or twelve events from when they were five to seven and eight to ten years old, after which they had to evaluate the adequacy of their childhood memory. Those who were instructed to retrieve more events paradoxically rated their childhood memory as worse than the groups who had to retrieve fewer events, presumably because they attributed the difficulty of the task to deficiencies in their memory. A later study showed that the effect of retrieving twelve events was abolished by telling participants that the task was difficult, consistent with the suggestion that without such explicit instructions participants used the difficulty of the task to make inferences about the quality of their memory.[57] These researchers suggested that psychotherapy patients' reports of incomplete childhood memory might be a mistaken consequence of difficulty in trying to recall large numbers of events, rather than reflecting genuine problems with memory. They warned that such processes might lead clients to infer, wrongly, that they were amnesic for parts of their childhood, and thus that they might have forgotten or repressed traumatic experiences.

These arguments imply that judgments about the adequacy of memory for childhood may bear no relation to actual memory performance, but this proposition had not been directly tested until recently. Louisa Stokou and I investigated whether ordinary individuals who judge themselves to have poor memory for their childhood do in fact score worse on a standardized memory test concerning their early life.[58] We found that a group who thought they had poor memory for childhood did indeed score worse than a control group on tests of memory for both the facts and events of their early years. Given the same standardized test, women with recovered memories of childhood abuse found it harder to recall facts about their childhoods, such as home addresses and names of teachers, friends, and neighbors, than did women who had never been abused.[59] Similar results have been obtained with traumatized adolescents.[60] Even more strikingly, a patient who suffered from dissociative identity disorder was unable to recall a single episode in her life from before age ten in response to numerous retrieval cues.[61] These studies suggest that some people have genuine deficits in their memory for their childhoods and that memory judgments do have some basis in reality.

Conclusions

The clinical and survey data reviewed indicate that at least some recovered memories may not correspond to actual events. A minority of memories contain unusual content or refer to events that occurred at an age preceding the development of verbal memories. Some memories occur within therapy after the use of a specific technique to aid recall and cannot be corroborated, and some practitioners appear to have important misconceptions about the nature of memory and adopt risky practices. Thus, false memories are a very real possibility that professionals in the field must guard against at all times. At the same time the data from these surveys suggest that many recovered memories are not amenable to this kind of explanation. Memory recovery appears to be a remarkably robust phenomenon, occurring both within and outside of therapy and involving a wide variety of different types of events. Many well-trained practitioners have encountered the phenomenon, often without using techniques to aid recall. Laboratory studies of hypnotic amnesia show that memories can be routinely lost and then recovered by ordinary hypnotized subjects when the appropriate instructions are given.[62]

To complicate matters further, memory theory and experimental research make the strong prediction that the recall of events that have not actually happened is more likely when there are similar events that have actually happened. That is, some false memories may have a basis in reality, even though details of events, people, and places may have gotten confused. Interestingly, trauma therapists have arrived at exactly the same conclusion on the basis of their experiences. Phil Mollon, a member of the BPS Working Party, commented: "Traumatised patients may be (a) very suggestible and (b) very compliant (in certain respects). Both qualities make the traumatised patient more likely to generate material that fits the therapist's expectations, theoretical assumptions, emotional prejudices, etc. This means that, paradoxically, traumatised and abused patients may be more likely to produce false memory narratives of trauma and abuse."[63]

This basic conclusion, that some recovered memories are almost certainly false and others almost certainly true, does not please the false memory societies, any more than the warnings about false memory pleased Saviors who were convinced of the value of digging for hidden memories of abuse. In part, this is understandable. Pressure groups exist to represent their members' interests rather than to advance knowledge, unless this is to their particular benefit. There is less excuse for those journalists, practitioners, and academics who wish to dismiss all the evidence for genuine recovered memories of multiple traumatic events and who recycle claims about false memory syndrome or accused families that are in every way as anecdotal as the therapists' case studies they are attacking.[64] It is tempting to argue that Loftus and Ketcham's division of the field into "True Believers" (in the accuracy of recovered memory) and "Skeptics" should now be expanded to include "True Disbelievers" who appear to share all the fervor and unshakable belief in their positions attributed to the True Believers.[65]

The idea that real life is muddy, complicated, and equivocal undermines the telling of a simple story about (on one hand) child victims and wicked parents or (on the other) innocent parents, inept therapists, and duped patients. Rather, some of the polemicists give the appearance of being primarily interested in creating controversy and not wanting to engage with the complexities of trying to help damaged families or resolve legal disputes in an equitable way. A particularly uninhibited example of this rejection of any balanced position is provided by English professor Frederick Crews: "The key question . . . is whether therapeutically generated memories of otherwise unknown and biographically anomalous early events tend to get corroborated by hard evidence. The answer is: Never! That is why the seeming rationality of [Theresa] Reid's moderate position—some memories are true and some are false—is deceptive. In view of the facts, it amounts to middle-of-the-road extremism."[66]

In contrast, most serious commentators now appear to accept that traumatic events can be forgotten and then remembered. For example, cognitive psychologists Lindsay and Read concluded: "In our reading, scientific evidence has clear implications . . . : memories recovered via suggestive memory work by people who initially denied any such history should be viewed with scepticism, but there are few grounds to doubt spontaneously recovered memories of common forms of child sexual abuse or recovered memories of details of never-forgotten abuse. Between these extremes lies a gray area within which the implications of existing scientific evidence are less clear and experts are likely to disagree."[67]

Similarly, the consensus view among independent commentators, repeated in the 1995 report of the BPS Working Party on Recovered Memories and the 1995 interim statement of the American Psychological Association's Working Group on Investigation of Memories of Childhood Abuse, is that memories may be recovered from total amnesia and they may sometimes be essentially accurate. Equally, such "memories" may sometimes be inaccurate in whole or in part.

In practical terms, the debate has had major effects on how psychotherapy is conducted, leading to greater safeguards for patients. The initial polarization between memory researchers and clinicians has now dissolved, so that both can largely endorse the same conclusions and recommendations.[68] Proponents of the idea that therapists should routinely try to recover abuse memories are now almost impossible to find within the ranks of leading psychiatrists and psychologists. Despite the lack of direct empirical support, there is widespread agreement that situations in which there is sustained suggestive influence, such as therapy, do have the potential to induce false memories of traumatic events. Active attempts to recover suspected forgotten memories may sometimes be appropriate in unusual or extreme cases, but both patient and therapist must be aware of the risk of false memories. Techniques such as hypnosis and guided imagery should not be used without safeguards against potential suggestive influence. Furthermore, good practice now requires therapist and patient to adopt a critical attitude toward *any* apparent memory that is recovered after a period of amnesia, whether or not this is within a therapeutic context, and not to assume that it necessarily corresponds to a true event. Even highly vivid traumatic memories (flashbacks) may be misleading or inaccurate in some cases. Clinical guidelines are now available to help the practitioner avoid the twin perils of uncritically accepting false memories as true or summarily dismissing genuine recovered memories.[69]

8

The Return of Repression?

Say, is there Beauty yet to find?
And Certainty? and Quiet kind?
Deep meadows yet, for to forget
The lies, and truths, and pain? . . . oh! yet
Stands the Church clock at ten to three?
And is there honey still for tea?

—Rupert Brooke, "The Old Vicarage, Grantchester"[1]

The memory wars centered almost entirely on a single concept, repression, that throughout its history has received more scorn and more impassioned defense than almost any other mental process. The title of the book by Elizabeth Loftus and Katherine Ketcham, *The Myth of Repressed Memory,* says it all.[2] Is repression a figment of psychoanalysts' and psychotherapists' imaginations, a fanciful notion contradicted by experimental data and unsupported by any proper scientific evidence? Or is repression actually consistent with modern discoveries about the human memory system? What other mechanisms could explain the evidence presented in the last chapter that people can indeed sometimes forget traumatic events for long periods of time? To answer these questions we will have to distinguish very carefully among different ways in which the term has been used and what different experts have said about it. We will examine the chain of reasoning that has led people to question it and the memory phenomena it is supposed to have produced. Finally, we will examine the more general claims that have been made about human memory and what the evidence shows. A hundred years after Sigmund Freud, it is clear that the whole area is characterized by confusion and obfuscation and that we know much less about human memory than we thought. Freud himself provides a useful starting point for our exploration of these murky depths.

Defining Repression

Freud and Repression

Repression is the one of the best-known of the various defense mechanisms Freud described. Throughout his life Freud claimed that the purpose of psychoanalytic therapy was to lift the repression that excluded unacceptable mental contents from awareness and "make the unconscious conscious." In 1893 he and Breuer argued that repression operated on memories of traumatic events and that allowing these memories back into consciousness, accompanied by their original affect (that is, emotion), could bring about a permanent cure for hysteria.[3] In 1896 Freud adapted this idea and claimed a unique role for early sexual traumas in the causation of later psychological disturbance.[4] Effectively, this was a trauma theory, but it is more usually referred to as his *seduction theory.* By the beginning of the new century he had already abandoned this stance in favor of the position that was to become part of mainstream psychoanalysis, namely, that repression operated primarily on infantile drives and wishes rather than on memories of actual events.

What did Freud mean by "repression"? In 1893 Breuer and Freud had noted "it was a question of things which the patient wished to forget, and therefore intentionally repressed from his conscious thought and inhibited and suppressed."[5] By 1915 he had come up with the following more elegant but equally ambiguous formula: "The essence of repression lies simply in turning something away, and keeping it at a distance, from the conscious."[6] Freud continued to use the term in two main ways and often failed to distinguish between them.[7] One usage referred to a completely unconscious process whereby unwanted material is turned away before it reaches awareness (Freud called this *primary repression*). Rather than quietly remaining in the unconscious, however, this material is likely to enter awareness in disguised ways via dreams and slips of the tongue. In his second usage of the term, Freud proposed that a person becomes aware of disturbing thoughts, impulses, or memories and then deliberately attempts to exclude them from consciousness (Freud called this *repression proper* or *after-expulsion*). In his later theorizing, repression proper was thought to operate mainly on disturbing thoughts or impulses that were unwanted derivatives of the material that had first been unconsciously repressed.

From a modern perspective, these two uses of the term have very different implications. Primary repression implies the need for unconscious mechanisms that block any conscious processing being accorded to the traumatic scene. Thus, forgetting is seen as arising from an initial failure to encode any information about the event into memory—it simply does not register, and the trauma, once over, leaves no trace. It is hard, therefore, to construct an explanation of how the trauma can subsequently be recalled to awareness, since no trace of conscious experience has existed.

In contrast, after-expulsion operates on sensations and experiences that have already received at least some conscious processing. Information has been encoded, and the focus is on a mechanism that interferes either with its storage or with the person's ability to retrieve it. Many examples of this conscious type of repression (or *suppression* as it is sometimes known) may be found in textbooks on cognitive psychology under the heading of "motivated forgetting." However, a lot of questions remain unanswered. For example, what happens if after-expulsion of some specific thought or memory is repeated time after time? Repetition often leads to processes becoming completely automatic and ceasing to require conscious deliberation. Can after-expulsion also become automatic, so that the mind blocks access to certain kinds of material without a person being aware that it is doing so?

Observation and Theory

We have seen that the Freudian theory of repression already contains a complication—the existence of one form (primary repression) that is disputed and barely understood versus another (after-expulsion) that does not seem to be greatly at variance with modern psychology or common experience. In progressing further, I am in agreement with others who have pointed out the fundamental distinction between *theory* of this kind and *observation*. If an argument is about observation, then the basic facts of what has been found are being disputed. If an argument is about theory, then the explanation of those facts is disputed. In much of the debate on the subject of repression, these two elements are hopelessly muddled. Jennifer Freyd has made the helpful suggestion that the more general term *knowledge isolation* might be usefully

employed to refer to all sorts of forgetting, without implying any specific mechanism.[8]

The trauma therapists' position is relatively straightforward, if
vaguely specified. Their concern is mainly with the observation that
patients sometimes appear to recover accurate memories of specific,
upsetting, past events. They typically describe patients as reporting an
intense, vivid, emotionally laden memory of an event that might have
occurred decades before and that a person had previously forgotten
about. The memory may be fragmented and experienced with a high
degree of shock and surprise. The trauma therapists are on the whole
less bothered about theory. They talk about "repression" or "dissociation" in an attempt to explain their observations, but with a few exceptions these theories mainly describe the data and do not add anything
significant to them.[9] Unlike the psychoanalytic community, who following Anna Freud have mainly used the term repression to refer to an
unconscious mechanism for avoiding unwanted thoughts and feelings,
trauma therapists rarely acknowledge or discuss the distinction between different types of repression, or between repression and dissociation, or the issue of whether these concepts are necessary at all. The
main concern is to provide a plausible account of the forgetting of
trauma, rather than to put forward a testable hypothesis about a specific causal mechanism.

In the last chapter we discussed some of the work that has supported these observations, for example, the studies that have examined
corroboration for supposed memories. The claims about the nature of
the memories and the way in which recovery is experienced have also
been investigated. In many of the reports, recovery was described as a
dramatic, emotional event.[10] And in their systematic survey of all
kinds of therapists with recovered memory clients, the BPS Working
Party found that the memories were overwhelmingly in the form of
specific, detailed personal episodes, often rather fragmented and usually accompanied by some degree of reliving of the original emotion.[11]
In other words, the memories often, but not always, resembled those of
patients with PTSD, as described in Chapter 5. As we have seen, therefore, some evidence supports the trauma therapists' observations, but
nothing rules out the possibility of some memories being false, nothing specifically supports the theory of repression, and nothing justifies

a political or therapeutic agenda that encourages the use of memory recovery techniques.

In contrast, the most trenchant Skeptics of recovered memories based their attacks on disputing both the observations and the theory. The first task was harder because they tended not to have access to people claiming to have recovered memories. Instead, they were more likely to have access to members of their families who contested their claims, or to retractors who had recovered a memory they subsequently came to believe was false.[12] They could also point with justification to claims that were clearly highly unlikely, such as conscious memories purporting to be from the first year of life, or to illustrative cases of people who had recovered memories after hypnosis or some form of sustained suggestion or interrogation. As we saw in the last chapter, all these points have some empirical support and can be used to assert that at least some patients were not recovering memories of an actual event. Beyond that, some Skeptics were unwilling to accept that there had been *any* demonstration of the forgetting and recovery of traumatic memories. They were also highly critical of the theory of repression, frequently citing a review by David Holmes of decades of experimental research that claimed no evidence had been found for the concept.[13] Repression was routinely denounced as unscientific, as unsupported by evidence, and as contrary to what was known about memory. We now examine these critiques in more detail.

Critiques of Repression

When outlining the critiques, it is vital that one specify exactly how repression is being defined. Despite periodic acknowledgment of the different senses in which the term repression has been used, those skeptical of the concept have generally assumed or tested the more extreme versions. Thus, in his review of the laboratory evidence, Holmes defined repression as being "not under voluntary control," rather than including studies relevant to intentional forgetting. Elizabeth Loftus, in a conversation with therapist Ellen Bass, described repression as a "magical homunculus in the unconscious mind that periodically ventures out into the light of day, grabs hold of a memory, scurries underground, and stores it in a dark corner of the insensible self, waiting a few decades before digging it up and tossing it back out again."[14] As well as appearing to opt for an unconscious version of repression (that is, Freud's primary repression), in this conversation Loftus went on to explicitly reject the possibility that repression could be recast in terms of scientifically acceptable theories about memory.

Another example comes from Frederick Crews. He brackets a large group of therapists together and offers sweeping generalizations, constantly referring to "the recovered memory movement" and using emotive terms such as "fanatics" and the "dogma of repression." However, he cites no sources for these supposed beliefs or evidence for their ubiquity. Psychotherapists are supposed to believe that repression is "strictly unconscious—so much so, indeed, that they can routinely regard a young incest victim as leading two parallel but independent lives, one in the warm daylight of normal family affection and the other in continually repressed horror."[15] Again, no evidence is provided that the majority of trauma therapists think about repression in this way. More generally, the whole argument against the scientific validity of repression is undermined when one realizes that what is being criticized is usually an extreme version of the theory that may not actually be needed to explain the forgetting of trauma. The claim that there is no experimental evidence for repression also depends on using the term in this extreme sense, and as we will see below, many laboratory studies support Freud's other notion of intentional repression. By failing to acknowledge the existence of another well-established type of repression, the debate became polarized, and common ground between Skeptics and therapists became harder to find.

Contesting Observations of Repression

Throughout the writing on this topic, little distinction frequently has been made between the phenomena that have been observed and their explanations. Thus studies that claim to offer examples of repression, and have been criticized as such,[16] in fact mainly provide observations of the forgetting of childhood sexual abuse. The confusion between observation and theory is one of the main reasons, in my view, for the sheer obscurity of much of this debate.

Two of the most well-known articles with a skeptical stance published in the professional literature—"Can Memories of Childhood Sexual Abuse Be Repressed?" and "Questionable Validity of 'Dissociative Amnesia' in Trauma Victims: Evidence From Prospective Studies"—have added considerably to this confusion.[17] In the text Harrison Pope and colleagues claimed that they were not concerned with the specific mechanisms involved in the forgetting and whether these were "repression," "dissociation," or "traumatic amnesia." However, they were not simply concerned with observations of *any* forgetting either, for in the two articles they required studies to demonstrate that the failure of memory exceeded "normal forgetfulness" (implying a special type of mechanism). Thus, both in the titles of the articles and in the criteria the researchers used to evaluate studies, the confusion between observation and theory or mechanism was perpetuated. Neither was any objective criterion offered for assessing "normal forgetfulness."

Pope and colleagues further argued that because they were not convinced by any of the existing evidence for repression, they would start from the default position that it did not exist unless the studies showed otherwise. This strategy neatly placed the burden of proof on those who believed memories could be recovered, ensuring that their evidence was subjected to the most stringent tests while the evidence that memories could not be recovered went unexamined and unchallenged. The authors then dismissed all the available studies offering evidence for memory recovery on various grounds, including that the events might have occurred before age six years, that the respondents might have been affected by suggestions from their therapists, that the corroboration of the trauma was not convincing enough, or that the events were not shown to be so traumatic that anyone could reasonably be expected to remember them. Case reports that addressed these issues were not examined.

The study that came closest to meeting their objections was Linda Williams's follow-up study of children taken to a hospital emergency department for investigation and treatment of sexual abuse.[18] Williams interviewed the children when they were grown up about their childhood experiences and failed to elicit an account of the previously documented abuse from 38 percent of her respondents. In an extremely carefully conducted investigation, she considered alternative

explanations for this finding and concluded that forgetting was probably responsible in most of the cases. In addition to their usual criticisms about childhood amnesia and ordinary forgetfulness, Pope and
colleagues argued that there were other studies suggesting that up to 72
percent of victims do not disclose their abuse on an initial interview
and that Williams's results could easily be explained by these various
factors.

Although Pope was right to point to some weaknesses in the
studies, there are counterarguments to all his criticisms. The studies
concluding that many victims do not disclose their abuse when asked
were themselves flawed and could easily be challenged on the grounds
of sample selection or on the quality of the data. As we have seen, the
justification for rejecting the recovery of memories for events before
age six could be disputed, since age three is a better established cutoff
for childhood amnesia.[19] The requirement that forgetting exceeded
"normal forgetfulness" could be regarded as unreasonable, since Pope
offered few suggestions for defining the characteristics of an event that
anyone could be expected to remember. In fact, he made it clear that
even events meeting research criteria for sexual abuse might not be very
memorable. Given the fact that the studies had not set out to assess repression as defined by Pope in the first place, together with the lack of
clarity about what was "memorable" and "nonmemorable" abuse, it
was not surprising that none of them lived up to these criteria.

As detailed in the last chapter, since Pope's review articles, many
more relevant studies have been published. These include community
surveys that get around the problem of therapist suggestion, and
closely documented case studies that address issues of corroboration
and forgetting in more detail than has been done before. The Skeptics
have not noticeably changed their position, however, which tells us
something important about the nature of many scientific debates.
Given the limitations applying to *any* sort of evidence, there seems little point in demanding that one side unequivocally prove its case to the
satisfaction of the other, or come up with an irrefutable study. Every
piece of research has flaws of some kind that can justify its being dis-
counted by people who wish to do so, and on the whole, scientific
progress is rarely made in this way. To take another example, tobacco
companies have argued that the harmful effects of smoking have not

yet been conclusively proved because individual studies were all flawed in various ways and competing explanations have not been entirely ruled out.

This kind of position is often hard to refute absolutely, and in complex areas, particularly those involving human health and behavior, there comes a point at which gathering evidence ceases to be a productive exercise. Rather, scientists may be forced to rely on somewhat less clear-cut criteria such as the weight and plausibility of the evidence. They may ask themselves how likely it is that *all* the observations of corroborated recovered memories can be rejected. Instead of letting one theory win by default, they will consider how good each opposing theory is at accounting for *all* the relevant data, and whether the predictions they make are upheld or contradicted. Similarly, scientists studying recovered memory need to consider what the alternatives are to the theory of repression, and whether other explanations can do a better job. In the last chapter we raised the possibility that apparent recovered memories might be produced by suggestion. This was shown to be only a partial explanation, because of evidence for the limited power of suggestion and the frequent absence of any apparent suggestive influences having been present. The only other explanation that has been put forward by the Skeptics is "ordinary forgetting."

An Alternative Theory—Ordinary Forgetting

The Circularity Problem
As we have seen, the reviews by Harrison Pope and colleagues were critical of the possibility of "repression" but accepted that some recovered memories might reflect "ordinary forgetting" of trauma. Without a clear distinction between the two, of course, there is a danger of circularity, such that verified or acceptable recovered memories are assumed to be due to ordinary forgetting, and unverified or unacceptable ones are more readily labeled as dubious examples of repression. Here is another extract from Elizabeth Loftus's conversation with Ellen Bass:

> I took a deep breath. "I am only interested in this isolated subset of memories that are labeled 'repressed.' All I want to

discuss, all I have the right to examine, is this relatively un-explored part of the survivor/recovery movement concerned with repression."

"But why do we even have to talk about repression?" Ellen asked. "Why can't we just get rid of that word? What if a person simply forgets about an abusive event and then remembers it later, in therapy? She's in a safe place; she feels, perhaps for the first time, that someone will believe her and validate her experience, and the memory suddenly returns. Isn't that a valid experience?"

"Of course it is," I said, "but that's simple forgetting and remembering . . ."

"But isn't it possible to redefine repression so that it falls more in line with the normal, scientifically accepted mechanisms of memory?" Ellen asked.

"But then it isn't repression," I said, "because repression isn't *normal* memory."[20]

Several points are interesting about this exchange. Loftus is clearly concerned about the subset of repressed memories and is happy to acknowledge the return of a genuine memory, caused by ordinary forgetting. But how are we (or therapists sitting in their offices) supposed to distinguish between the recall of a repressed memory and an ordinary memory? Could it be the length of time in therapy before recovery, the vividness of the memory, or the degree of reliving in the present? None of these factors has been found to be related to the degree of corroboration available for the memory.[21] No clues are provided by Loftus, apart from the hint that repressed memories are *by definition* not "normal."

Crews, citing Loftus, further argues that memory decays drastically over time unless it is rehearsed and so may disappear for reasons other than repression. This leads him to the following conclusions on Ross Cheit's recovery of his memories about being molested, which Crews accepts as proven: "But had that abuse been repressed in the first place? In a phone conversation with me on September 7, 1994, Cheit declared that while he takes no position on the existence of repression, he is inclined to doubt that he abruptly and completely consigned his experiences to oblivion. What Cheit does fervently believe is that this *forgotten* ordeal . . . is responsible for the anguish that he experienced

many years later as an adult. . . . The possibility—indeed, the likelihood—that Cheit lost track of the incident at issue through an ordinary process of atrophy renders the example of his restored memory
useless as a proof of repression."[22] Here, Crews clearly accepts the observations but disputes the theory.

The journalist Mark Pendergrast finds a similar solution to the
problem of Ross Cheit's testimony, arguing that the abuse was not really traumatic after all. According to him "there is overwhelming evidence that extreme trauma is remembered consciously all too well."[23]
But a few pages later he concludes rather confusingly: "I believe that
some form of repression may occur for one-time traumatic events. . . .
It is possible that single sexual abuse encounters—or those of limited
duration—may be intentionally forgotten or 'repressed,' only to be recalled later in life. If the event in question were truly traumatic, however, experimental evidence indicates that it would probably be remembered."[24] In other words, events that are forgotten are not "truly"
traumatic. Once again, the reader is given no clue as to how to discriminate events that are only apparently traumatic from those that are
"truly" traumatic, except by whether or not they are forgotten. Following this line of argument, Pendergrast would have to claim that all the
examples of forgotten events described in the last chapter, including
rape, physical assault, life-threatening medical procedures, and witnessing violence and death, were simply not traumatic enough.

There is a major problem here. How can we as adults judge what
a child finds traumatic, particularly in the context of a violent or inces-
tuous family, terrifying threats of what will happen if the child tells, or
the deliberate giving of misinformation about what is happening and
what it means? If this is the only reality a child has known, some of
these experiences will not contradict expectations and may indeed
seem part of what is "normal." Violence may occur intermixed with
caring and even at times considerate behavior. When it comes to sexually abusive behaviors, an adult may attempt to persuade a child that
they are "normal," a sign of love or special affection, and so on. Patterns of behavior that typify the response to public events such as the
bus kidnapping chronicled by Lenore Terr may be quite different from
behaviors that occur in response to family betrayals whose very existence the child is instructed to deny or cover up, and which have enor-

mous implications for safety and survival. The imposition of adult concepts such as "trauma" onto complex, interdependent family relationships is fraught with difficulty, and we may question whether it is at all possible to judge what events are so "memorable" as to be unable to be explained by ordinary forgetting. Certainly, confident claims of the kind "traumatic events are always remembered" appear out of place given the little that is known.

A Sufficient Explanation?

According to the "ordinary memory" position, forgetting is generally brought about by a normal process of decay of the memory trace, and perhaps on some occasions by interference from later, similar experiences. But do these processes provide a sufficient account of the observations of memory recovery? As noted above, Crews argued that ordinary atrophy could account for Ross Cheit's experience. The problem is that atrophy would surely have led to a weak, decayed memory trace that was unlikely to have returned. What Cheit actually described was a very powerful experience: "It was like he [the abuser] was in the room with me. I could picture him. I could hear his voice. I could remember him quite well. And it was very compelling."[25] Most of the detailed accounts of recovered memory experiences confirm that they are often, but not always, exceptionally strong and emotion-laden. The individuals described by Schooler used words and phrases such as "stunned," "complete chaos in my emotions," "just this extreme emotion of fear and disbelief," "it was literally like a brick wall just hit me. . . . I just started crying and screaming uncontrollably."[26] The BPS Working Party found that recovered memories were described by therapists as having numerous characteristics, such as reliving of the event in the present, that are commonly found in patients suffering from PTSD.[27] The "ordinary memory" hypothesis struggles to account for these observations.

From the "ordinary memory" argument we can also make a number of specific predictions. For example, it should be the case that the more distressing the event, the harder it would be to forget. The opposite has been found, however, in a community study of a wide range of traumatic events.[28] Focusing on child abuse, we would similarly predict that the less violent or threatening the experience, or the less the events were interpreted as sexual at the time, the easier the abuse should be to forget. Almost every study that has examined the influence of threats and violence has found the opposite, with greater forgetting being associated with more violence, with more threats of harm, and with a trend toward greater use of force.[29] Interestingly, however, events that were not thought about or were forgotten were *less* likely to have been interpreted as sexual.[30] Another prediction is that abuse by strangers or more distant relatives should be easier to forget than abuse occurring within the immediate family. This proposition has been examined in some detail by Jennifer Freyd, who found that three studies contradicted it and one gave no clear-cut result.[31]

Does the literature support any other predictions made by the "ordinary forgetting" hypothesis? If this factor is at work, the younger the age at which the trauma occurred, the greater should be the forgetting. This prediction has been confirmed in most studies that have examined the question.[32] The "ordinary memory" position that traumas are largely forgotten through decay of the memory trace is consistent with some of the evidence but is contradicted by other studies. A number of alternative explanations exist for the one prediction that is clearly upheld, about the effect of age.

A Modern View of Memory

Many of the most outspoken critics of repression relied on a particular set of assumptions about memory. Just as the notions of some therapists who put their faith in recovered memory techniques were hopelessly flawed, so many of the claims made by false memory society advocates, few of whom were actually experts in memory themselves, were equally mistaken. Thus, Sidney Brandon and his colleagues appeared to believe that "individual autobiographical memory is unreliable," "'flashbulb' memories . . . have been shown to be completely unreliable but held with absolute certainty," "suggestibility and confabulation increase with the length of time between the event and later attempts to recall it," and "memory is constructive and reconstructive rather than reproductive."[33] These claims grossly exaggerate the fallibility of memory and do not fairly reflect the wealth of research on the basic integrity of human memory.[34]

Confident statements of this kind by false memory advocates are particularly wide of the mark when it comes to forgetting. Thus Merskey suggested that "memories which are not refreshed or kept in mind repeatedly, or renewed as a result of rehearsal, or the occurrence of other events to reinforce them, will decay."[35] Similarly, Crews claimed "memory always fades with the passage of time."[36] But as we have seen in Chapter 5, memories for significant personal experiences are often vivid and persistent and do not seem to depend on rehearsal.[37] The wholly passive view of memory put forward by the Skeptics contrasts with an alternative view of forgetting as sometimes intentional. This tradition goes back at least as far as the nineteenth century[38] and in the past thirty years has generated new insights that are very relevant to the theory of repression.

The idea that unwanted or irrelevant mental contents are *actively* excluded from awareness has come back into fashion, supported by experimental research that has systematically attempted to rule out other, more straightforward explanations. Interestingly, an event does not have to be traumatic to be excluded from awareness. Rather, these are everyday processes designed to make our thinking more efficient and may have developed in response to evolutionary pressures. Without a way of screening out unwanted thoughts, memories, and associations, we would all become overwhelmed by the sheer volume of information available to us. Psychologists studying this topic have not generally used the term *repression* because of its many connotations, but have preferred the more neutral term *inhibition*. In many ways, however, the two concepts appear to be remarkably similar.

One illustrative experiment involved the naming of words that were related to alternative meanings of a homograph, that is, a word such as "mace," which has more than one distinct meaning.[39] On each of two successive trials, participants were presented with a homograph, followed by a target word that they had to name as quickly as possible. When participants were first shown a word pair illustrating one meaning of the homograph (for example, bank–stream), they were subsequently much slower to name a target related to the other meaning of the homograph (for example, bank–money). The previous context was effective in reducing the accessibility of words related to the second meaning of the homograph, even when this was the most common meaning. The experimenters concluded from the results of several studies that when the homograph is first shown, all its competing meanings are initially activated, but unwanted or irrelevant meanings are then suppressed.

In memory experiments, too, it has been argued that inhibition automatically improves the processing of selected (or "target") items by decreasing the processing of irrelevant items that might potentially interfere with the targets. This is shown by *retrieval-induced forgetting*.[40] In the first phase of a typical experiment, participants study several lists of words divided into a number of different categories (for example, Animals: Horse, Tiger, Sheep, Monkey; Fruit: Apple, Banana, Orange, Mango). In the second phase of the experiment, they practice retrieving half the items from some of the categories by completing category-plus-example clues derived from the first few letters of the word (for example, Animal–Ho____?; Animal–Ti____?). The remaining items are not retrieved. Later, there is an unexpected recall test in which participants are given the category name (Animal) and asked to remember as many words from the original list as possible. Under these conditions participants recall more of the practiced items (Horse, Tiger) but at the expense of unpracticed items from the same categories (Sheep, Monkey). Crucially, recall of these unpracticed items is *worse* than recall of items from other categories (for example, Fruit) in which no items were practiced. Subsequent experiments have provided evidence that this effect is likely to be the result of active inhibition interfering with recall of unpracticed words like Sheep and Monkey, and hence enhancing retrieval of the practiced (target) items.[41]

Inhibitory effects, however, are not limited to targets that are already associated, like the names of different animals or fruit. In *directed forgetting* experiments participants are instructed either to remember or to forget arbitrary lists of unrelated words.[42] Several methods are used to specify which targets are to-be-forgotten and which are to-be-remembered. In the list method, participants are presented with a list of words one at a time, and then midway through are instructed to forget the first half of the list and remember the second half of the list. In a surprise test in which participants have to recall *all* the items from both halves of the list without any retrieval cues, they remember fewer targets from the to-be-forgotten set than from the to-be-remembered set. Researchers have shown that this is not simply because of the position of the items in the list or because they have given extra rehearsal time to words participants were asked to remember.

A number of additional findings make these results even more interesting. If participants are asked to pick out the words they have been instructed to remember or forget from a longer list including new words they have not seen before, rather than recall them without any retrieval cues, the difference between to-be-forgotten and to-be-remembered targets disappears. The difference also disappears if participants are shown some of the to-be-forgotten words in another context; even presenting a few of the words appears to lift the inhibition on all the to-be-forgotten words. Finally, it can be shown that the to-be-forgotten words have been registered and can affect participants' behavior unconsciously, even though the words cannot be deliberately recalled. For example, two leading memory researchers, Robert and Elizabeth Bjork, had participants carry out a directed forgetting task and then try to solve a series of word fragment completion problems.[43] These involved being presented with a few initial letters (for example, Ord . . . ?) and having to find a word to complete the fragment (for example, Ordeal, Order, Ordinary). Some of the fragments corresponded to words that participants had previously been instructed to remember or forget. The Bjorks found that having seen a word before made it more likely that participants would complete the fragment with that word, even if it was one they had been told to forget and had been unable to recall when previously asked to do so.

Later experiments have pointed to the likelihood that the to-be-forgotten items are being actively inhibited. Because recognition performance is unimpaired in these studies, it has been concluded that the inhibition induced by the "forget" instruction takes the form of *retrieval inhibition*. That is, the to-be-forgotten targets are adequately encoded in memory in the first place and are later actively inhibited from being retrieved and entering consciousness by the "forget" instruction. These processes also may be involved in explaining posthypnotic amnesia, when participants are instructed to forget something while in a hypnotized state. After hypnosis has been lifted, they are unable to retrieve the forgotten item until their amnesia is reversed by a prearranged signal or cue.

In an even more direct demonstration of deliberate memory repression, Anderson and Green had their participants learn a series of word pairs such as "ordeal–roach" so that they could remember the right-hand word when shown the left-hand word.[44] They were then presented with the first word of a pair and were instructed either to retrieve and say aloud the second word of the pair ("think" condition) or to try to prevent the word from entering their consciousness at all ("no-think" condition). Other word pairs were not presented at this time to provide a comparison. At the end of the experiment participants were once again given the left-hand word of each pair and asked to recall the right-hand word. Anderson and Green found that, compared with the comparison pairs, recall was significantly better when participants were in the "think" condition and significantly worse when they were in the "no-think" condition. Moreover, the more often their participants practiced not thinking about a word, the harder it was for them to remember it later when asked to do so. The researchers concluded that they had identified an inhibitory control mechanism that was effective in keeping unwanted material out of consciousness, similar to that proposed by Freud.

What relevance do these experiments, which are largely based on word lists, have to clinical accounts of repression? The first thing to note is the close parallels between the organization of knowledge about the world (animals, fruit, and so on) and about ourselves. As we saw in Chapter 4, information in memory about the self is thought to be organized as a set of multiple, related memory records that capture important episodes and relationships. These overlapping records preserve some consistent features of the self but also contain information relating to the self at different ages and in the performance of different roles. They span the whole range of success and failure, stability and change, attachment and loss, acceptance and rejection. What is perhaps unique about the self is the potential for inconsistency and hence competition among alternative records containing contradictory information relating to the self and our relationships with important attachment figures. Just as simple words such as "bank" can have more than one meaning attached to them, so the same is true of our concepts of ourselves and others, only to an infinitely greater extent. Just as we saw in the homograph experiment, in real life we may frequently need to select the relevant memory record for our immediate purposes and inhibit what is irrelevant, contradictory, or unwanted. I will discuss some examples of this later in the chapter.

A few studies have begun to investigate these processes in people with PTSD, acute stress disorder, or recovered memories of trauma. Richard McNally and colleagues studied a different version of directed forgetting in which participants are shown a list of words and instructions to forget or remember are given after each one (item method). There is a similar tendency for people to find it difficult to remember words they have been told to forget, but this is thought to be due to the way the words are encoded in the first place rather than to retrieval inhibition operating on items stored in memory. In two studies using this method, McNally found no evidence that people with PTSD related to childhood sexual abuse, or with repressed or recovered memories of abuse, were any more able to forget trauma-related words than people who had not been abused.[45] In contrast, another recent study found that participants with acute stress disorder, who had very recently been traumatized and had numerous dissociative symptoms, were better at forgetting trauma words than control subjects.[46] What would be helpful now are similar studies using the list-method version of directed forgetting to provide a more direct test of the theory that people with dissociative symptoms or those who report memory recovery are particularly well able to inhibit unwanted material from coming to mind.

Natural Repressors

Experimental evidence for inhibitory processes has so far suggested that they are a feature of everyday mental life. In themselves, therefore, these processes are unable to explain why some people may be able to forget traumas whereas others always remember them. It would be of great interest to know whether there are people who are particularly good at forgetting unhappy experiences. Such a group has in fact been identified; they are individuals with the so-called *repressive coping style,* or *repressors* for short.

Repressors are usually defined in terms of scoring low on a measure of anxiety but high on a measure of psychological defensiveness.[47]

With this method, therefore, repressors are seen as people who tend to deny feeling anxious, fearful, angry, or jealous and who tend to deny possessing any antisocial habits. A series of studies with female undergraduate students has shown that repressors have problems recalling unhappy autobiographical memories. For example, given sixty seconds to recall as many childhood memories as possible, repressors in one of these studies recalled significantly fewer unhappy memories than nonrepressors, and their age at the time of the first unhappy memory they recalled was substantially greater. In contrast, there were no differences in the recalling of positive memories.[48]

The problem in the recall of unhappy events provided some justification for labeling this group of people as possessing a repressive coping style, except that there was a glaring alternative explanation of the results. The much more obvious possibility that had not been ruled out was that a person retrieving fewer unhappy memories might in fact have had a childhood that was happier than usual, and thus not constitute evidence for repression at all. Lynn Myers and I therefore used a semistructured interview for assessing early experience that allows raters to judge reports of childhood experiences according to their own predetermined criteria rather than relying simply on participants' own memories or on their judgments about the significance of various childhood experiences.[49] The interview has a number of specific questions such as "Did your parents praise (or criticize) you?" If participants answered "yes" to these questions, specific examples of praise and criticism were elicited and formed the basis of the interviewer ratings. Thus, to take this example, ratings were based not on the simple statement that participants were praised or criticized but on their ability to produce concrete examples of this. In this study ratings were checked by an independent judge blinded to whether participants were repressors. Crucially, our sample of repressors reported significantly more hostility, more indifference, and less closeness in their relationships with their fathers, thus making it extremely unlikely that they had in fact had happier childhoods than nonrepressors.

Because repressors in these studies might have been withholding unhappy personal memories intentionally, Myers and I carried out further experiments that showed much more widespread problems with learning and remembering negative information.[50] In one of these we had repressors and nonrepressors intentionally memorize a story about parental relationships. The story concerned a woman's childhood, with examples of each parent behaving in a positive and negative (critical and indifferent) way. As predicted, the female repressors did not differ from nonrepressors in their memory for neutral or positive phrases, but they recalled fewer examples of parents behaving in a negative way. In another study we also found that repressors were superior to nonrepressors in their ability to forget negative words when instructed to do so in a directed forgetting task, although they showed no differences in their forgetting of positive words.

These findings, which show that a group of individuals with more negative childhoods nevertheless had greater difficulty in learning and recalling negative information about childhood, are entirely contrary to standard psychological theories, which predict that the more experiences of a certain type a person has had, the easier it should be for that person to remember them. However, the precise relation of these findings to the Freudian view of traumatic early experiences leading to repression is not clear at this point. The childhood interview we used did not result in any dramatic instances of the lifting of repression, but this would have been unlikely given its brevity and the relatively small number of cues provided. At the same time it was not possible to rule out the Freudian hypothesis that there were additional repressed traumatic memories, involving either maternal or paternal behavior, that did not emerge in the interview and that might have accounted for the development of this coping style. An alternative possibility is that repressors may be socialized into stoically ignoring unpleasant events and feelings so that they are less well-represented in memory.

Mechanisms for Forgetting Trauma

These studies suggest, ironically, that the active exclusion of information from consciousness is an attribute of *normal* memory and *ordinary* forgetting. Inhibition (or repression) can be a healthy process, not a pathological one. Moreover, some people are better than others at selectively forgetting negative information of various kinds. Psychological disorders, in which people are bombarded by upsetting thoughts and memories, may reflect the breakdown of these inhibitory processes, and treating successfully the people who suffer from them may involve restoring inhibition so that the processes function effectively once again. But can these processes really be responsible for the dramatic forgetting of traumatic events? Although no conclusive answers are available to us at present, the possibilities are so intriguing that they are worth some speculation.

Studies of child abuse indicate that many victims deliberately try to forget the events after they happen, or are told by their abusers to do so and threatened with serious harm or death if they do not. Other adults whom a child may tell about the abuse may not believe the child. Even when adults know the truth of what has happened—whether it be abuse; witnessing violence, injury, or death; or some other event—they may deny the reality of these events or discourage the child from talking about them. In all these cases children may be left with little option but to try to forget what has happened. Few reminders may then occur to disrupt the inhibition and bring the event back to mind, particularly if the child no longer visits the place where the trauma happened. There is then some similarity with the intentional or directed forgetting experiments described above.

Studies of directed forgetting suggest that retrieval inhibition can be overcome by presenting a person with relevant reminders, such as examples of the to-be-forgotten targets. Reports of the circumstances under which traumatic memories are recovered are typically consistent with this, with triggers including TV programs and newspaper articles dealing with similar traumas, or the respondent's own children reaching an age at which the trauma originally occurred.[51] Of particular interest are accounts of instances in which people have previously been exposed to what seem to be highly relevant cues without triggering recall. For example, a memory of childhood sexual abuse was eventually triggered in one woman who had emigrated to the United Kingdom by media reports of sexual abuse in her home country; similar reports of abuse in the United Kingdom, to which she had been exposed for many years, were apparently not specific or powerful enough to have the same effect.

One possibility is that retrieval inhibition is strengthened by additional inhibitory processes that operate on other targets that are highly associated with the traumatic event. For example, abuse by a father who was a carpenter could lead to inhibition of words and concepts connected with woodworking, home improvement, furniture, and the like. The failure to process these associated concepts in any depth could lessen the risk of inadvertently triggering the spontaneous recall of traumatic memories. However, retrieval may not be protected by such inhibitory processes if either of two sets of circumstances occurs. One is that a particularly large number of retrieval cues are encountered at the same time; the other is when the cues are uncommon associates that previously have been only very rarely encountered.[52]

It is still hard to explain how repeated physical or sexual abuse by a caregiver could be forgotten, since the child would be constantly exposed to reminders of the abuser in different contexts. This situation corresponds more closely to Anderson's retrieval-induced forgetting experiments. Instead of different examples of a category such as "animals," there will be a range of memories corresponding to different examples of the category "mother" or "father." Anderson has argued that unwanted memories of abusive behavior could be inhibited by the child repeatedly retrieving competing examples of the parent being caring or loving.[53] In addition, there will be powerful incentives for children not to dwell on abusive incidents but to attempt to maintain a positive image of their parents. This is likely to be very important for safety and survival, particularly in a context of family violence where further abuse could easily be triggered or where the child fears the consequences of disclosure. Jennifer Freyd has presented evidence consistent with this idea in her book *Betrayal Trauma*, showing, for instance, that forgetting is more likely for abuse within the family than for stranger abuse.[54] Likewise, more forgetting occurs after rape by someone who is known to the victim than after rape by a stranger.[55]

Repression versus Dissociation Revisited

One of the most puzzling aspects of repression theory has been the notion of primary or unconscious repression. Even if information can be repressed before conscious encoding, critics have rightly questioned how it is then possible for a conscious memory to subsequently be recovered. One possible solution, following Janet, is to invoke the idea of a divided or dissociated consciousness with which a person is usually out of touch. For example, this could consist of a temporary alternative or fantasy world deliberately and repeatedly constructed by a frightened child seeking relief from pain or fear. Access to this alternative world might become more and more difficult after the trauma ceased and as the child grew older. Recall would involve spontaneous access, triggered by some reminder, to this area of the mind in which the experience *was* registered.

This explanation depends on the existence of a parallel consciousness, of the kind that used to be described as "multiple personality" and is now referred to as *dissociative identity.* For the memories to be retrieved, conscious encoding would have to occur in this alternative state. Some limited evidence from a detailed study of a patient with multiple personalities (HS) suggests that different autobiographical memories are retrieved by different personality states.[56] Whereas HS's host personality retrieved relatively more positive memories from the recent past, a child personality was found to retrieve predominantly negative memories from a period corresponding to her stated age (nine years). The pattern of memories was quite different from that of a control group, or from that of a group who were trying to simulate someone with a multiple personality.

This study is intriguing, and the results are largely consistent with the hypothesis of a divided consciousness. Apart from the limitations inherent in all case studies, however, the problem is that it is quite rare to come across dissociated identities, whereas the term *dissociative amnesia* is frequently used to account for memory loss during a traumatic event. As we have seen, it is generally used in the broader sense of there being some disturbance to consciousness such as a person being in a daze, being numb, or having an altered perception of him- or herself or reality. This broader usage, however, brings us back to the original problem of how a memory can be recovered when there was a disturbance during the original encoding.

There is also a second problem. As we saw in Chapter 3, dissociation occurring during the trauma itself (peritraumatic dissociation) is a risk factor for PTSD. It seems likely, therefore, that dissociation promotes the intrusion of unwanted trauma memories. Emily Holmes, Richard Hennessy, and I recently obtained more direct evidence for this in a series of laboratory experiments during which volunteers watched a film of upsetting scenes from car crashes.[57] The more participants reported an increase in dissociative experiences while they watched the film, the more likely they were to have intrusive memories of the film over the next week. In other words, dissociation appears to be an explanation both for having more memories of the film and for being unable to recall significant aspects of it.

Fortunately, the dual representation theory of PTSD that was discussed above provides a way around this apparent contradiction.[58] Emily Holmes suggested that dissociation during a traumatic event mainly blocks encoding into the verbally accessible memory system (VAM), so that a person has less-detailed conscious memories, but does not prevent encoding into the situationally accessible memory system (SAM), since this requires a minimal level of consciousness. As discussed in Chapter 6, the perceptual, image-based SAM system is thought to be mainly responsible for the intrusion of visual trauma memories and is inhibited by the existence of detailed memories in the VAM system. According to the theory, therefore, anything that blocks encoding into the VAM system (such as a disturbance in consciousness) should have two quite separate effects, making the trauma harder to recall deliberately and making spontaneous intrusive images more likely.

In contrast, the theory predicts that blocking encoding into the SAM system should reduce the frequency of intrusive images. In several trauma film experiments we have now tried to achieve this by having participants tap a predetermined pattern on a concealed keyboard while they are watching the film.[59] Because this task involves imagining spatial relationships on the keyboard, we expected it to compete for cognitive resources with the SAM system, and so interfere with the efficiency of encoding, leading to fewer spontaneous intrusions. In the experiments the tapping task did indeed reduce intrusions, compared with a control condition. Since then, we have shown that the effect cannot simply be due to distraction because a verbal task, designed to compete for resources with the VAM system, *increased* the number of later intrusive memories.[60]

It seems, then, that some kind of dissociative process other than an alternative personality state could be consistent with the existence of recovered memories. We would need to assume that the dissociation interfered with the creation of VAM memories but left SAM memories intact. Retrieval cues would subsequently lead to the intrusion of fragmented, sensory images from the SAM system, from which people could begin to reconstruct a conscious account of the events. Some trauma theorists have proposed that dissociation offers a better account of forgetting than does repression, in part because of the finding that recovered memories often come back in the form of unprocessed images.[61] According to this argument, it is the dissociation that occurs at the time of the trauma that is primarily responsible for the forgetting. In view of the evidence that not all recovered memories are of this kind, however, I think we must consider an alternative, albeit related, theory.

It is possible that dissociative reactions such as being in a daze or having out-of-body experiences may not in themselves *directly* lead to forgetting. For example, adult trauma victims can often remember and report only too well the depersonalization they experienced during a car crash or an assault. Rather, they may *indirectly* make forgetting easier, if the person wishes to intentionally inhibit the retrieval of unprocessed images stored in the SAM system or the retrieval of ordinary autobiographical memories stored in the VAM system. There are at least two ways in which dissociative reactions might have this effect. They might interfere with the encoding of detailed VAM memories of the trauma scene in the first place, so that there was less information to suppress and fewer details that might inadvertently trigger flashbacks when thought about consciously. Second, dissociation might reduce the emotional and physiological impact of the trauma, so that the normal boost to memory conveyed by the release of stress hormones was reduced or eliminated altogether, making forgetting easier.

Whether the memories are recovered in the form of fragmented images or as whole autobiographical memories depends, I would argue, on the degree of conscious processing that the events originally received. Dissociative responses of various kinds may simply be understood as a common response to trauma that can facilitate deliberate attempts to forget. Does this mean that forgetting is *always* intentional? Although I suspect it always starts off as intentional, it is likely that repeated efforts to forget a series of traumas may result in the forgetting itself becoming automatic. Forgetting may develop into a practiced coping strategy that no longer has to be put into effect deliberately when something unpleasant occurs. Like the natural repressors discussed above, certain people may come to abort processing of unpleasant events, whether by encoding them less effectively in the first place or by inhibiting the memory of them more strongly. Descriptions of immediate and effortless forgetting may be explained by this type of mechanism.

Before concluding this discussion, it is important to note that these various mechanisms leave plenty of opportunity for error. Ordinary autobiographical memories are partially reconstructed each time they are retrieved and may condense large quantities of information or large numbers of similar instances into a more manageable, but somewhat distorted, form. SAM memories may consist of isolated sensations or images that then form the basis for a constructed narrative account. Although this account may make sense of the sensations and images, it may also be inaccurate. The more fragmented and sparse the images, the greater the danger of this occurring. There is also the danger that images may be contaminated with information from similar experiences or from feared "worst-outcome" scenarios, so that composite pictures may be formed of events that never actually happened.[62]

Therefore, flashbacks may reflect the influence of several experiences rather than just one, and may have to be interpreted with caution. A dramatic example of this process was provided by a member of emergency services who was treated for PTSD after he attended the scene of a particularly brutal murder. Although he had not been present at the murder, he formed an image of this event that appeared to be influenced by a conscious memory of witnessing his father attack his mother when he was a teenager. Not only did he experience flashbacks based on this image, but he had intrusive imagery of himself attacking a woman in woods near his home using the same stereotyped motions. This image was so vivid that he visited the woods to confirm that he was not a murderer.

Conclusions

It is perhaps unfortunate that debate has centered so much on the concept of repression, which has never been clearly defined and for which there has never been much direct evidence, rather than on forgetting, which is what has actually been claimed to happen. It is also unfortunate that repression generally has been characterized by Skeptics in more extreme ways rather than other, more everyday possibilities being considered. It is likely that this has served the Skeptics' purposes in some way. For although the false memory societies could protest their members' innocence, criticize ill-advised therapeutic practices, and point to some bizarre and unlikely recovered memories, this kind of evidence was insufficient for making the argument that *all* cases of apparent recovered memory occurring in therapy must be false. Also, what was to be done with the small number of cases, such as that of Ross Cheit, in which there was strong corroborative evidence for an apparent recovered memory?

The solution the Skeptics appear to have adopted was to argue that recovered memories could not in the main be true because they depended on the theory of repression, which was unscientific, unsupported by evidence, and contrary to what was known about memory. Two final steps covered all eventualities. First, any therapist who had a patient recovering a memory could be labeled as a "recovered memory therapist" who believed in the most dubious form of unconscious repression and used inappropriate techniques; thus, the "memory" was "repressed," and both therapist and memory by definition were suspect. Second, any other cases of genuine recovered memories that could not be explained away could be attributed to a process other than repression. In effect, both Skeptics and some trauma therapists tended not to distinguish the observation and the theory of forgetting, which thoroughly confused most commentators.

As we have seen, the Skeptics' position was both logically flawed, because of the extreme way repression was defined and the circularity in the reasoning, and inconsistent with many facts for which suggestion or "ordinary forgetting" were inadequate explanations. Ironically for the "ordinary forgetting" argument, if repression is taken to include intentional forgetting, then a considerable amount of experimental literature actually supports the idea of a set of active processes keeping unwanted material out of consciousness. This means that repression no longer appears as an outlandish notion believed only by gullible clinicians, but is related to everyday processes serving an efficient and effective mental life. In effect, there need be no disagreement between clinicians and laboratory scientists, with both able to contribute to a greater understanding of memory, particularly under conditions of extreme stress.

The concepts of repression and dissociation have proved useful in carrying forward the idea of defensive strategies for forgetting trauma, but both have drawbacks when we attempt to explain recovered memories. Use of the term repression has led to confusion because it can be defined in two quite different ways, and dissociation, although often coexistent with traumatic forgetting, is concerned with alterations in consciousness rather than specifically with forgetting. The way forward is likely to depend on abandoning these clinical theories in favor of concepts derived from cognitive psychology. Although the gap between clinic and laboratory is still wide at present, it appears that progress is only a matter of time.

9

More Battlegrounds
Preventing and Treating PTSD

History, despite its wrenching pain,
Cannot be unlived, but if faced
With courage, need not be lived again.
—Maya Angelou, "On the Pulse of Morning"[1]

The previous chapters of this book have identified two separate processes that must be involved in recovery from PTSD. One is bringing under control the vivid reexperiencing of the trauma through flashbacks and nightmares, a reaction that seems to be mainly reported in the context of extreme fear, helplessness, or horror. The second is the conscious reappraisal of the event and its impact. In many cases negative beliefs about the self will reflect challenges to identity, a process that is not specific to PTSD but is encountered in many other psychiatric disorders such as depression. Corresponding to these two mechanisms are contrasting types of therapy for PTSD. One type, which involves prolonged exposure to upsetting images and trauma reminders, focuses primarily on the relief of flashbacks and nightmares, whereas the other type, which includes cognitive therapy, places greater emphasis on issues of belief, interpretation, and identity. Before describing preventive treatments and treatments for established PTSD in detail, however, we need to consider the fact that after most traumas, symptoms are common for the first few days or weeks but tend to diminish naturally in victims who do not go on to suffer from PTSD. What is happening in this group?

Normal and Interrupted Recovery

In Chapter 6 I proposed an analysis based on our dual representation theory of PTSD.[2] According to this, flashbacks and nightmares involve the activation of traces of the traumatic event recorded in the SAM system, a largely image-based system that encodes unattended sensory information but is unable to encode whether events belong to the present or the past. Immediately after the incident, far more detail, particularly about sights, sounds, smells, movements, and so on, is encoded in the SAM system than in the VAM system, which has recorded the corresponding conscious experience of the trauma. When the trauma survivor deliberately focuses and maintains attention on the content of the flashbacks, rather than trying to suppress them, information that is present only in the SAM system becomes reencoded into the VAM system, at which point the memories are assigned a spatial and temporal context.

This process has to be repeated numerous times because there may be a lot of extra information in the SAM system that has to be transferred to the VAM system. Eventually, providing the person is now safe, detailed memories in the SAM system that signaled the continuing presence of danger are matched by detailed memories in the VAM system that locate the danger in the past. When the person encounters trauma reminders, these VAM memories are accessed, preventing inappropriate amygdala activation and the accompanying return of fear.

Most contemporary explanations of PTSD propose that recovery involves changing the content or structure of trauma memories. In contrast, dual representation theory maintains that the original trauma memories are not altered in any way but remain intact and may be vividly reexperienced again in the future if the person unexpectedly comes across detailed and specific reminders of the trauma. Rather, recovery is seen in terms of creating new trauma memories in the VAM system that are made more permanent and more easily accessible by the person repeatedly going over them. This process produces competing memories of the trauma, an original one associated with extreme fear, helplessness, or horror, and more recent ones in which the trauma is recalled in a place of safety as something that belongs to the past. As long as these new memories are accessed when the person comes across reminders of the trauma, he or she will not feel in danger.

In addition to dealing with flashbacks, a separate task in the aftermath of trauma is evaluation of the implications of what has happened (see Chapter 4). The information provided by the trauma may initially produce catastrophic interference with existing knowledge about the self and its relation to the world, undermining positive identities and reinforcing previously established feared identities. Integrating the new information will be slow and gradual compared with the rapid realization of the occurrence of the traumatic event. As suggested in Chapter 6, this "working through" or "emotional processing" will depend on the reluctant trauma victim rehearsing interleaved pre- and posttrauma memories, repeatedly comparing the beliefs, plans, and goals that used to exist with those that have now been forced upon him or her. The repeated reinstatement of these contrasting hippocampally based memories will permit more complex neocortical knowledge structures to be gradually adjusted so that old and new data are combined in a more coherent way. This is essentially a process of construction, and the need many survivors feel to talk again and again about their trauma may reflect the ongoing work of putting together a version of events that is coherent and makes sense in all its details.

The proposals for the existence of fast and slow memory systems that we first reviewed in Chapter 6 have the potential to explain several interesting aspects of the response to trauma. The rapid formation of limited memories in the hippocampal system allows some acknowledgment of the event, but an absence of integration with knowledge already available in the neocortical system may contribute to a sense of unreality surrounding the event. Here, "unreality" reflects the comparative lack of neuronal connections between the initial hippocampal memory and other neocortical memory structures that are known to be closely related conceptually. "Denial" consists in the refusal of the trauma victim to consciously dwell on the traumatic experience and to initiate the process of interleaved learning. The existence of unchanged neocortical knowledge structures may be why certain traumatized people describe being able to "live in the past" and to pretend that the event never really happened. Their unwillingness or inability to update their memory systems may reflect the feeling that it is simply too painful to acknowledge the reality of their loss.

How is it that certain people can block what Horowitz suggested was an innate impulse toward resolving this kind of discrepancy?[3] As we reviewed in Chapter 4, Resick and Schnicke described two types of systematic distortion of the conscious memory of the event, one of which they called overassimilation.[4] By distorting the reality of what happened, the victim makes the discrepancy with previous beliefs and goals go away. My suggestion is that people have to actively construct and rehearse a distorted version of the event from which awkward elements have been removed.[5] Rehearsing this version often enough will lead to its becoming more accessible than the original memory that still contains the unwanted facts. But this strategy will work only if the person can limit his or her exposure to trauma reminders that have more in common with the original memory and that will, if unexpectedly encountered, cause this memory to spontaneously come to mind.

This proposal is illustrated diagrammatically in Figure 9.1. Assume that a memory consists of a number of features (F). In the top part of the diagram the VAM memory consists of a limited number of features (F1 to F6) and the SAM memory a larger number of features (F1 to F20). As long as trauma reminders only corresponding to the features F1 to F6 are encountered, this limited VAM memory will be sufficient to inhibit a fear response. In practice, trauma survivors can limit their exposure to trauma reminders in many ways—by avoiding anything to do with the incident, not talking about it, switching off related television programs, moving to a new home, or changing jobs or friends. Trauma survivors frequently do all of these things. But if they unexpectedly are confronted with additional trauma reminders from the set F7 to F20, the original trauma memory is likely to be automatically accessed in the form of flashbacks, and the body will once again sense itself to be in immediate danger. This is shown in the bottom part of Figure 9.1.

In this form of interrupted recovery, both the process of transferring information from the SAM to the VAM system and the process of allowing hippocampal and neocortical representations to interact and gradually change are prematurely blocked or inhibited. Another form

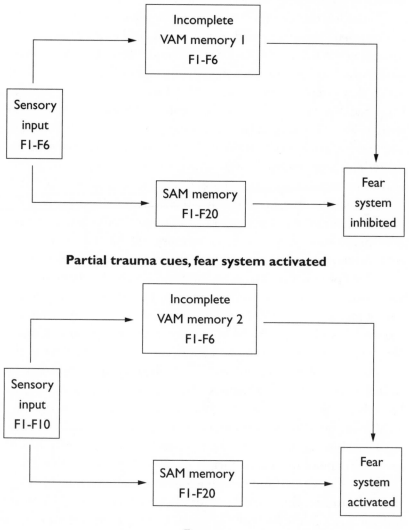

Figure 9.1

of interrupted recovery occurs when the survivor is unable to prevent trauma reminders from constantly activating negative images and thoughts and is engaged in an exhausting battle to stop them from entering consciousness. This is the situation of most people presenting with active PTSD. Here, the attempt to shore up positive identities and suppress feared identities has been ineffective, resulting in survivors labeling a wide variety of innocuous situations as potentially threatening, unpredictable, or unfair; labeling themselves as weak, bad, or inadequate; or labeling any positive goals as irrelevant or unattainable. This form of catastrophic interference has the effect of vastly increasing the number of cues that will potentially act as trauma reminders, thereby inducing a constant sense of current threat, inadequacy, or hopelessness.

Such an assault on the survivor's identity generates secondary emotions such as anger over others' betrayal, guilt over harming someone else, and shame over one's own perceived deficiencies, which in turn increase the unpleasantness of flashbacks and prompt a repetitive cycle of negative thoughts and memories (rumination). Rumination is associated with a poor outcome although we do not yet know why.[6] One possibility is that flashbacks, conscious memories of the trauma, and negative thoughts keep triggering each other in a vicious circle. The more accessible thoughts and vivid memories of the trauma are, the more likely the survivor is to feel that similar events are bound to occur again, thus maintaining the sense of threat.[7] Alternatively, the emotions generated by these negative evaluations may take up cognitive resources that would otherwise be used to block or inhibit unwanted memories. Can anything be done at an early stage to lessen the risk of these two forms of interrupted processing?

Can PTSD Be Prevented?

Psychological Debriefing

Rather than being the focus of constructive collaboration, attempts to prevent PTSD have tended to generate another set of ill-tempered arguments between Saviors and Skeptics. As with the "false memory" debate, semantic confusions and the promotion of unevaluated clinical procedures are gradually yielding to a more informed consensus on good practice. At the center of the debate has been a procedure called *critical incident stress debriefing* (CISD) described in a short article by Jeffrey Mitchell in 1983.[8] CISD was first used in the mid-1970s as a technique of reducing posttraumatic stress in emergency medical teams. Mitchell, then a paramedic, used the term CISD to refer to a general approach to stress management involving four elements: individual on-scene crisis intervention, an initial postincident small group discussion known as "defusing," a more extensive postincident small group discussion known as the "formal CISD," and follow-up psychological support services. It is the "formal CISD" element that has figured in most of the debates, with the new term *critical incident stress management* being introduced to identify the more comprehensive approach to postincident care.[9]

In this expanded model, CISD is a seven-phase small group discussion designed to help a person overcome an unhealthy fixation on a traumatic event. It takes place one to fourteen days after the incident and involves between three and twenty people over several hours. Following an introduction phase, group members describe factual details of what occurred during the incident, moving on to describe their thoughts during the incident, their reactions and feelings, and their symptoms during and after the incident. Finally, the debriefers provide information about normal posttraumatic reactions and coping strategies and close the meeting with a summary and recommendations to the group members.

The popularity and high face validity of CISD led to some variation of it being adopted by numerous organizations internationally, including the Federal Aviation Administration; the U.S. Air Force; the U.S. Coast Guard; the U.S. Secret Service; the Federal Bureau of Investigation; the Bureau of Alcohol, Tobacco, and Firearms; the Swedish National Police; the Defense Forces of Singapore; and the Australian Army and Navy. It is now common for survivors of all kinds of disasters to be offered CISD or some form of more generic psychological debriefing by counselors associated with the police or medical or social services immediately after an incident. Psychological debriefing, for both individuals and groups, has also been promoted vigorously by providers of counseling services to businesses such as banks whose employees might be faced with trauma in the course of their work. In some instances attendance at debriefings is a condition of employment.

Despite this unparalleled organizational and commercial success, the fact remains that the element of debriefing corresponding to "formal CISD," although enjoying a high degree of popularity among those who receive it, has never been shown to offer any protective effect against a person developing PTSD. Worse, a minority of studies have suggested that it may actually be harmful. Obviously, it is insufficient to simply follow up people who have been debriefed and see whether their symptoms reduce, as this could happen naturally with time. The critical test is to compare debriefing with some sort of comparison condition. The investigation conducted by Suzanna Rose, Bernice Andrews, Marilyn Kirk, and me is fairly typical of the majority of studies.[10] We randomly assigned assault victims within one month postincident to receive either individual debriefing, education about posttrauma responses, or no intervention and then gave everyone measures of posttraumatic symptoms and psychological distress six months and eleven months later. Although the debriefing was popular, there were no discernible differences between the groups in their liability for developing symptoms of PTSD or depression.

The findings of other randomized studies of individual debriefing have recently been reviewed.[11] Although most have simply suggested that debriefing is ineffective, several have now reported significantly worse outcomes for those who have been debriefed.[12] All these studies have been criticized on the grounds that the training of the debriefers may have been inadequate, that debriefing may have been offered at an inappropriately early stage, and that debriefing was intended to be a group not an individual intervention. Even if some of these criticisms are true, it must be borne in mind that the widespread and often commercially led promotion of debriefing means that these same conditions are sure to be repeated in the real world. There is therefore considerable value in seeing the effects of debriefing under less than optimal conditions. There are still no randomized studies of group debriefing, but it is striking that nobody who has implemented group debriefing shortly after a trauma and compared it with any kind of comparison condition has ever found it to be associated with significantly fewer symptoms.

There is now a fair degree of consensus that it is inappropriate to offer CISD or psychological debriefing except in the context of a more comprehensive approach such as critical incident stress management in which an overall framework exists for immediate and long-term support and people are followed up to see whether they require additional intervention.[13] But it is still the case that the "integrated, multi-component approach" of critical incident stress management with its ten separate elements has not been evaluated. Arguably, it is a considerable waste of resources to invest money in a complex, expensive set of procedures with no evidence of effectiveness. The data provide a strong hint that we need to rethink the question of early intervention in light of our knowledge of normal and interrupted recovery reviewed above.

Alternative Approaches: Psychological First Aid and Screen and Treat

We have seen that the normal processes of dealing with flashbacks and updating slow learning systems can take several days or weeks. Individual symptoms such as intrusive memories are relatively common in the immediate aftermath of a severe trauma and are not at that point predictive of long-term outcome.[14] For milder traumas such as some motor vehicle accidents, PTSD symptoms present after approximately one week predict later disorder.[15] A relatively extreme short-term reaction, acute stress disorder, also predicts vulnerability to later PTSD, but so far this has been measured only between a week and a month posttrauma.[16] Acute stress disorder primarily involves high levels of initial dissociative symptoms, but it is likely that high levels of other symptoms, such as reexperiencing and arousal, provide equally good prediction of the risk of later PTSD.[17]

From this it may be inferred that any intervention that is carried out within two or three days after a mild trauma, or within a month after a severe trauma, is probably coinciding with natural recovery processes. An obvious concern is that the intervention should interfere as little as possible with these processes, at least until some hindrance to recovery is evident. For this reason the approach known as *psychological first aid* concentrates on ensuring that the conditions necessary for promoting natural adjustment are in place.[18]

One of these conditions is the restoration of physical safety for victims. Until this is satisfactorily demonstrated, the body's responses to threat remain active, and victims cannot begin to process events in a way that discriminates between a past that involved threat and a present that does not. These considerations are particularly important for refugees, whose concerns about safety may realistically include the current whereabouts of their loved ones, their own housing and subsistence needs, and the probability that they will be returned to their country of origin. Until these issues are settled, it will likely be unhelpful and ineffective to begin any form of psychological intervention focused on their traumatic experiences.

Among the other conditions should be appropriate acknowledgment of the magnitude of the trauma, whether by family, friends, employers, or the community at large. Minimization of the trauma will give the message that no significant impact is likely and that adjustments to the person's routine, perhaps in the form of time away from work or other responsibilities, are unnecessary. If as a result of these messages no additional time is set aside by survivors, they may find it difficult to focus on flashbacks and go through the repeated cognitive appraisal that is part of normal recovery. This will make it easier for survivors who prefer to avoid thinking about the trauma by immersing themselves in other activities, a coping strategy that risks the later return of trauma-related symptoms.

Another condition is the availability of support, either from the victim's own social network or from professional sources. As we saw in Chapter 3, derogatory and critical comments by others are damaging, so the main value of support may be to shield the survivor from unhelpful influences. Arguably, support is most effective when it remains under the control of the survivor, who can choose whether and how to access it.

A final essential condition is the provision of information. Victims are often acutely concerned with knowing exactly what happened and who was involved, to supplement what may be imperfect conscious memories of the event, to assign appropriate responsibility, and to evaluate the implications for safety in the future. They may also require information about recovery from trauma in order to combat mistaken evaluations of their own reactions,[19] although there is little evidence that simply providing this information has any positive effect on trauma outcome.[20]

Special consideration is needed when children are direct or indirect victims of trauma. After major life-threatening incidents, as many as half of children directly involved may develop PTSD, and many more develop other, less persistent disorders.[21] Even if they are not direct victims, children may be affected by traumatized parents reducing physical contact and trying to shield them from facts about the event, at a time when children may be most in need of comfort, reassurance, and information.[22] Schools need to draw up plans that will guide them if confronted with serious injury or death to pupils or staff. These need to address such issues as what the relevant child agencies are and how they will work together, what burial practices are usual among the different faiths and cultures represented in the school, how best to inform children about what has happened, and how best to support them afterward.[23]

Apart from assisting natural recovery processes with the provision of safety, acknowledgment, support, and information, and seeing to the needs of children and families, there appears to be a strong case for not intervening more actively with trauma victims in the first few weeks after the event. The unpredictable unfolding of coping responses posttrauma, and the failure to demonstrate any effect of psychological debriefing, should enjoin caution. Doing too much may be as unhelpful as doing too little. An alternative, and perhaps more rational, strategy is called *Screen and Treat,* which involves careful monitoring of survivors' symptoms and referral for treatment only when symptoms are failing to subside naturally. To make this strategy work, it will almost certainly be important to have some initial contact with survivors postincident, providing them with reassurance, information, and a point of contact for them to seek further advice and support if required.

The Screen and Treat strategy requires an effective screening instrument. Ideally, this should be quick and simple to use by people with no specialist knowledge of trauma. We have recently developed an instrument of this kind and tested it on survivors of the Ladbroke Grove train crash that occurred outside a major London station in October 1999.[24] Many people died or were injured, both from the impact and from smoke inhalation. The ten Yes/No items, which correspond to the reexperiencing and arousal symptoms of PTSD (see Table 1.1), are shown in Table 9.1. Of the people who marked Yes to six or more of the items in our study, 86 percent were found to have PTSD when assessed with a structured clinical interview, whereas of the people who

Table 9.1. Trauma Screening Questionnaire:

Your Own Reactions Now to the Traumatic Event

Please consider the following reactions that sometimes occur after a traumatic event. This questionnaire is concerned with your personal reactions to the traumatic event that happened a few weeks ago. Please indicate whether or not you have experienced any of the following AT LEAST TWICE IN THE PAST WEEK:

	Yes, at least twice in the past week	No
1. Upsetting thoughts or memories about the event that have come into your mind against your will		
2. Upsetting dreams about the event		
3. Acting or feeling as though the event were happening again		
4. Feeling upset by reminders of the event		
5. Bodily reactions (such as fast heartbeat, stomach churning, sweatiness, dizziness) when reminded of the event		
6. Difficulty falling or staying asleep		
7. Irritability or outbursts of anger		
8. Difficulty concentrating		
9. Heightened awareness of potential dangers to yourself and others		
10. Being jumpy or being startled at something unexpected		

marked Yes to fewer than six questions, only 7 percent met criteria for PTSD. Similar results were obtained on a separate sample of assault victims. The measure therefore seems to be a useful and reasonably accurate way of detecting who may be in need of more detailed assessment and referral for treatment.

Trauma Treatments Old and New

At the end of the nineteenth century there was considerable optimism that psychological symptoms caused by trauma could be cured relatively simply by hypnosis and suggestion. In France, Pierre Janet pioneered the method of trying to recover dissociated memories by automatic writing or hypnosis, having the patient relive the event in all its intensity and then reintegrating the traumatic material with the contents of normal consciousness.[25] Freud also went through a phase of believing that hysterical symptoms produced by early sexual abuse could be cured in this way, although he rapidly lost confidence both in these methods and in the importance of traumatic events.

Trauma treatment first became established in the medical literature during World War I, when it was used with acutely shell-shocked soldiers in field units and hospitals close to the front. Myers described his approach to treating men who could be in a state of nervous collapse, shaking uncontrollably, mentally confused, stuporous, or displaying a variety of hysterical symptoms such as amnesia, blindness, deafness, and paralysis of one or more limbs. By his own account much of Myers's approach was unsystematic, combining reassurance over the symptoms soldiers were experiencing with firmness over the inevitability of their return to their unit in different degrees according to the individual case. The most specific part of the treatment involved attempting to overcome amnesia for the specific event that had triggered the collapse: "The physician's aim should be to restore by suggestion (aided, if necessary by hypnosis) the experiences of the 'emotional' personality in a chastened, controlled condition, able to be 'faced,' integrated with, and thus restoring, the normal personality."[26]

For Myers, it was important to revive memories that had been dissociated or repressed (residing in the "emotional" personality) and to mentally reintegrate or resynthesize them within the "normal" personality. Commonly, the soldier was hypnotized, induced to recall in detail the traumatic event, and told he would later be able to remember everything without fear or horror. The hypnotic state was then lifted and the soldier gave a second, detailed verbal account of his experiences in normal consciousness.

Many of Myers's colleagues adopted similar principles and firmly

believed that in the main these were real memories that had been repressed. Although no formal research was practical in the midst of the
chaos of war, the physicians at the front were highly educated and
acute observers who carefully considered different explanations for
what they saw. If their treatment did indeed involve the retrieval of forgotten memories and if it was successful in overcoming symptoms, this
may have been due to the very small amount of time that was allowed
to elapse between trauma and treatment. As we have seen in Chapter 7,
the recovery of memories long after the event, even if possible, is
fraught with difficult questions about separating the real from the
imagined. It would be of great interest to know whether this approach
was effective in simply returning men to the front or whether it actually produced lasting psychological benefits as well.

Whether or not traumatic events had been forgotten, there was
widespread agreement that the men's psychological problems were in
large part due to memories involving extreme fear, horror, or both and
that overcoming their problems required them to acknowledge these
experiences and talk about them, usually in detail. Writing about the
treatment of a soldier suffering from shell shock, Rows described his
discovery that the soldier was living with the secret knowledge that
while on sentry duty he had shot a wounded comrade by mistake. He
noted that "an examination back to this trying time which led to him
recounting this terrible secret was followed by a marked improvement."[27]

Today, standard treatment directed at PTSD symptoms generally
involves two elements, which may be used separately or together: the
detailed and repeated exposure to traumatic information, and the
modification of maladaptive beliefs about events, behaviors, or symptoms. Both exposure and cognitive methods have been demonstrated
to be clinically very effective although not all patients are able to toler-
ate them and not all patients become symptom-free as a result.[28]

Why have two different kinds of treatment evolved? One answer
may be that human reasoning is thought to be performed by two systems.[29] One is associative and automatic, making use of basic principles such as the similarity between elements or the closeness of two elements in time. It searches for and bases conclusions on patterns and
regularities between elements such as images and stereotypes. The sec-

ond system is rule-based and deliberate and tries to describe the world in more conceptual terms by capturing a structure that is logical or causal. Exposure treatments appear to draw on associative reasoning in that they attempt to produce new patterns and regularities involving the same elements that were part of the traumatic experience. Although the steps demanded by the treatment are deliberate, the processes by which change occurs are automatic. In contrast, cognitive methods involve the derivation of explicit rules that are then deliberately evaluated and modified verbally within therapy sessions.

Prolonged Exposure

Prolonged exposure is a treatment developed by Edna Foa and is in some ways a much more systematic and sophisticated version of the treatment used during World War I, without the element of hypnosis.[30] Patients typically close their eyes and are asked to relive the trauma as vividly as possible. This involves giving a very detailed narrative account of the trauma, reporting everything they recall seeing, hearing, touching, smelling, feeling, and thinking throughout the entire event. The reliving process often results in spontaneous flashbacks occurring, providing further more detailed, image-based information to be incorporated into the narrative. The account may be tape-recorded and the patient asked to listen to the tape every day until the next session. This provides an opportunity for further flashbacks and further elaborations of the narrative, as well as a gradual acclimatization to the most disturbing elements. The therapy requires that patients focus their attention on the traumatic material and not distract themselves with other thoughts or activities or deliberately skip over uncomfortable moments.

As well as this exposure in imagination to the traumatic memory, patients are encouraged to expose themselves to real-life situations linked to the trauma, such as the street in which they were attacked, the exact model and color of car that ran into them, or the hospital ward in which they nearly died. Again, the aim is to provoke fear reactions that patients can then extinguish by staying in the same place, focusing on the trauma reminders, and waiting for the realization of safety to overcome the expectation of danger. This is a demanding therapy, but if followed conscientiously it usually leads to a rapid reduction in levels of fear and in the extent to which memories are relived in the present.

As we saw in Chapter 6, the ease with which fear responses can be reinstated after extinction in animals or after successful therapy in patients provides a strong hint that fear memories encoded in the SAM system remain intact and are not directly modified by psychological therapy. From the perspective of dual representation theory, exposure treatment is a very good way of helping a person to construct detailed, consciously accessible memories in the VAM system that are then able to exert inhibitory control over amygdala activation. In my view, what suppresses flashbacks is the reencoding into the VAM system of critical retrieval cues that were previously encoded only in the SAM system.[31] These cues must be reencoded in a form that enables them to be deliberately recalled, and they must be associated with a past temporal context and a sense of current safety; that is, the cues must be identified as belonging to a specific past event that does not now constitute an ongoing threat. The value of adding real-life to imaginal exposure is that it provides an opportunity for a person to reencode additional retrieval cues that might not spontaneously come to mind.

Consistent with therapists who emphasize a graduated approach to trauma recall, particularly when the trauma has occurred early in life, dual representation theory suggests that arousal levels must be carefully managed during this process.[32] If arousal is too low, this may mean that traumatic images stored in the SAM system are not being accessed. If arousal becomes too high and the person starts to dissociate, becoming overabsorbed in the traumatic memory at the expense of contact with his or her immediate surroundings, frontal and hippocampal activity will again become impaired and the person will reexperience the trauma without transferring information from the SAM to the VAM system. With complex or long-lasting traumas it is likely that repeated episodes of recall will be necessary, with the process being terminated each time the person dissociates to the extent that he or she is no longer able to reflect consciously on the material coming to mind. In order to complete information transfer, it may be necessary for the therapist to divide the trauma episode or episodes into smaller units and to construct a hierarchy from less distressing to more distressing moments.

On the basis of the experimental studies discussed in the last chapter, which found that a tapping task reduced intrusive trauma memories, we can speculate that it may sometimes be useful to have someone perform a visuospatial task such as knitting or model-building while recalling the trauma.[33] This should lessen absorption by competing for resources in the image-based memory system. There is also evidence that typing the trauma narrative on a typewriter or computer may reduce levels of arousal compared with writing longhand, perhaps because typing requires more effort and once again limits absorption in the trauma memory.[34] If information transfer is being implemented successfully, the amount of the trauma narrative that the person is able to retrieve and reflect upon before beginning to dissociate should increase steadily.

Cognitive Therapy

In contrast to prolonged exposure, in which therapists have a clear-cut strategy but no direct control over the changes in the VAM and SAM systems, the cognitive approach is much more precisely targeted and involves a delicate dialogue between therapist and patient. The therapist's initial task is to find out as much as possible about how the patient has interpreted the trauma and the reactions that followed and about the chains of reasoning that support these interpretations. In some cases this reasoning will be in the form of explicit rules or assumptions that the patient can articulate. For example, he or she may comment, "It was my fault I was attacked because I knew this street was unsafe and I didn't look carefully enough before getting out of my car." At other times the reasoning may be associative, in the form of specific negative thoughts or images that come spontaneously to mind. The basic premise of cognitive therapy is that emotions are more the product of beliefs and interpretations than of events themselves, and that changing beliefs is the most effective way to reduce unwanted emotion.

On the basis of this knowledge it will be possible to hazard an educated guess about whether the trauma has had an effect on the patient's identity and whether positive identities have been undermined, negative identities reinforced, or both. Cognitive therapy requires a high degree of respect for patients' beliefs and the ability to motivate them to explore the puzzling inconsistencies and the "no-go" areas of their inner world. As the founder of cognitive therapy for depression, Aaron Beck, has insisted, it is a collaborative enterprise designed to uncover mental patterns, assumptions, and secrets, not a tool for browbeating patients who appear to hold irrational beliefs. Even the most irrational thoughts generally have a logic that makes sense when it is related to a particular personal history. The skill of the therapist lies in uncovering the logic while simultaneously helping the patient to discover an alternative way of reasoning about the same events that makes equally good if not better sense.

Resick and Schnicke developed a version of cognitive therapy for sexual assault victims that they called *cognitive processing therapy*.[35] After an educational session, patients are asked to write about what it means to them that the event happened. This provides an early opportunity for the therapist to identify negative beliefs and to explain the relationship between events, thoughts, and feelings. Patients then write a detailed account of the event; they are encouraged to relive their emotions in full and reread the account daily. They are then taught how to challenge their negative beliefs by asking themselves questions that have to do with how well their beliefs fit the facts and whether other beliefs can provide an equally good or better account of their reactions. There is a detailed manual with many suggestions about useful techniques for helping patients overcome unrealistic negative beliefs that are resistant to change.

In my own use of cognitive therapy I have found that it is quite often possible to make progress in reinstating positive identities by drawing people's attention to contradictions between their behavior and their goals. For example, people who have been in road accidents in which their vehicle was hit unexpectedly from behind may have lost their sense of being safe in the world and able to rely on others not to harm them, leading them to look constantly in their rear-view mirror to reassure themselves that it is not going to happen again. They may not have considered that this behavior, although apparently designed for their safety, may actually be endangering them because they are being distracted from more likely dangers ahead. The same logic can be applied to other "safety behaviors" such as hanging on to their seat or incessantly pointing out possible hazards to the driver.

Similarly, to escape at all costs the experience of being humiliated, people may adopt the safety behaviors of avoiding being assertive and standing up for their rights (in case they are put down) or alternatively being overaggressive when it is not necessary (to dissuade another person from challenging them). Both strategies are likely to be equally self-defeating, making it less likely that people will achieve what they want and more likely that they will experience further humiliation. Safety behaviors are very common in the victims of all kinds of traumas and tend to block recovery because they signal that the person is still in danger and that defensive reactions still need to be mobilized.[36] In this respect safety behaviors often have the opposite effect of what is intended—they keep people anxious but don't keep them safe.

I have found that negative beliefs are sometimes experienced by people with PTSD as being "spoken" by internal "voices" in their heads that reinforce and make concrete feared identities by telling them they are weak, incompetent, worthless, guilty, and so forth. Sometimes the voice is the person's main evidence for the reality of the identity he or she is trying to avoid. It may be possible to identify what this voice sounds like or who in the person's past said things that were similar. Consistent with the principles of associative reasoning, the voice is typically highly predictable, uttering criticisms or warnings that are black and white, are always couched in similar terms, and never seem to take much account of the person's actual circumstances. These are not like the voices that people with major psychotic disorders describe. In psychoses such as schizophrenia the voices are experienced as messages from an outside source, like God or the devil, whereas in the vast majority of cases in which there is no psychosis people are perfectly aware that they are their own thoughts.

People with depression and anxiety disorders like PTSD frequently say that they feel as though two or more parts of themselves are in conflict, offering different advice or different comments. Often, one part is more reasonable and one more critical or punitive so that their subjective experience appears to directly reflect the existence of multiple identities, one able to employ rule-based reasoning and the other much more reliant on associative reasoning. It also makes sense to see the problem as one of multiple identities rather than as one of multiple thoughts because the negative or self-critical thoughts are not completely stereotyped but appear able to adapt their content somewhat to each situation while maintaining a consistent theme. People can even sometimes describe the kind of relationship they have with their internal voices. They remain for the most part fully aware of the existence of their different identities, although they may not have thought of them in these terms. Only in the rare cases of dissociative identity disorder are there amnesic barriers so that some identities remain completely unaware of the thoughts and actions of other identities. This can have the result that people repeatedly find themselves in a place they don't remember going to or wearing clothes they don't remember putting on or even owning.

Many people with PTSD readily respond to the suggestion that these internal voices are produced by a not-very-intelligent computer program that gets triggered very predictably in specific types of situations. Some like to give the voice or the program a name to help them think about it as a distinct part of themselves. The first task is to distance themselves from the voice, treating it as an interesting phenomenon rather than as an authoritative guide on what they are *really* like and what they should think. The second task is to evaluate carefully the evidence for what the voice is saying, which often turns out to be based on a biased interpretation of a few incidents or on the opinion of someone important in the family. After repeated testing and rule-based reasoning of this kind, the person effectively begins to construct a new positive identity, or to reinforce an existing one, that is more coherent and more convincing than the one that has been feared for so long.

Cognitive therapy is sometimes criticized for not being sufficiently based in reality. Skeptics will point to thoughts that appear not to be distorted but to be reality-based, such as the refusal to travel by some means of transport that has risk attached to it, the negative expectations of the person who has been severely disabled in an assault, or the guilt of someone who has run over and killed a child in a motor vehicle accident. It is quite true that not all negative beliefs are irrational, but the cognitive therapist will be on the lookout for beliefs that are so extreme as to be harmful or to close down opportunities for positive change. For example, the train crash survivor who will no longer travel by train may be exposing himself or herself to greater risks on the highway. The aim of therapy is to help the survivor overcome any anxiety about trains so that he or she can make a rational choice, unconstrained by fear, about how to travel given the various degrees of actual risk.

Similarly, the aim of therapy in a disabled assault survivor is not to argue that life will be just as enjoyable and rewarding but to combat the belief that *nothing* will ever again afford any pleasure and that a disabled life is one that has *no* value whatsoever. The driver's actions in killing a child can never be minimized, but what can be addressed is the belief that he or she is and always will be a *uniquely* bad person and that he or she can *never* be forgiven in any degree no matter how much and for how long he or she attempts to make reparation for what has happened. Therapy aimed at such extreme beliefs must at the same time always take into account the reality that some places or jobs are not worth returning to, some conditions are painful and demoralizing, and some actions require punishment and the making of reparation.

New Ideas for Treatment

Closer study of people reliving traumatic events has identified that most have a small number of "hot spots," often quite brief moments when emotions are exceptionally intense,[37] and it has been proposed that these hot spots correspond to the content of the flashbacks that people with PTSD experience.[38] Ehlers and Clark suggested that these moments might be associated with important meanings and that exposure treatment could be more efficient if it focused specifically on hot spots rather than on the entire event. Although these moments usually involve intense fear, other emotions such as anger and shame do sometimes figure in them, particularly when the trauma has been prolonged.[39] From the perspective of dual representation theory, hot spots may correspond to moments when encoding into the VAM system was maximally impaired and there was consequently a large discrepancy between the contents of the respective VAM and SAM memories. In other words, these are the moments when there are many potential retrieval cues that need reencoding into the VAM system if they are not to trigger flashbacks.

As survivors recover, trauma reminders they come across will have the potential to trigger both new memories in the VAM system and older memories created at the time of the trauma in the SAM system. These two types of memory will compete to determine which is retrieved and whether the body's alarm systems will be activated. To begin with, the older SAM memories may enjoy a retrieval advantage as they have already been spontaneously retrieved many times in the weeks and months following the trauma. The capacity to prevent the amygdala from initiating alarm reactions should be improved by incorporating into the new VAM memories features that will make them more likely to be retrieved than the old trauma memories in the SAM system. Theoretically, such an advantage might be gained from making the new memories highly distinctive.

It has long been known that the encoding of unusual or distinctive features makes retrieval more likely if some of those features are available when the time comes to recall what has been learned. For example, in trying to learn a word paired with train (such as train–cloud), a person will probably find it easier to remember cloud if he or she forms a bizarre image of a train flying through the air above the clouds. In other words, the memory has become highly discriminable.[40] More recent evidence goes further in showing that the encoding of unique features with the target memory improves retrieval even when these features are not available at recall. Even general reminders or cues can access these distinctive encodings.[41] Extrapolating to a trauma context, this would suggest that the more distinctive the new VAM memory, the more likely any trauma reminder would be to access it.

Interestingly, a number of therapeutic procedures may be effective in incorporating distinctive attributes into VAM representations of trauma. Eye movement desensitization and reprocessing (EMDR) is a treatment for PTSD that has been claimed to yield benefits similar to those of prolonged exposure but in a significantly shorter time or with significantly less homework for the patient.[42] The core of the method involves three simultaneous elements: the patient visualizing the worst moments of the trauma, holding in mind a current negative thought concerning the event, and following with his or her eyes the therapist's fingers as they are moved back and forth in front of the patient's face. This last element may be replaced by looking alternately at lights flashing on the left and right or attending to the therapist tapping alternately on each of the patient's hands.[43] Patients try to distance themselves from the traumatic images; allow new thoughts, images, and associations to come to mind; and report on their mental contents and level of distress at regular intervals. There is also provision for some cognitive intervention, although not in such a structured way as in cognitive therapy.

Francine Shapiro, the originator of EMDR, suggested that people have an innate tendency to process disturbing information in such a way that they reach an adaptive and healthy resolution, but that this mechanism may sometimes be blocked. She speculated that eye movements or hand-tapping might trigger a physiological mechanism that activates the information-processing system and unblocks the processing of trauma memories; but she also considered that it simply might be the concentrated attention on the trauma memory that initiated the processing. Current explanations for the effects of EMDR are very controversial.[44]

If the claims for the effectiveness of EMDR are shown to be soundly based, dual representation theory suggests an alternative mechanism that so far has not been considered. The real-time stimulus provided by the therapist's actions, which impinge directly on the person's senses as he or she is attending to the traumatic image, might have the effect of encoding a very distinctive set of features with the new VAM memory of the trauma. After all, it will almost certainly be the first time the person has ever tried to think about something important while following someone else's hand moving back and forth just in front of the eyes. Trauma reminders would then tend to lead to the rapid reinstatement of this memory, created in a safe context, in preference to the older SAM memories, thereby producing a reduction in fear.

This explanation implies that there is nothing essential about eye movements, hand-tapping, or stimulation on alternate sides of the body. Rather, the critical feature of EMDR is that it is encouraging the reencoding of detailed sensory aspects of the trauma memory, those when most emotion was experienced, into the VAM system, and doing so in a highly distinctive way. This is consistent with the finding that the precise nature of the visual or tactile stimulation does not seem to be vital to the success of EMDR.[45] Eye movements may also be a good choice because they are relatively easy to perform even when a person is very emotional, and the requirement to perform this simple action helps to prevent the person from getting too absorbed in the trauma memory. What EMDR does not do is provide exposure to real-life situations that are also able to trigger trauma memories, or systematically address recurrent vulnerable identities, and for this reason it would be surprising if its long-term effectiveness was equivalent to prolonged exposure or cognitive therapy.

Other forms of therapy involving the reconstruction of traumatic events in the imagination have also obtained encouraging results.[46] For example, people sexually abused as children may replay traumatic moments and imagine their adult self intervening to comfort the child and prevent the occurrence of harmful and frightening acts. Typically, the therapist encourages the person to produce his or her own ideas and images as much as possible rather than instructing the person exactly what to imagine. Most kinds of trauma-related images can similarly be manipulated in the imagination to produce a different or more reassuring outcome. Once again, these techniques are claimed to bring about a relatively rapid reduction in anxiety, without requiring a repetitive and lengthy reworking of the trauma narrative.

What is striking is that the new images are not more "realistic" or "believable" in the sense of being consistent with the facts. To the contrary, they are often physically impossible and at all times known to be wholly false. However, in encoding highly distinctive and sometimes bizarre attributes paired with the original trauma images, imaginal reconstruction is consistent with the principle of trying to confer a retrieval advantage onto consciously accessible memories in the VAM system. The distinctiveness and retrievability of the new images is likely to be further enhanced by the so-called generation effect, a well-established tendency for items that are generated by people themselves to be better remembered than items suggested by someone else.[47]

We turn now to new ideas for strengthening associative links between the more adaptive beliefs and ways of thinking introduced through therapy and the original memory structures containing various kinds of negative content. As discussed above in the chapter, some people with PTSD have internal critical voices that are the source of many of their negative thoughts. Often, these voices are experienced as omnipotent, authoritative, and persecutory. At the same time that the therapist is exploring alternative, more positive beliefs with the patient, these voices may be providing a running commentary in the background that is dismissing what is being suggested or telling the person not to entertain specific thoughts or dwell on specific memories. Rather than having to compete with this hidden adversary, I have sometimes found it helpful to have patients themselves conduct internal dialogues in which they put my questions and arguments to their critical voices and see what kind of response the voices make. This technique of confronting internal voices can have the effect of greatly weakening the relentless criticism and sometimes reducing the voices to helpless silence. As a result, people seem to feel much more in control and less likely to be intimidated by their voices in the future.

Ehlers and Clark recently proposed another method for enhancing the effectiveness of cognitive restructuring that involved incorporating the more adaptive cognitions into a reliving of the traumatic event.[48] This idea has been elaborated by Nick Grey, Kerry Young, and Emily Holmes, who suggested that trying to restructure people's beliefs as part of standard cognitive therapy may fail to access important memories coded in the SAM system.[49] As a result, patients might end up agreeing with the therapist's logic but failing to feel any different. Their intellectual beliefs or "cold" cognitions might have changed, but not their emotional beliefs or "hot" cognitions. Like Ehlers and Clark, Grey and colleagues proposed that cognitive restructuring should be carried out first in the normal way but then repeated within the context of a reliving session in which strong feelings and vivid images from the SAM system are activated. They give a number of interesting case examples illustrating this method and its potential advantages over standard cognitive therapy.

Conclusions

I have argued that the current overemphasis by some Saviors on preventive techniques such as CISD has led to the risk of a serious misuse of resources, with ineffective interventions being delivered to people who do not need them, and effective interventions not being delivered to those who do need them. Although different approaches may meet with better success in the future, an alternative and at this time more soundly based strategy for survivors of disaster is what we have called Screen and Treat. This involves careful monitoring of survivors' symptoms and referral for treatment only when symptoms are failing to subside naturally. Immediate posttrauma intervention should be limited to demonstrating safety, acknowledging the trauma, making support available to those who want it, and providing information, above all with a focus on supporting natural recovery. This means there should be no compulsory procedures that impose a particular model of recovery on victims. Second, trauma victims should be systematically monitored so that one can detect any failure of victims to adapt at four to six weeks posttrauma. Third, scientifically established interventions should be used at that point with those victims who have not adapted. They are an important group whose needs risk being neglected if too much attention and too many resources are devoted to early intervention.

The failure to prevent PTSD in unselected groups of trauma survivors stands in contrast to the much greater effectiveness of treatment when it is targeted at people with extreme reactions or in whom symptoms have become established. The psychiatric crises of combat troops were, it is claimed, effectively defused during World War I and during many subsequent conflicts where frontline psychiatry was provided, although there is little in the way of hard evidence for this. In more recent times patients who become severely affected soon after a trauma and meet diagnostic criteria for acute stress disorder have responded very positively to five ninety-minute sessions of cognitive-behavioral therapy in two studies.[50] These findings stand in contrast to the majority of studies of brief one-session interventions that have had equivocal results.[51] The most clear-cut evidence is for the effectiveness of longer and more systematic therapies, principally prolonged exposure and cognitive therapy, applied to established PTSD.

This review has suggested that trauma treatment addresses two tasks, in principle separate but usually occurring together. One is the abolition of flashbacks and nightmares, brought about by the patient focusing attention on detailed sensory images of the traumatic scenes and reencoding the information into the VAM system. This creates alternative trauma memories that in the presence of trauma reminders then compete with the original memories in the SAM system to determine which one will be retrieved. Techniques such as EMDR that make the new memories more distinctive may improve the chance that they will be retrieved in preference to the original ones. As we saw in Chapter 3, however, the effectiveness of some kinds of treatment may be reduced when the patient is angry or has experienced mental defeat.

The second task, I have argued, is the reestablishment of positive beliefs and identities and the deactivation of negative beliefs and feared identities that the trauma has evoked. In some cases giving detailed attention to the trauma memories may lead a patient to recall additional information that spontaneously results in this happening. For example, a rape survivor may remember that she did struggle and try to defend herself when attacked, or that she failed to do so only because she was being threatened with a knife. Cognitive therapy provides a more structured framework for addressing these issues, in which alternative beliefs and the chain of reasoning behind them are systematically explored and evaluated. Some of the new ideas for treatment I have discussed involve trying to integrate the new cognitions more effectively with existing mental contents.

The undermining of negative thoughts and feared identities and the establishment of new and stable positive identities depends at least in part on interleaved learning. This process of repeated information review and comparison between pre- and posttrauma states may be severely impeded by negative emotions or "stuck points," resulting in avoidance or in the rehearsal of partial and/or distorted versions of the trauma. These overassimilated trauma memories require identification, challenge, and modification.[52] Otherwise, the person will have alternative, competing representations in the VAM system, some containing and some omitting important information about the event. Such knowledge systems are inherently unstable.[53] Inputs such as unexpected trauma reminders may cause a switch in the version currently in consciousness, accompanied by strong emotional reactions.

Before leaving the topic of treatment, it is appropriate to ask what recovery means in the case of PTSD. As other authors have noted, unlike with many purely physical disorders, it does not imply that trauma survivors return to some pretrauma state.[54] For survivors, it is unlikely that life will be exactly the same again. In some cases, their circumstances will change dramatically. Even when this is not the case, there are likely to be changes, perhaps subtle ones, in their view of themselves, of other people, of death, or of the role of chance in life. Some positive illusions will have gone for good, and the trauma is always likely to loom large in their personal history. Therapists, however, can aspire to helping such people return to normal hopes, normal pleasures, and normal feelings and experience the freedom to think, behave, and make choices unconstrained by fear.

10

Ancient Malady
or Modern Myth?

Macbeth: Canst thou not minister to a mind diseased,
  Pluck from the memory a rooted sorrow,
  Raze out the written troubles of the brain,
  And with some sweet oblivious antidote
  Cleanse the stuffed bosom of that perilous stuff
  Which weighs upon the heart?
Doctor: Therein the patient must minister to himself.
    —William Shakespeare, *Macbeth*[1]

According to Shakespeare it would appear that the helping professions were powerless to treat PTSD during Macbeth's reign in the eleventh century, or perhaps recognized their limitations when the patient was a powerful ruler with a guilty conscience. Only since the middle of the nineteenth century have doctors and scientists begun to write specifically about stress arising from a single class of traumatic incidents, and ever since then the topic has seen numerous skirmishes and several pitched battles between Saviors and Skeptics. What cannot help but strike the reader is the way so many of these conflicts have continued essentially unchanged over this period. Among the most prominent are the debates over the legitimacy of the symptoms, the importance of the trauma itself versus prior vulnerability, the reliability of traumatic memory, the ability of a person to forget horrible events, and the value of psychological treatments. Saviors and Skeptics have both scored some wins and suffered some defeats, with reality as ever turning out to be more complicated and far more interesting than had been imagined. We are now in a position to synthesize the insights of the past 150 years and the scientific findings of the past 20 years, with the aim of resolving at least some of these conflicts. Intensive study in the laboratory, clinic, and community is at last pointing the way toward realistic conclusions about traumatic memory, the nature of PTSD and how to diagnose it, and the practical implications for prevention and treatment.

Traumatic Memory and the Nature of PTSD

Skeptics have sometimes claimed that there is no clinical or laboratory evidence to suppose traumatic memories are special or that they can be repressed or dissociated.[2] The studies we have reviewed paint a very different picture, in which memories for traumatic experiences are repeatedly found to show contradictory qualities, sometimes being better recalled than memories for neutral events and sometimes being worse recalled. There is also convincing evidence that memories for many different kinds of highly disturbing events can sometimes be completely forgotten and later recovered, although we do not yet understand how this happens. It seems increasingly likely, however, that some kind of active inhibitory mechanism may be involved, related to the intentional type of repression described by Freud.

Does this mean that traumatic memories are entirely different from other memories? It seems more likely that they are based on everyday mechanisms that are responding in an unusual way owing to the physiological effects of high levels of sustained arousal on the different brain structures involved in memory. One consequence may be to alter the normal balance between verbal and image-based memory systems, making the former less efficient and the latter more efficient. It is likely, though, that other kinds of extremely emotional events, such as positive events, could have similar effects. Several authors have noted the existence of vivid, intrusive memories of positive experiences,[3] and there are good grounds for thinking that the same brain structure, the amygdala, may be activated in response to positive as well as negative events.[4] Most of our knowledge has come from the study of negative events, however, and our understanding of traumatic memory has been inseparably linked with research into recovered memories of childhood abuse and into PTSD.

Reactions to a traumatic event, including those captured by the

PTSD diagnosis, are complicated because these reactions may incorporate two quite separate sets of processes. One of these is concerned with specific reactions to extreme threat, including the activation of the hypothalamic-pituitary-adrenal axis and the effect of increased levels of catecholamines and stress hormones on critical brain structures such as the prefrontal cortex, hippocampus, and amygdala. Closely associated with the subjective responses of fear, helplessness, horror, and dissociation, the effects on these brain structures have predictable consequences for the formation of different types of trauma memory. I have suggested that a useful way of describing these different memories is in terms of a higher-level, VAM system containing a record of information that has had a relatively greater degree of conscious processing and a lower-level, image-based SAM system containing a much more detailed record of sensory information that was largely unattended and received little conscious processing. Whether these memories are actually stored in anatomically distinct locations or represent different types of encoding within a common location is a matter for future research.

Some evidence already supports this idea that the interplay between brain processes supporting sensory images and conscious verbal processes will turn out to be of central importance in PTSD. As reviewed in Chapter 6, ordinary memory for visual stimuli such as faces or colors is made worse if study participants are asked to describe those faces or colors in words. One explanation is that the verbal description leads to a new and only partially accurate memory that interferes with people's ability to access the original visual image.[5] In this research, image-based memory is supporting better recognition, which is made worse by interference from verbal memories, whereas in the case of PTSD, image-based memory appears to support unwanted flashbacks that can similarly be reduced by interference from verbal memories or from competing images.

In Chapter 8 I described our findings that a person carrying out a competing imagery-based task while watching a stressful film had a reduced number of later memory intrusions, whereas that person carrying out a competing verbal or consciousness-altering task increased such intrusions. Also, as we saw in Chapter 3, the ability of someone to hold a greater number of words in mind while solving math problems is related to the ability to suppress unwanted thoughts. It is therefore of considerable interest that in PTSD it is the hippocampus, a presumed site of verbal memory formation, that is thought to be compromised, that verbal memory is consistently impaired,[6] and that the ability to encode meaningful verbal material predicts a more positive response to treatment.[7]

In traumatic situations, specific reactions to extreme threat are shaped by prior experience, social and intellectual resources, subjective interpretation, and biological vulnerability, as well as the nature of the event itself. It cannot be sufficiently emphasized that two people's accounts of what they actually experienced, witnessed, or believed during the same event may have very little in common. Therefore, the extent of any discrepancy between what is encoded in the VAM and SAM systems will vary considerably among individuals. Mental defeat, helplessness, and dissociative reactions such as confusion, blankness, and numbing may all interfere with effective encoding into the VAM system. In the vast majority of cases these encoding discrepancies will be produced at the time of trauma, but occasionally, later reinterpretation of events as highly threatening may act in a similar way. Under these circumstances high levels of fear or horror may temporarily suppress the functioning of the prefrontal cortex and hippocampus, leading to new "memories" being created in the SAM system based on either remembered scenes, internally generated images, or some combination of both. These "memories" may then be reexperienced in the form of flashbacks, providing an opportunity for a great deal of confusion over whether they correspond to actual events.

The other set of processes involved in reactions to a traumatic event is concerned with the challenge the event poses to the victim's beliefs and identity. These processes are not specific to trauma but are encountered in other types of nontraumatic adversity, hence the overlap between symptoms of PTSD and symptoms of depression, generalized anxiety disorder, and so on. Repeated exposure to physical or sexual threat over an extended period of time will lead to the longer-term establishment of identities that have lost much of the capacity for optimism, trust, and intimacy. But even a single event that is merely upsetting for one person may fatally undermine the positive aspirations of another or provide apparently convincing evidence for an unwanted identity as weak, incompetent, worthless, or bad. As we saw in Chapter 4, negative reactions to trauma go beyond thoughts and include impulses, imagined pictures of what might have happened, emotions such as anger and shame, a feeling of being more than one person, and a sense of disconnection from others. These individual responses are also highly varied and yet at the same time contain their own internal organization, suggesting that a helpful framework for understanding them is the social-psychological approach to identity involving multiple selves.

In addition to the subjectivity involved in all but the most overwhelming traumas, what has become clear about PTSD in the past decade or so is that it represents a failure of normal adaptation. The symptoms described in the DSM-IV are clearly not all pathological precisely because in the beginning they are part of a normal response to overwhelming threat. As in many other psychiatric disorders, the pathology lies not so much in the symptoms themselves as in their persistence and the amount of distress they cause. This realization brings with it a number of important implications. One is that vulnerability may have as much or more to do with what happens after trauma as it does with what happened before. Although the meta-analysis discussed in Chapter 3 found three pretrauma factors to be the most consistent predictors of risk, posttrauma factors such as social support and other adverse posttrauma events tended to have stronger, albeit more variable, effects. It is also clear that negative interpretations of what happened, why it happened, and how the victim has been affected by it, as well as choice of coping strategy, are critical in helping or hindering the successful resolution of posttraumatic stress.

There will of course be many connections between pretrauma and posttrauma risk factors, with some pretrauma factors such as childhood maltreatment likely to express themselves through posttrauma factors such as negative interpretations of trauma behavior and symptoms. Importantly, though, our analysis suggests that it is far too narrow to think of vulnerability in nineteenth-century terms as some kind of inherent weakness. Rather, vulnerability to PTSD may consist in a person's difficulty or reluctance to adapt to new and unforeseen circumstances by changing established patterns of thought, habitual methods of coping, and cherished goals. Such a difficulty is sometimes shown by highly determined, effective, moral, or responsible people who have made major contributions to their employers, families, or communities through these very habits. What they may not immediately find easy is being patient, attending to internal signs of the speed at which recovery is progressing, and accepting that they must adapt to the changes and symptoms the trauma brought about.

Another implication is that the biological changes of most importance in understanding the effects of trauma are not just those that occur during the event. This point has been made most clearly by Israeli psychiatrist Arieh Shalev.[8] He notes that initially, extreme environmental demands engage a general stress response that includes activation of the sympathetic nervous system, secretion of the hormones adrenaline and cortisol, and activation of brain areas involved with perception and action. Within a relatively short period of time, this response moves through the phases of alarm, resistance, and either return to equilibrium or exhaustion. These reactions are followed by a cascade of neuronal and genomic events that function, among other things, to lay down long-term memories of the stressful event. There may also be separate long-term biological effects brought about by loss, separation, and grief, such as changes in the reactivity of the hypothalamic-pituitary-adrenal axis. Shalev suggests that PTSD follows when normal stress responses are exacerbated by depression, the disruption of plans, the existence of negative meanings, or the absence of appropriate social support. Under these conditions there is no positive resolution, but instead, prolonged expressions of distress have the effect of progressively sensitizing the central nervous system to further threat.

A third implication is that any attempts at prevention or early intervention will be taking place against a background of natural recovery processes. At this stage symptoms will be quite varied and are unlikely to have settled into stable patterns. It is perhaps not surprising, then, that it has been so hard to demonstrate that early interventions such as CISD, although popular and appreciated by some survivors, have any effect on the development of posttraumatic stress. Even more intensive interventions undertaken in the first month after a trauma have not always shown consistent benefits. Together with the strong disinclination of many survivors to talk to counselors and thereby (in their view) demonstrate an inability to cope on their own, these find-ings strongly suggest that early interventions for adult survivors be lim-ited to the restoration of a sense of safety and the provision of informa-tion and arms-length support. Families and children, however, may require additional input to ensure that natural recovery processes are not inadvertently blocked by parents and teachers trying (but failing) to do the right thing. Finally, the fact that PTSD symptoms are going to resolve only gradually makes it imperative to follow up survivors and ensure that recovery is proceeding or arrange for more specialist help.

Summarizing, we can conclude that both Saviors and Skeptics are right about the nature of PTSD. As Skeptics have claimed, the "symptoms" described in the DSM-IV *are* part of a normal reaction to a traumatic event and *do* largely overlap with those of other disorders. PTSD is like depression in that as far as one part of memory is con-cerned, there is a past event that has brought with it all sorts of negative implications for identity and for future goals. PTSD is also like other anxiety disorders in that as far as another part of memory is concerned, the event does not yet belong to the past and the victim feels ongoing danger. It is no surprise, then, to find such high levels of comorbidity. But this is not the whole story. Consistent with the Saviors' position, several psychological and biological features of PTSD seem to be spe-cific to extreme stress, such as dissociation, flashbacks, high levels of forgetting, and low resting levels of cortisol. Moreover, the symptoms may persist long past the period of normal recovery and follow their own distinct course. Confusion arises because PTSD, like all trauma reactions, is a hybrid in which specific responses to extreme threat co-exist with processes that are the familiar accompaniment of normal problems in living. We now have to consider whether and how these new insights can be reflected in our diagnostic systems.

The Future of the PTSD Diagnosis

The political imperatives that were successful in shaping the original view of PTSD and providing a solution to the needs of Vietnam veter-ans, battered women, and other survivors of extreme trauma have, not surprisingly, been insufficient scientifically and clinically. The attempt to tie PTSD to an objectively stressful event meeting Criterion A of

Table 1.1 has been an interesting exercise but despite numerous revisions is still throwing up anomalies. It is clear that a minority of people have all the symptoms of PTSD without a Criterion A event and that very few of the symptoms of PTSD are exclusively caused by such events. Nor, in many cases, does the event provide a complete explanation for the development of PTSD.

These anomalies are only to be expected given the consistent evidence for the importance of subjectivity in determining responses to trauma. If such events breach mental defenses and interact in complex ways with prior identities, then clearly, except in overwhelming circumstances, the prior state of such defenses and identities is going to be critical. In psychological and biological terms, there is no reason why someone may not respond to an apparently minor event as though it had all the Criterion A features, provided there is sufficient prior sensitization that leads to the event being perceived as highly threatening. Equally, there are strong scientific grounds for believing that the formation of enduring memories in the SAM system is not solely caused during the traumatic moments themselves but can also sometimes be produced when mildly or moderately stressful events are subsequently reinterpreted in a much more threatening light.

Trying to specify objectively what constitutes a traumatic event has been important politically to draw attention to enduring and previously overlooked stress responses. If Criterion A had been drawn more widely in 1980, the justification for regarding PTSD as a distinct disorder would have been greatly undermined. PTSD has also played a unique role in legal contexts because of the explicit link that was claimed between a causal event and specific symptoms such as intrusive memories. Again, concern has been expressed that too lax a definition of Criterion A would permit a deluge of compensation claims for all sorts of trivial events. It is unrealistic, however, to expect that the same set of rules will solve all political, legal, clinical, and scientific problems. Arguably, a major political battle was won with the inclusion of PTSD in the DSM and with the scientific evidence that it forms a distinct disorder, while the courts are perfectly capable of coming up with their own solutions to the claims for compensation. The focus now should be on a definition that is consistent with what is known scientifically and that captures clinical reality.

The current way of diagnosing PTSD has at least two problems. If reactions to traumatic events are so frequently subjective, it makes little sense to try to define a Criterion A event in objective terms. An alternative solution might be to widen the definition of a qualifying event and embrace the inevitable subjectivity, but with the option of specifying different subtypes of PTSD corresponding to the different ways in which the diagnosis might be earned. So, for example, the current Criterion A might be widened to include any event in which the person *either* experienced, witnessed, or was confronted by death, serious injury, or threats to physical integrity *or* responded with intense fear, helplessness, or horror. This would enable several groups of people to be diagnosed with PTSD who would not at present qualify: those who have been repeatedly stalked, intimidated, or emotionally abused; those who have had major traumatic events in the past and for whom a comparatively minor event acts as the proverbial "last straw"; and those who are confronted with severe threats but who do not respond at the time with intense emotions. At present, there are no scientific reasons for classing their reactions as being any different from standard DSM-IV PTSD, nor would they be treated any differently in clinical practice.

The second problem is that under the current diagnostic rules, no core symptom or symptoms immediately distinguish PTSD and correspond, for instance, to hand-washing in obsessive-compulsive disorder or panic attacks in panic disorder. At present, according to the DSM-IV, someone can be diagnosed with PTSD if he or she has general symptoms reflecting anxiety, depression, and a threat to identity but no features thought to be specific to extreme threat such as the frequent reexperiencing of the trauma in flashbacks or nightmares. For example, a diagnosis could be based on distress when ruminating about the traumatic event coupled with social withdrawal, loss of interest in activities, concentration problems, and so on.

This curious absence of any unique defining symptoms, and the substitution of an exceptionally complex "committee" definition of PTSD, is understandable given that up until now the event itself has provided the justification for the diagnosis. Arguably, this association of PTSD with a specific event has introduced unfortunate distortions into the DSM. As we have seen, other disorders such as depression, health anxiety, and social phobia are also often associated with specific negative experiences that repeatedly intrude in the form of memories or images that have become divorced from their context. This is likely to be true of other anxiety disorders, too. In the majority of cases, PTSD is similar to other disorders in that disturbing events become the focus of highly individual interpretations and coping strategies. Not infrequently these interpretations and coping strategies provide partial, temporary solutions that later prove to be inadequate in the face of additional adversity.

If the objectivity of the traumatic event is often unsustainable and little is unique about the relationship between the event and the disorder anyway, an alternative solution would be to dispense completely with Criterion A and define PTSD solely in terms of its symptoms. Ultimately, the goal would be to specify the smallest possible number of unique biological or psychological features that differentiate it from other psychiatric disorders. A good starting point would be to identify a small number of core symptoms and specify how many other related symptoms would be required to support the diagnosis and provide a severity threshold. This approach is used in the DSM-IV with major depression, where the diagnosis requires the presence of at least five of nine symptoms, at least one of which must be a core symptom (depressed mood, or loss of interest or pleasure).

Applied to PTSD, this approach might restrict the currently wide scope of Criterion B. The reexperiencing items are in any case unsatisfactory because the questions on intrusive recollection, flashbacks, psychological distress, and physiological reactivity are not necessarily independent and may reflect different aspects of a single symptom. Instead, the diagnosis could require the vivid reexperiencing of trauma memories during either wakefulness or sleep, accompanied by strong emotions of fear or horror. Given the evidence that conscious avoidance and emotional numbing are separate processes, this core symptom could be supplemented by a minimum of five additional symptoms from Criteria C and D, to include at least one symptom of avoidance, one of numbing, and one of hyperarousal.

It might reasonably be objected that some patients with PTSD would not report flashbacks or nightmares because they were successfully able to avoid specific reminders of the trauma. Given the ubiquitous role of avoidance in all psychological disorders, and the resulting inaccessibility of certain emotion-laden thoughts and memories, it is probably unrealistic to assume that clinical interviews or question-naires are always going to be adequate for diagnostic purposes. Just as physical examinations and laboratory tests are required in the rest of medicine, psychiatric diagnosis must also recognize that in some cases more powerful psychological or biological tools may be needed to provide definitive answers when the symptoms are ambiguous. In the case of PTSD, for example, it might be necessary to assess the presence of flashbacks in the context of having the person give a detailed oral or written narrative of the traumatic event.

Another possible objection is that there would be a pool of patients without the core symptom or symptoms who were now bereft of a diagnosis. However, in the absence of any concrete evidence that their symptoms included a specific reaction to extreme threat, or met the criteria for major depression or other anxiety disorders, they could be assigned an alternative diagnosis that reflected a general long-term problem in adjustment to adverse events. Here we would expect to find identity disturbances arising not only from events involving intense fear or horror but also from events that were exceptionally frustrating or humiliating.

Research is challenging traditional psychiatric classifications, con-tradicting assumptions about the role of events and symptoms and re-vealing hitherto unexpected similarities among disorders that are usu-ally studied and treated as though they were distinct. Although this does not mean a return to the old categories of hysteria and neurasthe-nia, it does suggest that the current system of diagnosis is out of step with scientific observations and needs changing. To accomplish such change it will be necessary to understand more about the underlying biological and psychological mechanisms at work and to build diagno-sis around a fuller assessment of these processes. The intensive study of PTSD since 1980 may prove to be a catalyst for liberating thinking across the entire psychiatric spectrum.

Treatment of PTSD

Although the Skeptics have so far been correct about the redundancy of widespread counseling and debriefing in the immediate aftermath of a trauma, Saviors who have insisted on the need to identify and treat PTSD also have been vindicated. Once symptoms are established there is ample evidence that effective help is often possible. Recent research is consistent with early twentieth-century ideas in pointing toward treatment addressing two separate issues, one specific to trauma (the reintegration of dissociated material in memory) and one common to other disorders (the successful bringing about of longer-term adjustments to identity). This has a number of implications for how treatment for PTSD should best be conducted and offers a new way of seeing psychotherapy in general.

In this book I have argued against the standard idea that the telling of a narrative has its therapeutic effect because it transforms a disorganized, fragmented trauma memory into a more streamlined and organized version of the same memory. Instead, I proposed that during the narrative the attention that is paid to detailed, emotion-laden images (flashbacks) results in the information they contain being reencoded into the VAM system. Here, all those details are classified for the first time as belonging to the past, so that they are less likely to trigger further flashbacks when trauma reminders are encountered. The original memory, however, remains intact. Whether or not flashbacks occur depends on the specific match between the trauma reminders and the details encoded in the VAM and SAM systems.

If the global organization of the entire trauma memory is not critical, then it may not be necessary to have patients recall the entire event during a series of sessions and then repeatedly review the material during homework practice, which is a standard element of many types of reliving or exposure therapy. Rather, it may be possible to terminate flashbacks before patients achieve a coherent, streamlined narrative. Like other recent models of PTSD, dual representation theory suggests a modification to standard methods involving a more specific focus on critical retrieval cues associated with very high levels of distress in the narrative.[9] Having identified these "hot spots" during the initial account of the trauma, therapists can help patients focus and maintain their attention on these specific moments, recoding the events and images into VAM memory such that they can later be intentionally retrieved. Their attentional focus should include both the external events represented in the traumatic images and internal events such as fleeting thoughts and bodily changes.

Although many traumas are over so quickly that interpretation tends to happen afterward, others, like natural disasters or extended assaults, may allow a variety of interpretations and emotions to occur as the event is in progress and therefore be partially represented in the SAM system as well as the VAM system. It is worth asking whether cognitive restructuring of the VAM system undertaken during therapy will generalize when other emotions are encoded in the SAM system, or whether patients may be left agreeing with the logic of the therapist's argument but being unable to prevent the unwanted cognitions and emotions from being reinstated during reliving episodes. The informational isolation of the SAM system suggests that the latter could well be the case.

Grey and colleagues have suggested, consistent with dual representation theory, that when negative interpretations and emotions occurred during the trauma rather than exclusively after the trauma, standard cognitive therapy techniques might not be enough.[10] Rather, cognitive interventions have to be implemented in such a way that they make contact with the SAM representations. Their patient LC was a refugee from Afghanistan who had been hiding in her uncle's cellar when Taliban soldiers learned of her presence and killed him. At the beginning of therapy she believed 100 percent in her own responsibility for her uncle's murder, although after standard cognitive intervention this went down to 50 percent, the patient saying that although she believed in the therapist's argument, she still felt guilty. The next stage was to have her vividly relive the murder while prompting her to challenge any guilty feelings as they occurred with the arguments that had already been practiced. Over the course of therapy, her beliefs in her own responsibility went down to 10 percent and she ceased to meet diagnostic criteria for PTSD.

The approach I have outlined does not just provide a different perspective on how trauma memories are changed but is also relevant to the general work on identity issues that is part of psychotherapy for other conditions such as social phobia or depression. There, treatment is normally described as a process of replacing negative with positive associations or of changing maladaptive thoughts and beliefs in a more positive direction. Of course, successful therapy does create more positive associations and beliefs, but it is becoming increasingly implausible that they actually replace the original negative ones. Partly this is because, as we saw in Chapter 6, even after fear has been successfully extinguished, it readily returns when people or animals find themselves in an unfamiliar context or are presented with unexpected signals of threat.

What seems much more likely is that psychotherapy helps in the construction of new and more positive beliefs and identities, makes existing positive mental contents more memorable and easily accessed, reinforces associations between possible threat cues and positive mental contents, and weakens associations between possible threat cues and negative mental contents. Later, in the presence of disturbing events or reminders, these different sorts of contents compete to determine which will come to mind. The therapist's job is to ensure that as far as possible, the positive mental contents are more memorable and more able to incorporate the unwanted or unexpected information provided by challenging situations. It rarely will be possible to eliminate all tendencies for the negative mental contents to come to mind, particularly when there are strong associations between the nature of present and past adversity, but the aim is to have them replaced as quickly as possible with more positive thoughts emphasizing competence, security, and a sense of personal value.

Afterword

For most of the nineteenth century and up until the early twentieth century, traumatic reactions generally were considered to be the result of neurological damage or inherent character flaws, and fears were widespread that listening to victims encouraged a weakness of moral fiber, thereby threatening the family and society. Not until World War I was treatment for "nervous shock" systematically implemented on a large scale. By the end of the twentieth century, attitudes had shifted dramatically because of the sheer amount of exposure through the mass media to the realities of war, the Holocaust, childhood abuse, and other telling examples of horror and cruelty. For the first time the mass media provided a platform for the public to witness the liberation of concentration camps, to see the effects of mass bombings, to participate at third hand in disasters happening on the other side of the world, and to hear the stories of victims spoken in their own words. The similarities in reactions to many different kinds of trauma were rediscovered and resulted in the birth of PTSD, lending additional depth to media coverage.

With mental health professionals systematically identifying and treating civilian trauma reactions for the first time, and with the public exposed to an ever greater amount of coverage of victims and their stories, an at times naïve belief appeared to develop about the overwhelming power of almost any kind of "trauma" to destroy people's lives. Media coverage confined to people in the immediate aftermath of bombings and shootings provided a simplistic impression of emotional devastation, and at times journalists inadvertently provided a platform for people to claim a totally undeserved victim status. An unquestioning acceptance of the literal reality of any experience claimed to be traumatic was matched by the assumption that any symptoms should be if possible prevented, certainly treated, and at any rate compensated. The discovery that trauma was a risk factor for problems such as depression and eating disorders was sometimes misunderstood to mean that it was legitimate to assume traumatic origins in patients with these symptoms.

Not surprisingly, this led to a moral backlash of the kind that would be instantly recognizable to a nineteenth-century observer. Unable to sustain the news value of trauma victims except in the context of major disasters, the media gave space to features about the new "victim culture" in which traditional virtues of fortitude were being eroded, lawyers were encouraging people to obtain compensation they did not deserve, and therapists were conjuring up trauma that never existed. Of course, there is nothing particularly new about complainers, malingerers, deluded patients, and wrong-headed therapists. But the claims that combat-related PTSD was a politically inspired invention of antiwar psychiatrists, that counseling and psychotherapy threatened the population's innate resilience to stress, and that an epidemic of false memories was destroying family life were all classic examples of the perennial struggle to uphold the interests of society's institutions against too great an erosion by individual rights.

Why these debates regularly explode out of a professional context into the public arena seems to have something to do with the combination of a clearly identifiable causal event and a universal willingness to imagine the consequences for one's own identity. In other words, observers' reactions are impelled by the same interweaving of trauma with issues of identity that we have found in victims. Whereas journalists and the public would have little reason to compare themselves to people suffering from disorders of obscure origin such as obsessive-compulsive disorder or agoraphobia, observers cannot help but evaluate victims' reactions to a traumatic event according to their own personal assumptions and standards. Well-publicized mass disasters affecting high-status individuals will almost invariably fit in with the stereotypic view of trauma as a devastating blow to innocent victims and will elicit widespread, and wholly appropriate, sympathy.

In contrast, poorly publicized or selectively reported events experienced by victims with little credibility will be met with greater caution. Ignorant of the powerful nature of reactions to extreme fear, possessed of few details about what was actually experienced or witnessed, and challenged by these events to preserve their own sense of personal invulnerability and good character, observers may not only question the reality of the event but denigrate victims' actions and cast doubt on the legitimacy of their responses. One prominent example is childhood sexual abuse within the family of origin, which rarely receives the same publicity as sexual abuse perpetrated by public officials or ministers of religion. What was notable in the 1990s was the widespread positive media coverage given to claims of false allegations of abuse by the False Memory Syndrome Foundation, without the appropriate balance provided by accusers, therapists, or independent research data. As we saw in Chapter 7, some journalists were quite explicit about their identification with the accused parents.

Another example is provided by the experiences of war zone refugees and displaced people looking to be resettled. Large numbers seeking asylum in the United Kingdom are dismissed as "bogus" claimants or "economic migrants" by politicians and in the media although in the main no evidence is offered for this view. In the United Kingdom national guidelines on evaluating asylum claims state that "discrepancies, exaggerated accounts, and the addition of new claims of mistreatment may affect credibility" and that such discrepancies may be used as a reason for refugees being refused asylum. What evidence there is from the laboratory repeatedly indicates that people asked to remember the same material on several occasions frequently recall more with each telling. This is particularly marked when they are recalling images, as is likely to be the case if they have been traumatized.[11] Nevertheless, asylum seekers do sometimes give accounts of persecution that differ with each telling and have their claims refused on the grounds that their account was false or exaggerated and that is why it could not be recalled clearly.

In a recent study investigators obtained memories of traumatic and nontraumatic events at two points in time up to seven months apart from refugees who had been granted leave to remain in the United Kingdom under the U.N. High Commissioner for Refugees group programs.[12] None of the participants had given accounts of their experiences to gain their asylum status. As would be expected from laboratory studies of the inconsistency of memory, the researchers found numerous discrepancies between accounts given on the two occasions, and these were particularly marked in those refugees suffering from PTSD. This is a good example of how decisions affecting victims' lives are sometimes made on the basis of inaccurate scientific knowledge, and of how people with PTSD may be at greater risk of injustice. A Skeptical attitude may correctly identify some malingerers, victims of inappropriate therapy, and undeserving asylum seekers but runs the risk of overlooking, minimizing, and frequently exacerbating much genuine suffering.

If we are to apply wisely our new understanding of this nineteenth-century malady, we must avoid all forms of myth-making and embrace the insights of both Saviors and Skeptics. These two stances are in any case not incompatible but should be viewed rather as alternative and equally useful identities with which to approach the troublesome topic of trauma. The challenge we face in furthering scientific knowledge of PTSD and deploying it in the real world demands something of the same flexibility and resourcefulness shown by survivors suddenly confronted with the unexpected, the unwanted, and the unimaginable.

Notes

Chapter 1. Saviors and Skeptics

1. Stone, 1993, 23.
2. Bracken, 2002; Burkett and Whitley, 1998; Ellard, 1997; Young, 1995.
3. Creswell et al., 2002.
4. Freud, 1920, 29–30.
5. Janoff-Bulman, 1992.
6. Bolton and Hill, 1996, 359.
7. American Psychiatric Association, 1980, 1987, 1994.
8. Green, 1990.
9. Resick, 2001.
10. Kessler et al., 1995.
11. Resick, 2001.
12. Gelles and Straus, 1988.
13. van Dijk, 1997, cited in Resick, 2001.
14. Resick, 2001.
15. Keane, 1993.
16. Horowitz, 1976.
17. Horowitz, 1976; Brett and Ostroff, 1985.
18. Breslau and Davis, 1987a; Kasl, 1990.
19. Young, 1995.
20. Lembcke, 1998.
21. Frankel, 1994.
22. Burkett and Whitley, 1998, 158.
23. Ibid., 232.
24. McNally, 1999.
25. Weiner, 1986.
26. Janoff-Bulman, 1992, 74–75.
27. Ibid., 148.
28. Pyszczynski et al., 2000.
29. Solomon et al., 2000.
30. Harber and Pennebaker, 1992.
31. Coates et al., 1979.
32. Felman, 1995.
33. Herman, 1992; Solomon, 1995; Shephard, 2000.
34. Solomon, 1995.

Chapter 2. Postraumatic Stress Disorder:
Discovery or Invention?

1. Young, 1995, 10.
2. Beard, 1890.
3. Clark, 1981, 299.
4. Page, 1883, 172–73.
5. Ibid., 143.
6. Janet, 1904.
7. Myers, 1940, 25–26.
8. Wiltshire, 1916.
9. Rows, 1916, 441.
10. Ibid., 443.
11. Culpin, 1931, 28.
12. Ibid., 27.
13. Ibid., 50.
14. Young, 1995; Double, 2002.
15. Summerfield, 2001, 96.
16. Freyd, 1996; Reynolds and Brewin, 1999.
17. Field, 1999.
18. Berntsen, 1996; Brewin, Christodoulides, and Hutchinson, 1996.
19. Reynolds and Brewin, 1998.
20. Mendelson, 1995.
21. Rothbaum and Foa, 1993.
22. Kessler et al., 1995.
23. Pitman et al., 2000.
24. Shin et al., 1997, 1999.
25. Pitman et al., 2000.
26. Bracken, 2002; Summerfield, 2001.
27. Norris et al., 2001.
28. Nijenhuis, Spinhoven et al., 1998; Nijenhuis, Vanderlinden et al., 1998.
29. Field, 1999, 36.
30. Summerfield, 2001, 97.
31. Bowlby, 1980.
32. Kilpatrick et al., 1998.
33. Breslau and Davis, 1987a.
34. With the exception of acute stress disorder, a short-term response to trauma introduced for the first time in the DSM-IV and discussed later in this book.
35. Reynolds and Brewin, 1999.
36. Kilpatrick et al., 1998; Reynolds and Brewin, 1998.
37. Wells and Hackmann, 1993.
38. Hackmann et al., 2000.
39. Keane, 1993.
40. Green, 1993.
41. Foa, Riggs, and Gershuny, 1995.
42. Kilpatrick et al., 1998.

43. King et al., 1998.
44. Resick, 2001.
45. Kessler et al., 1995.
46. Herman, 1993.
47. Yehuda, Resnick et al., 1993; Yehuda, Southwick et al., 1993.
48. Yehuda, Southwick et al., 1993.
49. Resnick et al., 1995.
50. Young, 1995.
51. Ruscio et al., 2002.
52. Birchwood and Jackson, 2001.

Chapter 3. Is Posttraumatic Stress Disorder Caused by Trauma?

1. Caruth, 1995, 5.
2. Resick, 2001.
3. Breslau and Davis, 1987a; Kasl, 1990.
4. Yehuda and McFarlane, 1995.
5. Brewin, Andrews, and Valentine, 2000.
6. Bromet et al., 1982; Pynoos and Nader, 1988.
7. Kilpatrick and Resnick, 1993.
8. Kilpatrick et al., 1998.
9. Helzer et al., 1987.
10. Scott and Stradling, 1994.
11. Pathé and Mullen, 1997.
12. Wiltshire, 1916.
13. Kessler et al., 1995; Kilpatrick et al., 1998.
14. Dunmore et al., 2001; Kilpatrick and Resnick, 1993.
15. Bernat et al., 1998; Girelli et al., 1986.
16. Brewin, Andrews, and Rose, 2000.
17. Breslau and Davis, 1987b.
18. Mayou et al., 2001.
19. The exception is in combat and war situations, in which men and women tradition-
    ally have different roles and are selected for different tasks, so the risks are hard to
    compare.
20. Resick, 2001.
21. Macklin et al., 1998; Pitman et al., 1991.
22. Rosen and Engle, 1998.
23. Wenzlaff and Wegner, 2000.
24. Brewin and Beaton, 2002.
25. Brewin and Smart, 2002.
26. See Frueh et al., 1998, and Resick, 2001, for reviews.
27. Spiegel and Cardeña, 1991.
28. Myers, 1940, 66.
29. van der Kolk et al., 1996.

30. Morgan et al., 2001.
31. Marmar et al., 1997.
32. Griffin et al., 1997.
33. Holman and Silver, 1998; Morris et al., 2000; Reynolds and Brewin, 1999.
34. Ehlers, Mayou, and Bryant, 1998; Koopman et al., 1994; Murray et al., 2002; Shalev et al., 1996; Ursano et al., 1999.
35. Holman and Silver, 1998.
36. Brewin et al., 1999; Classen et al., 1998; Harvey and Bryant, 1998, 1999a.
37. Brewin, Andrews, and Rose, in press.
38. Ehlers et al., 2000, 45.
39. Ehlers et al., 2000.
40. Başoğlu et al., 1997.
41. Dunmore et al., 2001.
42. Ehlers, Clark et al., 1998.
43. Bryant et al., 2000; Shalev et al., 1998.
44. McFarlane, 1997.
45. See Brewin, Andrews, and Valentine, 2000, for a review.
46. Andrews et al., in press; Zoellner et al., 1999.
47. Dunmore et al., 2001; Ullman and Filipas, 2001; Zoellner et al., 1999.
48. Andrews et al., in press.
49. Tarrier et al., 1999.
50. Butzlaff and Hooley, 1998.
51. Andrews, Brewin, Rose, and Kirk, 2000, 71.
52. Ibid., 72.
53. Ehlers, Mayou, and Bryant, 1998.
54. Andrews, Brewin, Rose, and Kirk, 2000.
55. Ehlers and Clark, 2000.
56. Dunmore et al., 1999; Ehlers et al., 2000; Steil and Ehlers 2000.
57. Dunmore et al., 2001; Ehlers, Mayou, and Bryant, 1998.
58. Wenzlaff and Wegner, 2000.
59. Dunmore et al., 1999; Steil and Ehlers, 2000.
60. Dunmore et al., 2001; Ehlers, Mayou, and Bryant, 1998.
61. De Bellis, Baum et al., 1999; De Bellis, Keshavan et al., 1999.
62. Perry et al., 1995.
63. Holman and Silver, 1998; Kisiel and Lyons, 2001; Morgan et al., 2001; Resnick et al., 1995.
64. Andrews, 1997a.

Chapter 4. A Crisis of Identity

1. Keenan, 1993,76.
2. Andrews, 1997a; Brown et al., 1995; Gilbert, 1992.
3. Young, 1995.
4. Rows, 1916, 442.
5. Horowitz, 1976.
6. Blank, 1993; McFarlane, 1997.

7. Janoff-Bulman, 1992.

8. Bracken, 2002.

9. Herman, 1992; Freyd, 1996.

10. Beck et al., 1979.

11. Padesky, 1994.

12. Young, 1990.

13. Brewin, 1989; Teasdale and Barnard, 1993.

14. Segal, 1988.

15. Kihlstrom and Cantor, 1984; Markus and Sentis, 1982.

16. Markus and Nurius, 1986; Ogilvie, 1987.

17. Strauman and Higgins, 1988.

18. Strauman, 1990; Strauman et al., 1993.

19. Carver et al., 1999.

20. Brewin and Vallance, 1997.

21. Resick and Schnicke, 1993.

22. Brewin and Power, 1999.

23. Van Velsen et al., 1996.

24. Reynolds and Brewin, 1999.

25. Joseph et al., 1991, 1993.

26. Shay, 1995.

27. Andrews, 1998.

28. Rows, 1916; Ehlers and Clark, 2000.

29. Swan and Andrews, in press.

30. Lee et al., 2001, 460.

31. Shay, 1995.

32. Keenan, 1993, 67.

33. Ibid., 68.

34. Freyd, 1996.

35. Brown et al., 1986.

36. Janoff-Bulman and Frantz, 1997.

37. Herman, 1992, 213.

38. Bolton and Hill, 1996.

Chapter 5. The Puzzle of Emotional Memory

1. Terr, 1990, 170.

2. Brown and Kulik, 1977, 74.

3. Ibid., 74.

4. Pillemer, 1984.

5. Conway, 1995; Brewer, 1992.

6. Neisser and Harsch, 1992.

7. Neisser, 1982.

8. Brewer, 1992.

9. Conway, 1995; Conway et al., 1994.

10. Conway et al., 1994.

11. Rubin and Kozin, 1984.

12. Pillemer, 1998a.

13. Pillemer and White, 1989, 326.

14. Pillemer, 1998a, 158.

15. Neisser, 1982.

16. Loftus and Burns, 1982.

17. Kassin et al., 1989.

18. Kuehn, 1974.

19. Koss et al., 1996; Tromp et al., 1995.

20. Mechanic et al., 1998.

21. Christianson, 1992.

22. Christianson and Loftus, 1990; Wessel and Merckelbach, 1994.

23. Yerkes and Dodson, 1908.

24. Mandler, 1992.

25. Butler and Wolfner, 2000.

26. van der Kolk, 1996; van der Kolk and Fisler, 1995.

27. Pitman, 1989.

28. Schwarz et al., 1993; Southwick et al., 1997.

29. Foa, Molnar, and Cashman, 1995; Harvey and Bryant, 1999b.

30. Terr, 1990; van der Kolk and van der Hart, 1991; Brewin, Dalgleish, and Joseph, 1996.

31. Hellawell and Brewin, 2002b.

32. Ibid.

33. Estes, 1997.

34. Herman, 1992.

35. Ehlers and Steil, 1995.

36. Hellawell and Brewin, 2002b.

37. For example, Bremner et al., 1995; Ehlers and Clark, 2000; Janet, 1904.

38. Reynolds and Brewin, 1998.

39. Hellawell and Brewin, 2002a.

40. Treisman and Gelade, 1980.

41. Treisman and DeSchepper, 1996.

42. For example, Porter and Birt, 2001; Byrne et al., 2001.

43. Horowitz and Reidbord, 1992.

Chapter 6. Trauma, Memory, and the Brain

1. Eliot, 1963, 26.

2. Lang, 1979, 1985.

3. Chemtob et al., 1988; Creamer et al., 1992; Foa and Rothbaum, 1998.

4. Foa, Molnar, and Cashman, 1995.

5. Murray et al., 2002.

6. Teasdale and Barnard, 1993.

7. Brown and Kulik, 1977; Pillemer, 1998a.

8. Janet, 1904.

9. For example, van der Hart and Horst, 1989; van der Kolk and van der Hart, 1991.

10. Terr, 1990, 171.

11. Brewin, Dalgleish, and Joseph, 1996.

12. Grey et al., 2001.

13. Mack and Rock, 1998.

14. Wheeler and Treisman, 2002.

15. For example, Paivio, 1986.

16. Schooler and Engstler-Schooler, 1990; Schooler, Fiore, and Brandimonte, 1997.

17. Hellawell and Brewin, 2002a, 2002b.

18. Pillemer et al., 1998.

19. Rachman, 1989.

20. Bouton and Swartzentruber, 1991; Jacobs and Nadel, 1985.

21. For example, LeDoux, 1998.

22. Morris et al., 1999.

23. Douglas, 1972; McCormick and Thompson, 1982.

24. Conway and Pleydell-Pearce, 2000; Wheeler et al., 1997.

25. Hariri et al., 2000; LeDoux, 1998.

26. See Davey, 1993.

27. Eichenbaum, 1997; Squire, 1994.

28. Kesner, 1998.

29. Eichenbaum, 1997.

30. Moscovitch, 1995.

31. For example, Squire and Alvarez, 1995; but see Nadel and Moscovitch, 1997, for an alternative position.

32. McClelland et al., 1995.

33. McCloskey and Cohen, 1989.

34. For example, Gabrieli et al., 1995.

35. Tulving and Schacter, 1990.

36. Brown and Kulik, 1977; Pillemer, 1998a.

37. Cahill and McGaugh, 1998.

38. Bremner et al., 1995; Metcalfe and Jacobs, 1998.

39. Newcomer et al., 1999.

40. Pitman et al., 2000.

41. Amaral et al., 1992.

42. Bremner, 2001, 2002.

43. Sapolsky, 2000.

44. Yehuda, 2001.

45. Pitman et al., 2000.

46. Gilbertson et al., 2002.

47. Ehlers and Clark, 2000.

48. Herman, 1992; van der Kolk, 1996.

49. Schwarz et al., 1993; Southwick et al., 1997.

50. Conway and Pleydell-Pearce, 2000.

Chapter 7. Myths, Memory Wars, and Witch-hunts

1. Wiltshire, 1916, 1,210.

2. Mollon, 1998.

3. Bass and Davis, 1988, 70.

4. Ibid., 87.

5. For example, Blume, 1990; Fredrickson, 1992.

6. Freyd, 1996.

7. Kihlstrom, cited in Pope, 1996, 959.

8. Loftus, 1993.

9. Lindsay and Read, 1994, 1995.

10. Reviewed in Hyman and Loftus, 1998.

11. Hyman et al., 1995.

12. Pezdek, 2001; Pezdek et al., 1997.

13. Lindsay and Read, 1995.

14. Clancy et al., 1999, 2000.

15. Freyd and Gleaves, 1996.

16. For example, Leavitt, 1997.

17. Crews, 1997; Ofshe and Watters, 1994; Pendergrast, 1996.

18. Kitzinger and Reilly, 1997, 332–33.

19. Ibid., 336.

20. Crews, 1997; Pendergrast, 1996.

21. Pope, 1996.

22. Gudjonsson, 1997.

23. See Freyd, 1996, and Mollon, 1998, for reviews.

24. Joslyn et al., 1997.

25. Morton et al., 1995.

26. Andrews et al., 1995.

27. Andrews et al., 1999.

28. Elliott, 1997; Feldman-Summers and Pope, 1994; Melchert, 1996.

29. Howes et al., 1993; Usher and Neisser, 1993.

30. Morton et al., 1995.

31. Gudjonsson's figure of 7 percent is reduced to 3 percent if missing cases are included in the calculations (Andrews, 1997b).

32. Andrews et al., 1999.

33. Brewin et al., 1993.

34. Pope and Hudson, 1995.

35. Cheit, 1998.

36. Schooler, 1994, 2001; Schooler, Bendiksen, and Ambadar, 1997.

37. Schooler, Bendiksen, and Ambadar, 1997, 273.

38. Ofshe and Watters, 1994; Pendergrast, 1996.

39. See Cheit, 1998, or the Web site at http://www.brown.edu/Departments/Taubman_Center/Recovmem/Archive.html.

40. Corwin and Olafson, 1997.

41. Williams 1994, 1995.

42. Feldman-Summers and Pope, 1994.

43. Gudjonsson, 1997.

44. Andrews et al., 1999.

45. Chu et al., 1999.

46. Feldman-Summers and Pope, 1994.

47. Andrews et al., 1995.

48. Elliott and Briere, 1995.
49. Harvey and Herman, 1994.
50. Andrews et al., 1999; Elliott and Briere, 1995; Gold et al., 1994; Loftus et al., 1994.
51. Yapko, 1994.
52. Poole et al., 1995.
53. Andrews et al., 1995.
54. Andrews et al., 1999; Andrews, Brewin, Ochera et al., 2000.
55. Schooler, 2001.
56. Belli et al., 1998; Read and Lindsay, 2000.
57. Winkielman et al., 1998.
58. Brewin and Stokou, 2002.
59. Hunter and Andrews, 2002.
60. Meesters et al., 2000.
61. Schacter et al., 1989.
62. Kihlstrom, 1985.
63. Mollon, 1998, 175.
64. For example, Brandon et al., 1998; Crews, 1997; Kihlstrom, 1995; Merskey, 1995; Pendergrast, 1996; Pope et al., 1998; Weiskrantz, 1995.
65. Loftus and Ketcham, 1994.
66. Crews, 1997, 249.
67. Lindsay and Read, 1995, 894.
68. For example, Lindsay and Briere, 1997.
69. Courtois, 1997; Mollon, 1998; Pope and Brown, 1996.

Chapter 8. The Return of Repression?

1. Brooke, 1918, 57.
2. Loftus and Ketcham, 1994.
3. Breuer and Freud, 1893.
4. Freud, 1896.
5. Breuer and Freud, 1893, 10.
6. Freud, 1915, 147.
7. Erdelyi, 1990.
8. Freyd, 1996.
9. For exceptions see, for example, Herman and Schatzow, 1987; van der Kolk and Fisler, 1995.
10. Corwin and Olafson, 1997; Herman and Schatzow, 1987; Schooler, 1994, 2001; Schooler, Bendiksen, and Ambadar, 1997.
11. Andrews, Brewin, Ochera et al., 2000.
12. For example, de Rivera, 1997.
13. Holmes, 1990.
14. Loftus and Ketcham, 1994, 214.
15. Crews, 1997, 162.
16. For example, Briere and Conte, 1993; Herman and Schatzow, 1987.
17. Pope and Hudson, 1995; Pope et al., 1998.

18. Williams, 1994.

19. Pillemer, 1998b.

20. Loftus and Ketcham, 1994, 214.

21. Andrews, Brewin, Ochera et al., 2000.

22. Crews, 1997, 165–66.

23. Pendergrast, 1996, 90.

24. Ibid., 99–100.

25. Cheit, cited in Freyd, 1996, 7.

26. Schooler, 2001.

27. Andrews, Brewin, Ochera et al., 2000.

28. Elliott, 1997.

29. Briere and Conte, 1993; Herman and Schatzow, 1987; Elliott and Briere, 1995; Williams, 1994.

30. Joslyn et al., 1997.

31. Freyd, 1996.

32. Briere and Conte, 1993; Herman and Schatzow, 1987; Elliott, 1997; Williams, 1994.

33. Brandon et al., 1998, 298–99.

34. See, for example, Brewin et al., 1993.

35. Merskey, 1995, 283.

36. Crews, 1997, 172.

37. Conway, 1995.

38. Erdelyi, 1990; Brewin and Andrews, 1998.

39. Simpson and Kang, 1994.

40. Anderson, Bjork, and Bjork, 1994.

41. Anderson and Spellman, 1995.

42. See Bjork and Bjork, 1996, for a review.

43. Bjork and Bjork, 1996.

44. Anderson and Green, 2001.

45. McNally et al., 1998, 2001.

46. Moulds and Bryant, 2002.

47. Weinberger et al., 1979.

48. Davis and Schwartz, 1987.

49. Myers and Brewin, 1994.

50. Myers and Brewin, 1995; Myers et al., 1998.

51. Andrews, Brewin, Ochera et al., 2000.

52. Dalenberg et al., 1995.

53. Anderson, 2001.

54. Freyd, 1996.

55. Mechanic et al., 1998.

56. Bryant, 1995.

57. Holmes et al., 2002.

58. Brewin, Dalgleish, and Joseph, 1996.

59. Brewin and Saunders, 2001; Holmes et al., 2002.

60. Holmes et al., 2002.

61. For example, van der Kolk and Fisler, 1995.

62. Merckelbach et al., 1998; Reynolds and Brewin, 1998.

Chapter 9. More Battlegrounds: Preventing and Treating PTSD

1. Angelou, 1994, 272.
2. Brewin, Dalgleish, and Joseph, 1996.
3. Horowitz, 1976.
4. Resick and Schnicke, 1993.
5. Brewin, 2001.
6. Ehlers, Mayou, and Bryant, 1998.
7. MacLeod and Campbell, 1992.
8. Mitchell, 1983.
9. Everly and Mitchell, 1999.
10. Rose et al., 1999.
11. Bisson et al., 2000; Rose et al., 2002.
12. Bisson et al., 1997; Mayou et al., 2000.
13. Dyregrov, 2001; Everly and Mitchell, 1999; Everly et al., 2001.
14. Greenberg, 1995; Rothbaum and Foa, 1993; Shalev, 1992.
15. Koren et al., 1999.
16. Brewin et al., 1999; Classen et al., 1998; Harvey and Bryant, 1998.
17. Brewin et al., 1999.
18. Pynoos and Nader, 1988; Shalev, 2002.
19. Ehlers and Clark, 2000.
20. Rose et al., 1999.
21. Bolton et al., 2000; Pynoos et al., 1993; Yule et al., 2000.
22. Dyregrov, 2001.
23. La Greca et al., 2002; Yule, 2001; Yule and Gold, 1993.
24. Brewin, Rose et al., 2002.
25. Janet, 1925/1976.
26. Myers, 1940, 68.
27. Rows, 1916, 442.
28. Foa et al., 1991, 1999; Marks et al., 1998; Resick and Schnicke, 1993; Resick et al., 2002; Tarrier et al., 1999.
29. Sloman, 1996.
30. For example, Foa and Rothbaum, 1998.
31. Brewin, 2001.
32. For example, Herman, 1992.
33. Holmes et al., 2002.
34. Brewin and Lennard, 1999.
35. Resick and Schnicke, 1993.
36. See also Ehlers and Clark, 2000.
37. Ehlers and Clark, 2000; Richards and Lovell, 1999.
38. Grey et al., 2002.
39. Grey et al., 2001.
40. Eysenck, 1979; Lockhart et al., 1976.
41. Hunt and McDaniel, 1993; Hunt and Smith, 1996.

42. Van Etten and Taylor, 1998.

43. Shapiro, 1995.

44. McNally, 1999.

45. Cahill et al., 1999.

46. Hackmann, 1998; Layden et al., 1993; Smucker et al., 1995.

47. Hunt and McDaniel, 1993.

48. Ehlers and Clark, 2000.

49. Grey et al., 2002.

50. Bryant et al., 1998, 1999.

51. Rauch et al., 2001.

52. Resick and Schnicke, 1993.

53. McClelland et al., 1995.

54. For example, Janoff-Bulman, 1992.

Chapter 10. Ancient Malady or Modern Myth?

1. William Shakespeare, *Macbeth,* Act V, scene 3.

2. Shobe and Kihlstrom, 1997.

3. Berntsen, 2001; Pillemer, 1998a.

4. Hamann and Mao, 2002; Kesner et al., 1989.

5. Schooler and Engstler-Schooler, 1990.

6. Bremner et al., 1999.

7. Wild et al., 2002.

8. Shalev, in press.

9. For example, Ehlers and Clark, 2000.

10. Grey et al., 2002.

11. Hunt and McDaniel, 1993.

12. Herlihy et al., 2002.

References

Amaral, D. G., Price, J. L., Pitkänen, A., and Carmichael, S. T. (1992). Anatomical organization of the primate amygdaloid complex. In J. P. Aggleton (Ed.), *The amygdala: Neurobiological aspects of emotion, memory, and mental dysfunction* (pp. 1–66). New York: Wiley-Liss.

American Psychiatric Association (1980). *Diagnostic and statistical manual* (3rd ed.). Washington, D.C.: American Psychiatric Association.

———(1987). *Diagnostic and statistical manual* (3rd, revised ed.). Washington, D.C.: American Psychiatric Association.

———(1994). *Diagnostic and statistical manual* (4th ed.). Washington, D.C.: American Psychiatric Association.

Anderson, M. C. (2001). Active forgetting: Evidence for functional inhibition as a source of memory failure. *Journal of Aggression, Maltreatment, and Trauma, 4,* 185–210.

Anderson, M. C., and Green, C. (2001). Suppressing unwanted memories by executive control. *Nature, 410,* 366–69.

Anderson, M. C., and Spellman, B. A. (1995). On the status of inhibitory mechanisms in cognition: Memory retrieval as a model case. *Psychological Review, 102,* 68–100.

Anderson, M. C., Bjork, R. A., and Bjork, E. L. (1994). Remembering can cause forgetting: Retrieval dynamics in long-term memory. *Journal of Experimental Psychology: Learning, Memory and Cognition, 20,* 1063–87.

Andrews, B. (1997a). Early adversity and the creation of personal meaning. In M. Power and C. R. Brewin (Eds.), *The transformation of meaning in psychological therapies: Integrating theory and practice* (pp. 75–89). Chichester: Wiley.

———(1997b). Can a survey of British False Memory Society members reliably inform the recovered memory debate? *Applied Cognitive Psychology, 11,* 19–23.

———(1998). Shame and childhood abuse. In P. Gilbert and B. Andrews (Eds.), *Shame: Interpersonal behavior, psychopathology, and culture* (pp. 176–90). New York: Oxford University Press.

Andrews, B., Brewin, C. R., and Rose, S. (in press). Gender, social support and PTSD in victims of violent crime. *Journal of Traumatic Stress.*

Andrews, B., Brewin, C. R., Ochera, J., Morton, J., Bekerian, D. A., Davies, G. M., and Mollon, P. (1999). Characteristics, context and consequences of memory recovery among adults in therapy. *British Journal of Psychiatry, 175,* 141–46.

————(2000). The timing, triggers and qualities of recovered memories in therapy. *British Journal of Clinical Psychology, 39*, 11–26.

Andrews, B., Brewin, C. R., Rose, S., and Kirk, M. (2000). Predicting PTSD symptoms in victims of violent crime: The role of shame, anger, and childhood abuse. *Journal of Abnormal Psychology, 109*, 69–73.

Andrews, B., Morton, J., Bekerian, D. A., Brewin, C. R., Davies, G. M., and Mollon, P. (1995). The recovery of memories in clinical practice: Experiences and beliefs of British Psychological Society practitioners. *Psychologist, 8*, 209–14.

Angelou, M. (1994). *The complete collected poems of Maya Angelou.* London: Virago Press.

Alpert, J. L., Brown, L. S., and Courtois, C. A. (1996). *Symptomatic clients and memories of childhood abuse: What the trauma and child sexual abuse literature tells us (Final Report).* Washington, D.C.: American Psychological Association Working Group on Investigation of Memories of Childhood Abuse.

Başoğlu, M., Mineka, S., Paker, M., Aker, T., Livanou, M., and Gök, Ş. (1997). Psychological preparedness for trauma as a protective factor in survivors of torture. *Psychological Medicine, 27*, 1421–33.

Bass, E., and Davis, L. (1988). *The courage to heal: A guide for women survivors of child sexual abuse.* New York: Harper and Row.

Beard, G. M. (1890). *A practical guide on nervous exhaustion.* London: H. K. Lewis.

Beck, A. T., Rush, A. J., Shaw, B. F., and Emery, G. (1979). Cognitive therapy of depression. New York: Wiley.

Belli, R. F., Winkielman, P., Read, J. D., Schwarz, N., and Lynn, S. J. (1998). Recalling more childhood events leads to judgments of poorer memory: Implications for the recovered/false memory debate. *Psychonomic Bulletin and Review, 5*, 318–23.

Bernat, J. A., Ronfeldt, H. M., Calhoun, K. S., and Arias, I. (1998). Prevalence of traumatic events and peritraumatic predictors of posttraumatic stress symptoms in a nonclinical sample of college students. *Journal of Traumatic Stress, 11*, 645–64.

Berntsen, D. (1996). Involuntary autobiographical memories. *Applied Cognitive Psychology, 10*, 435–54.

Berntsen, D. (2001). Involuntary memories of emotional events: Do memories of traumas and extremely happy events differ? *Applied Cognitive Psychology, 15*, S135–58.

Birchwood, M., and Jackson, C. (2001). *Schizophrenia.* Hove: Psychology Press.

Bisson, J. I., Jenkins, P. L., Alexander, J., and Bannister, C. (1997). Randomized controlled trial of psychological debriefing for victims of acute burn trauma. *British Journal of Psychiatry, 171*, 78–81.

Bisson, J. I., McFarlane, A. C., and Rose, S. (2000). Psychological debriefing. In

E. B. Foa, T. M. Keane, and M. J. Friedman (Eds.), *Effective treatments for PTSD* (pp. 39–59). New York: Guilford.

Bjork, E. L., and Bjork, R. A. (1996). Continuing influences of to-be-forgotten information. *Consciousness and Cognition, 5*, 176–96.

Blank, A. S. (1993). The longitudinal course of posttraumatic stress disorder. In J. R. T. Davidson and E. B. Foa (Eds.), *Posttraumatic stress disorder: DSM-IV and beyond* (pp. 3–22). Washington, D.C.: American Psychiatric Press.

Blume, E. S. (1990). *Secret survivors: Uncovering incest and its aftereffects in women.* New York: Ballantine.

Bolton, D., and Hill, J. (1996). *Mind, meaning, and mental disorder.* Oxford: Oxford University Press.

Bolton, D., O'Ryan, D., Udwin, O., Boyle, S., and Yule, W. (2000). The long-term psychological effects of a disaster experienced in adolescence: II. General psychopathology. *Journal of Child Psychology and Psychiatry, 41*, 513–23.

Bouton, M. E., and Swartzentruber, D. (1991). Sources of relapse after extinction in Pavlovian and instrumental learning. *Clinical Psychology Review, 11*, 123–40.

Bowlby, J. (1980). *Attachment and loss. Vol. 3: Loss, sadness, and depression.* London: Hogarth Press.

Bracken, P. J. (2002). *Trauma: Culture, meaning, and philosophy.* London: Whurr Publishers.

Brandon, S., Boakes, J., Glaser, D., and Green, R. (1998). Recovered memories of childhood sexual abuse—Implications for clinical practice. *British Journal of Psychiatry, 172*, 296–307.

Bremner, J. D. (2001). Hypotheses and controversies related to effects of stress on the hippocampus: An argument for stress-induced damage to the hippocampus in patients with posttraumatic stress disorder. *Hippocampus, 11*, 75–81.

Bremner, J. D. (2002). *Does stress damage the brain?: Understanding trauma-related disorders from a neurological perspective.* New York: W. W. Norton.

Bremner, J. D., Krystal, J. H., Southwick, S. M., and Charney, D. S. (1995). Functional neuroanatomical correlates of the effects of stress on memory. *Journal of Traumatic Stress, 8*, 527–53.

Bremner, J. D., Southwick, S. M., and Charney, D. S. (1999). The neurobiology of posttraumatic stress disorder: An integration of animal and human research. In P. A. Saigh and J. D. Bremner (Eds.), *Posttraumatic stress disorder: A comprehensive text* (pp. 103–43). Boston: Allyn and Bacon.

Breslau, N., and Davis, G. C. (1987a). Posttraumatic stress disorder: The stressor criterion. *Journal of Nervous and Mental Disease, 175*, 255–64.

———(1987b). Posttraumatic stress disorder: The etiologic specificity of wartime stressors. *American Journal of Psychiatry, 144*, 578–83.

Brett, E. A., and Ostroff, R. (1985). Imagery and posttraumatic stress disorder: An overview. *American Journal of Psychiatry, 142*, 417–24.

Breuer, J., and Freud, S. (1893/1955). On the psychical mechanism of hysterical phenomena: Preliminary communication. In J. Strachey (Ed.), *Standard Edition* (Vol. 2). London: Hogarth Press.

Brewer, W. F. (1992). The theoretical and empirical status of the flashbulb memory hypothesis. In E. Winograd and U. Neisser (Eds.), *Affect and accuracy in recall: Studies of flashbulb memories* (pp. 274–305). Cambridge: Cambridge University Press.

Brewin, C. R. (1989). Cognitive change processes in psychotherapy. *Psychological Review, 96*, 379–94.

———(2001). A cognitive neuroscience account of posttraumatic stress disorder and its treatment. *Behaviour Research and Therapy, 39*, 373–93.

Brewin, C. R., and Andrews, B. (1998). Recovered memories of trauma: Phenomenology and cognitive mechanisms. *Clinical Psychology Review, 18*, 949–70.

Brewin, C. R., and Beaton, A. (2002). Thought suppression, intelligence, and working memory capacity. *Behaviour Research and Therapy, 40*, 923–30.

Brewin, C. R., and Lennard, H. (1999). Effects of mode of writing on emotional narratives. *Journal of Traumatic Stress, 12*, 355–61.

Brewin, C. R., and Power, M. J. (1999). Integrating psychological therapies: Processes of meaning transformation. *British Journal of Medical Psychology, 72*, 143–57.

Brewin, C. R., and Saunders, J. (2001). The effect of dissociation at encoding on intrusive memories for a stressful film. *British Journal of Medical Psychology, 74*, 467–72.

Brewin, C. R., and Smart, L. (2002). Working memory capacity and suppression of obsessional thoughts. Manuscript submitted for publication.

Brewin, C. R., and Stokou, L. (2002). Validating reports of poor childhood memory. *Applied Cognitive Psychology, 16*, 509–14.

Brewin, C. R., and Vallance, H. (1997). Self-discrepancies in young adults and childhood violence. *Journal of Interpersonal Violence, 12*, 600–06.

Brewin, C. R., Andrews, B., and Gotlib, I. H. (1993). Psychopathology and early experience: A reappraisal of retrospective reports. *Psychological Bulletin, 113*, 82–98.

Brewin, C. R., Andrews, B., and Rose, S. (in press). Diagnostic overlap between acute stress disorder and posttraumatic stress disorder in victims of violent crime. *American Journal of Psychiatry.*

———(2000). Fear, helplessness, and horror in posttraumatic stress disorder: Investigating DSM-IV criterion A2 in victims of violent crime. *Journal of Traumatic Stress, 13*, 499–509.

Brewin, C. R., Andrews, B., and Valentine, J. D. (2000). Meta-analysis of risk factors for posttraumatic stress disorder in trauma-exposed adults. *Journal of Consulting and Clinical Psychology, 68*, 748–66.

Brewin, C. R., Andrews, B., Rose, S., and Kirk, M. (1999). Acute stress disorder and posttraumatic stress disorder in victims of violent crime. *American Journal of Psychiatry, 156,* 360–66.

Brewin, C. R., Christodoulides, J., and Hutchinson, G. (1996). Intrusive thoughts and intrusive memories in a nonclinical sample. *Cognition and Emotion, 10,* 107–12.

Brewin, C. R., Dalgleish, T., and Joseph, S. (1996). A dual representation theory of post traumatic stress disorder. *Psychological Review, 103,* 670–86.

Brewin, C. R., Rose, S., Andrews, B., Green, J., Tata, P., McEvedy, C., Turner, S. W., and Foa, E. B. (2002). A brief screening instrument for posttraumatic stress disorder. *British Journal of Psychiatry, 181,* 158–62.

Briere, J., and Conte, J. (1993). Self-reported amnesia for abuse in adults molested as children. *Journal of Traumatic Stress, 6,* 21–31.

Bromet, E. J., Parkinson, D. K., Schulberg, H. C., Dunn, L. O., and Gondek, P. C. (1982). Mental health of residents near the Three Mile Island reactor: A comparative study of selected groups. *Journal of Preventive Psychiatry, 1,* 225–74.

Brooke, R. (1918). *The collected poems of Rupert Brooke.* London: Sidgwick and Jackson.

Brown, R., and Kulik, J. (1977). Flashbulb memories. *Cognition, 5,* 73–99.

Brown, G. W., Andrews, B., Harris, T., Adler, Z., and Bridge, L. (1986). Social support, self-esteem and depression. *Psychological Medicine, 16,* 813–31.

Brown, G. W., Harris, T. O., and Hepworth, C. (1995). Loss, humiliation and entrapment among women developing depression—a patient and non-patient comparison. *Psychological Medicine, 25,* 7–21.

Bryant, R. A. (1995). Autobiographical memory across personalities in dissociative identity disorder: A case report. *Journal of Abnormal Psychology, 104,* 625–31.

Bryant, R. A., Harvey, A. G., Dang, S. T., Sackville, T., and Basten, C. (1998). Treatment of acute stress disorder: A comparison of cognitive-behavioral therapy and supportive counseling. *Journal of Consulting and Clinical Psychology, 66,* 862–66.

Bryant, R. A., Harvey, A. G., Guthrie, R. M., and Moulds, M. (2000). A prospective study of psychophysiological arousal, acute stress disorder, and posttraumatic stress disorder. *Journal of Abnormal Psychology, 109,* 341–44.

Bryant, R. A., Sackville, T., Dang, S. T., Moulds, M., and Guthrie, R. (1999). Treating acute stress disorder: An evaluation of cognitive behavior therapy and supportive counseling techniques. *American Journal of Psychiatry, 156,* 1780–86.

Burkett, B. G., and Whitley, G. (1998). *Stolen valor: How the Vietnam generation was robbed of its heroes and its history.* Dallas, Tex.: Verity Press.

Butler, L. D., and Wolfner, A. L. (2000). Some characteristics of positive and negative ("most traumatic") event memories in a college sample. *Journal of Trauma and Dissociation, 1,* 45–68.

242

References

Butzlaff, R. L., and Hooley, J. M. (1998). Expressed emotion and psychiatric relapse—A meta-analysis. *Archives of General Psychiatry, 55, 547–52*.

Byrne, C. A., Hyman, I. E., and Scott, K. L. (2001). Comparisons of memories for traumatic events and other experiences. *Applied Cognitive Psychology, 15*, S119–33.

Cahill, L., and McGaugh, J. L. (1998). Mechanisms of emotional arousal and lasting declarative memory. *Trends in Neurosciences, 21, 294–99*.

Cahill, S. P., Carrigan, M. H., and Frueh, B. C. (1999). Does EMDR work? And if so, why?: A critical review of controlled outcome and dismantling research. *Journal of Anxiety Disorders, 13, 5–33*.

Caruth, C. (Ed.) (1995). *Trauma: Explorations in memory.* Baltimore: Johns Hopkins University Press.

Carver, C. S., Lawrence, J. W., and Scheier, M. F. (1999). Self-discrepancies and affect: Incorporating the role of feared selves. *Personality and Social Psychology Bulletin, 25, 783–92*.

Cheit, R. E. (1998). Consider this, skeptics of recovered memory. *Ethics and Behavior, 8, 141–60*.

Chemtob, C., Roitblat, H. L., Hamada, R. S., Carlson, J. G., and Twentyman, C. T. (1988). A cognitive action theory of post-traumatic stress disorder. *Journal of Anxiety Disorders, 2, 253–75*.

Christianson, S.-A. (1992). Emotional stress and eyewitness memory: A critical review. *Psychological Bulletin, 112, 284–309*.

Christianson, S.-A., and Loftus, E. F. (1990). Some characteristics of people's traumatic memories. *Bulletin of the Psychonomic Society, 28, 195–98*.

Chu, J. A., Frey, L. M., Ganzel, B. L., and Matthews, J. A. (1999). Memories of childhood abuse: Dissociation, amnesia, and corroboration. *American Journal of Psychiatry, 156, 749–55*.

Clancy, S. A., McNally, R. J., and Schacter, D. L. (1999). Effects of guided imagery on memory distortion in women reporting recovered memories of childhood sexual abuse. *Journal of Traumatic Stress, 12, 559–69*.

Clancy, S. A., Schacter, D. L., McNally, R. J., and Pitman, R. K. (2000). False recognition in women reporting recovered memories of sexual abuse. *Psychological Science, 11, 26–31*.

Clark, M. J. (1981). The rejection of psychological approaches to mental disorder in late nineteenth-century British psychiatry. In A. Scull (Ed.), *Madhouses, mad-doctors, and madmen* (pp. 271–312). London: Athlone Press.

Classen, C., Koopman, C., Hales, R., and Spiegel, D. (1998). Acute stress disorder as a predictor of posttraumatic stress symptoms. *American Journal of Psychiatry, 155, 620–24*.

Coates, D., Wortman, C. B., and Abbey, A. (1979). Reactions to victims. In I. H. Frieze, D. Bar-Tal, and J. S. Carroll (Eds.), *New approaches to social problems* (pp. 21–52). San Francisco: Jossey-Bass.

Conway, M. A. (1995). *Flashbulb memories.* Hove: Erlbaum.

Conway, M. A., and Pleydell-Pearce, C. W. (2000). The construction of autobi ographical memories in the self-memory system. *Psychological Review, 107,* 261–88.

Conway, M. A., Anderson, S. J., Larsen, S. F., Donnelly, C. M., McDaniel, M. A., McClelland, A. G. R., Rawles, R. E., and Logie, R. H. (1994). The formation of flashbulb memories. *Memory and Cognition, 22,* 326–43.

Corwin, D. L., and Olafson, E. (1997). Videotaped discovery of a reportedly unrecallable memory of child sexual abuse: Comparison with a childhood interview videotaped 11 years before. *Child Maltreatment, 2,* 91–112.

Courtois, C. A. (1997). Delayed memories of child sexual abuse: Critique of the controversy and clinical guidelines. In M. A. Conway (Ed.), *Recovered memories and false memories* (pp. 206–29). Oxford: Oxford University Press.

Creamer, M., Burgess, P., and Pattison, P. (1992). Reaction to trauma: A cognitive processing model. *Journal of Abnormal Psychology, 101,* 452–59.

Creswell, C., Holmes, E., and O'Connor, T. G. (2002). Post-traumatic stress symptoms in London school children following terrorist attacks on 11 September 2001. Manuscript submitted for publication.

Crews, F. (1997). The revenge of the repressed. In F. Crews (Ed.), *The memory wars: Freud's legacy in dispute* (pp. 157–223). London: Granta Books.

Culpin, M. (1931). *Recent advances in the study of the psychoneuroses.* London: J. A. Churchill.

Dalenberg, C., Coe, M., Reto, M., Aransky, K., and Duvenage, C. (1995). The prediction of amnesiac barrier strength as an individual difference variable in state-dependent learning paradigms. Paper presented at the conference on Responding to Child Maltreatment, San Diego, Calif.

Davey, G. C. L. (1993). Trauma revaluation, conditioning and anxiety disorders. *Behavior Change, 10,* 131–40.

Davis, P. J., and Schwartz, G. E. (1987). Repression and the inaccessibility of affective memories. *Journal of Personality and Social Psychology, 52,* 155–62.

De Bellis, M. D., Baum, A. S., Birmaher, S., Keshavan, M. S., Eccard, C. H., Boring, A. M., Jenkins, F. J., and Ryan, N. D. (1999). Developmental traumatology Part I: Biological stress systems. *Biological Psychiatry, 45,* 1259–70.

De Bellis, M. D., Keshavan, M. S., Clark, D. B., Casey, B. J., Giedd, J. N., Boring, A. M., Frustaci, K., and Ryan, N. D. (1999). Developmental traumatology Part II: Brain development. *Biological Psychiatry, 45,* 1271–84.

de Rivera, J. (1997). The construction of false memory syndrome: The experience of retractors. *Psychological Inquiry, 8,* 271–92.

Double, D. (2002). The limits of psychiatry. *British Medical Journal, 324,* 900–04.

Douglas, R. J. (1972). Pavlovian conditioning and the brain. In R. A. Boakes and M. S. Halliday (Eds.), *Inhibition and learning* (pp. 529–53). London: Academic Press.

Dunmore, E., Clark, D. M., and Ehlers, A. (1999). Cognitive factors involved in the onset and maintenance of posttraumatic stress disorder (PTSD) after physical or sexual assault. *Behaviour Research and Therapy, 37,* 809–29.

———(2001). A prospective investigation of the role of cognitive factors in persistent posttraumatic stress disorder (PTSD) after physical or sexual assault. *Behaviour Research and Therapy, 39,* 1063–84.

Dyregrov, A. (2001). Early intervention: A family perspective. *Advances in Mind-Body Medicine, 17,* 168–74.

Ehlers, A., and Clark, D. M. (2000). A cognitive model of posttraumatic stress disorder. *Behaviour Research and Therapy, 38,* 319–45.

Ehlers, A., and Steil, R. (1995). Maintenance of intrusive memories in posttraumatic stress disorder: A cognitive approach. *Behavioural and Cognitive Psychotherapy, 23,* 217–49.

Ehlers, A., Clark, D. M., Dunmore, E., Jaycox, L., Meadows, E., and Foa, E. B. (1998). Predicting response to exposure treatment in PTSD: The role of mental defeat and alienation. *Journal of Traumatic Stress, 11,* 457–71.

Ehlers, A., Maercker, A., and Boos, A. (2000). Posttraumatic stress disorder following political imprisonment: The role of mental defeat, alienation, and perceived permanent change. *Journal of Abnormal Psychology, 109,* 45–55.

Ehlers, A., Mayou, R. A., and Bryant, B. (1998). Psychological predictors of chronic posttraumatic stress disorder after motor vehicle accidents. *Journal of Abnormal Psychology, 107,* 508–19.

Eichenbaum, H. (1997). Declarative memory: Insights from cognitive neurobiology. *Annual Review of Psychology, 48,* 547–72.

Eliot, T. S. (1963). *Collected poems 1909–1962.* London: Faber.

Ellard, J. H. T. (1997). The epidemic of post-traumatic stress disorder: A passing phase? *Medical Journal of Australia, 166,* 84–87.

Elliott, D. M. (1997). Traumatic events: Prevalence and delayed recall in the general population. *Journal of Consulting and Clinical Psychology, 65,* 811–20.

Elliott, D. M., and Briere, J. (1995). Posttraumatic stress associated with delayed recall of sexual abuse: A general population study. *Journal of Traumatic Stress, 8,* 629–47.

Erdelyi, M. H. (1990). Repression, reconstruction, and defense: History and integration of the psychoanalytic and experimental frameworks. In J. L. Singer (Ed.), *Repression and dissociation* (pp. 1–31). Chicago: University of Chicago Press.

Estes, W. K. (1997). Processes of memory loss, recovery, and distortion. *Psychological Review, 104,* 148–69.

Everly, G. S., and Mitchell, J. T. (1999). *Critical incident stress management: A new era and standard of care in crisis intervention* (2nd ed.). Ellicott City, Md.: Chevron.

Everly, G. S., Flannery, R. B., Eyler, V., and Mitchell, J. T. (2001). Sufficiency analysis of an integrated multicomponent approach to crisis intervention: Critical Incident Stress Management. *Advances in Mind-Body Medicine, 17,* 174–83.

Eysenck, M. W. (1979). Depth, elaboration, and distinctiveness. In L. S. Cermak and F. I. M. Craik (Eds.), *Levels of processing in human memory* (pp. 89–118). Hillsdale, N.J.: Lawrence Erlbaum.

Feldman-Summers, S., and Pope, K. S. (1994). The experience of forgetting childhood abuse: A national survey of psychologists. *Journal of Consulting and Clinical Psychology, 62,* 636–39.

Felman, S. (1995). Education and crisis, or the vicissitudes of teaching. In C. Caruth (Ed.), *Trauma: Explorations in memory* (pp. 13–60). Baltimore: Johns Hopkins University Press.

Field, L. H. (1999). Post-traumatic stress disorder: A reappraisal. *Journal of the Royal Society of Medicine, 92,* 35–37.

Foa, E. B., and Rothbaum, B. O. (1998). *Treating the trauma of rape.* New York: Guilford Press.

Foa, E. B., Dancu, C. V., Hembree, E. A., Jaycox, L. H., Meadows, E. A., and Street, G. P. (1999). A comparison of exposure therapy, stress inoculation training, and their combination for reducing posttraumatic stress disorder in female assault victims. *Journal of Consulting and Clinical Psychology, 67,* 194–200.

Foa, E. B., Molnar, C., and Cashman, L. (1995). Change in rape narratives during exposure to therapy for posttraumatic stress disorder. *Journal of Traumatic Stress, 8,* 675–90.

Foa, E. B., Riggs, D. S., and Gershuny, B. S. (1995). Arousal, numbing, and intrusion: Symptom structure of PTSD following assault. *American Journal of Psychiatry, 152,* 116–20.

Foa, E. B., Rothbaum, B. O., Riggs, D. S., and Murdock, T. B. (1991). Treatment of posttraumatic-stress-disorder in rape victims—a comparison between cognitive-behavioral procedures and counseling. *Journal of Consulting and Clinical Psychology, 59,* 715–23.

Frankel, F. H. (1994). The concept of flashbacks in historical perspective. *International Journal of Clinical and Experimental Hypnosis, 42,* 321–35.

Fredrickson, R. (1992). *Repressed memories: A journey to recovery from sexual abuse.* New York: Simon and Schuster.

Freud, S. (1896/1962). The aetiology of hysteria. In J. Strachey (Ed.), *Standard Edition* (Vol. 3). London: Hogarth Press.

———(1915/1957). Repression. In J. Strachey (Ed.), *Standard Edition* (Vol. 14). London: Hogarth Press.

———(1920/1955). Beyond the pleasure principle. In J. Strachey (Ed.), *Standard Edition* (Vol. 18). London: Hogarth Press.

Freyd, J. J. (1996). *Betrayal trauma: The logic of forgetting childhood abuse.* Cambridge, Mass.: Harvard University Press.

Freyd, J. J., and Gleaves, D. H. (1996). "Remembering" words not presented in lists: Relevance to the current recovered/false memory controversy. *Journal of Experimental Psychology—Learning, Memory and Cognition, 22,* 811–13.

Frueh, B. C., Brady, K. L., and de Arellano, M. A. (1998). Racial differences in combat-related PTSD: Empirical findings and conceptual issues. *Clinical Psychology Review, 18,* 287–305.

Gabrieli, J. D. E., Fleischman, D. A., Keane, M. M., Reminger, S. L., and Morrell, F. (1995). Double dissociation between memory systems underlying explicit and implicit memory in the human brain. *Psychological Science, 6,* 76–82.

Gelles, R., and Straus, M. (1988). *Intimate violence.* New York: Simon and Schuster.

Gilbert, P. (1992). *Depression: The evolution of powerlessness.* Hove: Lawrence Erlbaum.

Gilbertson, M. W., Shenton, M. E., Ciszewski, A., Kasai, K., Lasko, N. B., Orr, S. P., and Pitman, R. K. (2002). Smaller hippocampal volume predicts pathologic vulnerability to psychological trauma. *Nature Neuroscience, 5,* 1242–47.

Girelli, S. A., Resick, P. A., Marhoefer-Dvorak, S., and Hutter, C. K. (1986). Subjective distress and violence during rape: Their effects on long-term fear. *Victims and Violence, 1,* 35–46.

Gold, S. N., Hughes, D., and Hohnecker, L. (1994). Degrees of repression of sexual abuse memories. *American Psychologist, 49,* 441–42.

Green, B. L. (1990). Defining trauma—Terminology and generic stressor dimensions. *Journal of Applied Social Psychology, 20,* 1632–42.

Green, B. L. (1993). Disasters and posttraumatic stress disorder. In J. R. T. Davidson and E. B. Foa (Eds.), *Posttraumatic stress disorder: DSM-IV and beyond* (pp. 75–97). Washington, D.C.: American Psychiatric Press.

Greenberg, M. A. (1995). Cognitive processing of traumas: The role of intrusive thoughts and reappraisals. *Journal of Applied Social Psychology, 25,* 1262–96.

Grey, N., Holmes, E., and Brewin, C. R. (2001). Peritraumatic emotional "hotspots" in traumatic memory: A case series of patients with posttraumatic stress disorder. *Behavioural and Cognitive Psychotherapy, 29,* 367–72.

Grey, N., Young, K., and Holmes, E. (2002). Hot spots in emotional memory and the treatment of posttraumatic stress disorder. *Behavioural and Cognitive Psychotherapy, 30,* 37–56.

Griffin, M. G., Resick, P. A., and Mechanic, M. B. (1997). Objective assessment of peritraumatic dissociation: Psychophysiological indicators. *American Journal of Psychiatry, 154,* 1081–88.

Gudjonsson, G. H. (1997). Accusations by adults of childhood sexual abuse: A survey of the members of the British False Memory Society (BFMS). *Applied Cognitive Psychology, 11,* 3–18.

Hackmann, A. (1998). Working with images in clinical psychology. In A. S. Bellack and M. Hersen (Eds.), *Comprehensive clinical psychology* (Vol. 6, pp. 301–18). New York: Elsevier.

Hackmann, A., Clark, D. M., and McManus, F. (2000). Recurrent images and early memories in social phobia. *Behaviour Research and Therapy, 38,* 601–10.

Hamann, S., and Mao, H. (2002). Positive and negative emotional verbal stimuli elicit activity in the left amygdala. *Neuroreport, 13,* 15–19.

Harber, K. D., and Pennebaker, J. W. (1992). Overcoming traumatic memories. In S.-A. Christianson (Ed.), *The handbook of emotion and memory* (pp. 359–87). Hillsdale, N.J.: Erlbaum.

Hariri, A. R., Bookheimer, S. Y., and Mazziotta, J. C. (2000). Modulating emotional responses: Effects of a neocortical network on the limbic system. *Neuroreport, 11,* 43–48.

Harvey, A. G., and Bryant, R. A. (1998). The relationship between acute stress disorder and posttraumatic stress disorder: A prospective evaluation of motor vehicle accident survivors. *Journal of Consulting and Clinical Psychology, 66,* 507–12.

———(1999a). The relationship between acute stress disorder and posttraumatic stress disorder: A 2-year prospective evaluation. *Journal of Consulting and Clinical Psychology, 67,* 985–88.

———(1999b). A qualitative investigation of the organization of traumatic memories. *British Journal of Clinical Psychology, 38,* 401–05.

Harvey, M. R., and Herman, J. L. (1994). Amnesia, partial amnesia, and delayed recall among adult survivors of childhood trauma. *Consciousness and Cognition, 3,* 295–306.

Hellawell, S. J., and Brewin, C. R. (2002a). A comparison of flashbacks and ordinary autobiographical memories of trauma: Cognitive resources and behavioural observations. *Behaviour Research and Therapy, 40,* 1139–52.

———(2002b). A comparison of flashbacks and ordinary autobiographical memories of trauma: Content and language. Manuscript submitted for publication.

Helzer, J. E., Robins, L. N., and McEvoy, L. (1987). Posttraumatic stress disorder in the general population: Findings of the Epidemiologic Catchment Area survey. *New England Journal of Medicine, 317,* 1630–34.

Herlihy, J., Scragg, P., and Turner, S. (2002). Discrepancies in autobiographical memories—Implications for the assessment of asylum seekers: repeated interviews study. *British Medical Journal, 324,* 324–27.

Herman, J. L. (1992). *Trauma and recovery.* London: Pandora Books.

———(1993). Sequelae of prolonged and repeated trauma: Evidence for a complex posttraumatic syndrome (DESNOS). In J. R. T. Davidson and E. B. Foa (Eds.), *Posttraumatic stress disorder: DSM-IV and beyond* (pp. 213–28). Washington, D.C.: American Psychiatric Press.

Herman, J. L., and Schatzow, E. (1987). Recovery and verification of memories of childhood sexual trauma. *Psychoanalytic Psychology, 4,* 1–14.

Holman, E. A., and Silver, R. C. (1998). Getting "stuck" in the past: Temporal orientation and coping with trauma. *Journal of Personality and Social Psychology, 74,* 1146–63.

Holmes, D. S. (1990). The evidence for repression: An examination of sixty years of research. In J. L. Singer (Ed.), *Repression and dissociation* (pp. 85–102). Chicago: University of Chicago Press.

Holmes, E., Brewin, C. R., and Hennessy, R. (2002). Trauma films, information processing, and intrusive memory development. Manuscript submitted for publication.

Horowitz, M. J. (1976). *Stress response syndromes.* New York: Aronson.

Horowitz, M. J., and Reidbord, S. P. (1992). Memory, emotion, and response to trauma. In S.-A. Christianson (Ed.), *Handbook of emotion and memory: Research and theory* (pp. 343–57). Hillsdale, N.J.: Erlbaum.

Howes, M., Siegel, M., and Brown, F. (1993). Early childhood memories: Accuracy and affect. *Cognition, 47,* 95–119.

Hunt, R. R., and McDaniel, M. A. (1993). The enigma of organization and distinctiveness. *Journal of Memory and Language, 32,* 421–45.

Hunt, R. R., and Smith, R. E. (1996). Accessing the particular from the general: The power of distinctiveness in the context of organization. *Memory and Cognition, 24,* 217–25.

Hunter, E. C. M., and Andrews, B. (2002). Memory for autobiographical facts and events: A comparison of women reporting childhood sexual abuse and non-abused controls. *Applied Cognitive Psychology, 16,* 575–88.

Hyman, I. E., and Loftus, E. F. (1998). Errors in autobiographical memory. *Clinical Psychology Review, 18,* 933–47.

Hyman, I. E., Husband, T. H., and Billings, F. J. (1995). False memories of childhood experiences. *Applied Cognitive Psychology, 9,* 181–97.

Jacobs, W. J., and Nadel, L. (1985). Stress induced recovery of fears and phobias. *Psychological Review, 92,* 512–31.

Janet, P. (1904). L'amnesie et la dissociation des souvenirs par l'emotion. *Journal de Psychologie, 1,* 417–53.

———(1925/1976). *Psychological healing: A historical and clinical study.* New York: Arno Press.

Janoff-Bulman, R. (1992). *Shattered assumptions: Towards a new psychology of trauma.* New York: Free Press.

Janoff-Bulman, R., and Frantz, C. M. (1997). The impact of trauma on meaning: From meaningless world to meaningful life. In M. Power and C. R. Brewin (Eds.), *The transformation of meaning in psychological therapies* (pp. 91–106). Chichester: Wiley.

Joseph, S. A., Brewin, C. R., Yule, W., and Williams, R. (1991). Causal attributions and psychiatric symptoms in survivors of the Herald of Free Enterprise disaster. *British Journal of Psychiatry, 159,* 542–46.

————(1993). Causal attributions and posttraumatic stress in adolescents. *Journal of Child Psychology and Psychiatry and Allied Disciplines, 34,* 247–53.

Joslyn, S., Carlin, L., and Loftus, E. F. (1997). Remembering and forgetting childhood sexual abuse. *Memory, 5,* 703–24.

Kasl, S. V. (1990). Some considerations in the study of traumatic stress. *Journal of Applied Social Psychology, 20,* 1655–65.

Kassin, S. M., Ellsworth, P. C., and Smith, V. L. (1989). The "general acceptance" of psychological research on eyewitness testimony: A survey of the experts. *American Psychologist, 44,* 1089–98.

Keane, T. M. (1993). Symptomatology of Vietnam veterans with posttraumatic stress disorder. In J. R. T. Davidson and E. B. Foa (Eds.), *Posttraumatic stress disorder: DSM-IV and beyond* (pp. 99–111). Washington, D.C.: American Psychiatric Press.

Keenan, B. (1993). *An evil cradling.* London: Vintage.

Kesner, R. P. (1998). Neural mediation of memory for time: Role of the hippocampus and medial prefrontal cortex. *Psychonomic Bulletin and Review, 5,* 585–96.

Kesner, R. P., Walser, R. D., and Winzenried, G. (1989). Central but not basolateral amygdala mediates memory for positive affective experiences. *Behavioural Brain Research, 33,* 189–95.

Kessler, R. C., Sonnega, A., Bromet, E., Hughes, M., and Nelson, C. B. (1995). Posttraumatic stress disorder in the National Comorbidity Survey. *Archives of General Psychiatry, 52,* 1048–60.

Kihlstrom, J. F. (1985). Posthypnotic amnesia and the dissociation of memory. In G. H. Bower (Ed.), *The psychology of learning and motivation* (Vol. 19, pp. 131–78). Orlando, Fla.: Academic Press.

————(1995). The trauma memory argument. *Consciousness and Cognition, 4,* 63–67.

Kihlstrom, J. F., and Cantor, N. (1984). Mental representations of the self. In L. Berkowitz (Ed.), *Advances in experimental social psychology* (Vol. 17, pp. 1–47). Orlando, Fla.: Academic Press.

Kilpatrick, D. G., and Resnick, H. S. (1993). Posttraumatic stress disorder associated with exposure to criminal victimization in clinical and community populations. In J. R. T. Davidson and E. B. Foa (Eds.), *Posttraumatic stress disorder: DSM-IV and beyond* (pp. 113–43). Washington, D.C.: American Psychiatric Press.

Kilpatrick, D. G., Resnick, H. S., Freedy, J. R., Pelcovitz, D., Resick, P., Roth, S., and van der Kolk, B. (1998). Posttraumatic stress disorder field trial: Evaluation of the PTSD construct—Criteria A through E. In T. Widiger, A. Frances, H. Pincus, R. Ross, M. First, W. Davis, and M. Kline (Eds.), *DSM-IV sourcebook* (Vol. 4, pp. 803–44). Washington, D.C.: American Psychiatric Press.

King, D. W., Leskin, G. A., King, L. A., and Weathers, F. W. (1998). Confirmatory factor analysis of the Clinician-Administered PTSD Scale: Evidence for the dimensionality of posttraumatic stress disorder. *Psychological Assessment, 10,* 90–96.

Kisiel, C. L., and Lyons, J. S. (2001). Dissociation as a mediator of psychopathology among sexually abused children and adolescents. *American Journal of Psychiatry, 158,* 1034–39.

Kitzinger, J., and Reilly, J. (1997). The rise and fall of risk reporting—Media coverage of human genetics research, "False Memory Syndrome" and "Mad Cow Disease." *European Journal of Communication, 12,* 319–50.

Koopman, C., Classen, C., and Spiegel, D. (1994). Predictors of posttraumatic stress symptoms among survivors of the Oakland/Berkeley, California, firestorm. *American Journal of Psychiatry, 151,* 888–94.

Koren, D., Arnon, I., and Klein, E. (1999). Acute stress response and posttraumatic stress disorder in traffic accident victims: A one-year prospective, follow-up study. *American Journal of Psychiatry, 156,* 367–73.

Koss, M. P., Figueredo, A. J., Bell, I., Tharan, M., and Tromp, S. (1996). Traumatic memory characteristics: A cross-validated mediational model of response to rape among employed women. *Journal of Abnormal Psychology, 105,* 421–32.

Kuehn, L. L. (1974). Looking down a gun barrel: Person perception and violent crime. *Perceptual and Motor Skills, 39,* 1159–64.

La Greca, A. M., Silverman, W. K., Vernberg, E. M., and Roberts, M. C. (2002). *Helping children cope with disasters and terrorism.* Washington, D.C.: American Psychological Association.

Lang, P. J. (1979). A bio-informational theory of emotional imagery. *Psychophysiology, 16,* 495–512.

———(1985). The cognitive psychophysiology of emotion: Fear and anxiety. In A. H. Tuma and J. D. Maser (Eds.), *Anxiety and the anxiety disorders* (pp. 131–70). Hillsdale, N.J.: Erlbaum.

Layden, M. A., Newman, C. F., Freeman, A., and Morse, S. B. (1993). *Cognitive therapy of borderline personality disorder.* Boston: Allyn and Bacon.

Leavitt, F. (1997). False attribution of suggestibility to explain recovered memory of childhood sexual abuse following extended amnesia. *Child Abuse and Neglect, 21,* 265–72.

LeDoux, J. E. (1998). *The emotional brain.* London: Weidenfeld and Nicolson.

Lee, D. A., Scragg, P., and Turner, S. (2001). The role of shame and guilt in traumatic events: A clinical model of shame-based and guilt-based PTSD. *British Journal of Medical Psychology, 74,* 451–66.

Lembcke, J. (1998). The "right stuff" gone wrong: Vietnam veterans and the social construction of post-traumatic stress disorder. *Critical Sociology, 24,* 37–64.

Lindsay, D. S., and Briere, J. (1997). The controversy regarding recovered memories of childhood sexual abuse—Pitfalls, bridges, and future directions. *Journal of Interpersonal Violence, 12,* 631–47.

Lindsay, D. S., and Read, J. D. (1994). Psychotherapy and memories of child-

hood sexual abuse: A cognitive perspective. *Applied Cognitive Psychology,*
8, 281–338.

———(1995). "Memory work" and recovered memories of childhood sexual
abuse: Scientific evidence and public, professional, and personal issues.
Psychology, Public Policy, and Law, 1, 846–908.

Lockhart, R. S., Craik, F. I. M., and Jacoby, L. L. (1976). Depth of processing,
recognition and recall. In J. Brown (Ed.), *Recall and recognition* (pp. 75–
102). New York: Wiley.

Loftus, E. F. (1993). The reality of repressed memories. *American Psychologist, 48,*
518–37.

Loftus, E. F., and Burns, T. (1982). Mental shock can produce retrograde amnesia. *Memory and Cognition, 10,* 318–23.

Loftus, E. F., and Ketcham, K. (1994). *The myth of repressed memory.* New York:
St. Martin's Press.

Loftus, E. F., Polonsky, S., and Fullilove, M. T. (1994). Memories of childhood
sexual abuse: Remembering and repressing. *Psychology of Women Quar-
terly, 18,* 67–84.

Mack, A., and Rock, I. (1998). *Inattentional blindness.* Cambridge, Mass.: MIT
Press.

Macklin, M. L., Metzger, L. J., Litz, B. T., McNally, R. J., Lasko, N. B., Orr, S.
P., and Pitman, R. K. (1998). Lower precombat intelligence is a risk factor
for posttraumatic stress disorder. *Journal of Consulting and Clinical Psychology, 66,* 323–26.

Macleod, C., and Campbell, L. (1992). Memory accessibility and probability
judgments: An experimental evaluation of the availability heuristic. *Journal of Personality and Social Psychology, 63,* 890–902.

Mandler, G. (1992). Memory, arousal, and mood: A theoretical integration. In
S.-A. Christianson (Ed.), *Handbook of emotion and memory* (pp. 93–110).
Hillsdale, N.J.: Erlbaum.

Marks, I., Lovell, K., Noshirvani, H., and Livanou, M. (1998). Treatment of
posttraumatic stress disorder by exposure and/or cognitive restructuring
—a controlled study. *Archives of General Psychiatry, 55, 317–25.*

Markus, H., and Nurius, P. (1986). Possible selves. *American Psychologist, 41,*
954–69.

Markus, H., and Sentis, K. (1982). The self in social information processing. In
J. Suls (Ed.), *Psychological perspectives on the self* (Vol. 1, pp. 41–70). Hillsdale, N.J.: Lawrence Erlbaum.

Marmar, C. R., Weiss, D. S., and Metzler, T. J. (1997). The Peritraumatic Disso-
ciative Experiences Questionnaire. In J. P. Wilson and T. M. Keane
(Eds.), *Assessing psychological trauma and PTSD* (pp. 412–28). New York:
Guilford Press.

Mayou, R., Bryant, B., and Ehlers, A. (2001). Prediction of psychological outcomes one year after a motor vehicle accident. *American Journal of Psychiatry, 158,* 1231–38.

Mayou, R. A., Ehlers, A., and Hobbs, M. (2000). Psychological debriefing for road traffic accident victims: Three-year follow-up of a randomised controlled trial. *British Journal of Psychiatry, 176,* 589–93.

McClelland, J. L., McNaughton, B. L., and O'Reilly, R. C. (1995). Why there are complementary learning systems in the hippocampus and neocortex: Insights from the successes and failures of connectionist models of learning and memory. *Psychological Review, 102,* 419–57.

McCloskey, M., and Cohen, N.J. (1989). Catastrophic interference in connectionist networks: The sequential learning problem. In G. H. Bower (Ed.), *The psychology of learning and motivation* (Vol. 24, pp. 109–65). New York: Academic Press.

McCormick, D. D., and Thompson, R. F. (1982). Locus coeruleus lesions and resistance to extinction of a classically conditioned response: Involvement of the neocortex and hippocampus. *Brain Research, 245,* 239–49.

McFarlane, A. C. (1997). The prevalence and longitudinal course of PTSD. *Annals of the New York Academy of Sciences, 821,* 10–23.

McNally, R. J. (1999). EMDR and mesmerism: A comparative historical analysis. *Journal of Anxiety Disorders, 13,* 225–36.

McNally, R. J., Clancy, S. A., and Schacter, D. L. (2001). Directed forgetting of trauma cues in adults reporting repressed or recovered memories of childhood sexual abuse. *Journal of Abnormal Psychology, 110,* 151–56.

McNally, R. J., Metzger, L. J., Lasko, N. B., Clancy, S. A., and Pitman, R. K. (1998). Directed forgetting of trauma cues in adult survivors of childhood sexual abuse with and without posttraumatic stress disorder. *Journal of Abnormal Psychology, 107,* 596–601.

Mechanic, M. B., Resick, P. A., and Griffin, M. G. (1998). A comparison of normal forgetting, psychopathology, and information-processing models of reported amnesia for recent sexual trauma. *Journal of Consulting and Clinical Psychology, 66,* 948–57.

Meesters, C., Merckelbach, H., Muris, P., and Wessel, I. (2000). Autobiographical memory and trauma in adolescents. *Journal of Behavior Therapy and Experimental Psychiatry, 31,* 29–39.

Melchert, T. P. (1996). Childhood memory and a history of different forms of abuse. *Professional Psychology—Research and Practice, 27,* 438–46.

Mendelson, D. (1995). Legal and medical aspects of liability for negligently occasioned nervous shock—a current perspective. *Journal of Psychosomatic Research, 39,* 721–35.

Merckelbach, H., Muris, P., Horselenberg, R., and Rassin, E. (1998). Traumatic intrusions as "worse case scenario's." *Behaviour Research and Therapy, 36,* 1075–79.

Merskey, H. (1995). Multiple personality disorder and false memory syndrome. *British Journal of Psychiatry, 166,* 281–83.

Metcalfe, J., and Jacobs, W. J. (1998). Emotional memory: The effects of stress on "cool" and "hot" memory systems. In D. L. Medin (Ed.), *The psychology of learning and motivation* (Vol. 38, pp. 187–222). New York: Academic Press.

Mitchell, J. T. (1983). When disaster strikes . . . The Critical Incident Stress Debriefing process. *Journal of the Emergency Medical Services, 8,* 36–39.

Mollon, P. (1998). *Remembering trauma: A psychotherapist's guide to memory and illusion.* Chichester: Wiley.

Morgan, C. A., Hazlett, M. G., Wang, S., Richardson, E. G., Schnurr, P., and Southwick, S. M. (2001). Symptoms of dissociation in humans experiencing acute, uncontrollable stress: A prospective investigation. *American Journal of Psychiatry, 158,* 1239–47.

Morris, M. K., Kaysen, D., and Resick, P. A. (2000). Peritraumatic responses and their relationship to perceptions of threat in female crime victims. Manuscript submitted for publication.

Morris, J. S., Öhman, A., and Dolan, R. J. (1999). A subcortical pathway to the right amygdala mediating "unseen" fear. *Proceedings of the National Academy of Sciences, 96,* 1680–85.

Morton, J., Andrews, B., Bekerian, D., Brewin, C. R., Davies, G. M., and Mollon, P. (1995). *Recovered memories.* Leicester: British Psychological Society.

Moscovitch, M. (1995). Recovered consciousness: A hypothesis concerning modularity and episodic memory. *Journal of Clinical and Experimental Neuropsychology, 17,* 276–90.

Moulds, M. L., and Bryant, R. A. (2002). Directed forgetting in acute stress disorder. *Journal of Abnormal Psychology, 111,* 175–79.

Murray, J., Ehlers, A., and Mayou, R. (2002). Dissociation and posttraumatic stress disorder: Two prospective studies of motor vehicle accident survivors. *British Journal of Psychiatry, 180,* 363–68.

Myers, C. S. (1940). *Shell shock in France, 1914–1918.* Cambridge: The University Press.

Myers, L. B., and Brewin, C. R. (1994). Recall of early experience and the repressive coping style. *Journal of Abnormal Psychology, 103,* 288–92.

———(1995). Repressive coping and the recall of emotional material. *Cognition and Emotion, 9,* 637–42.

Myers, L. B., Brewin, C. R., and Power, M. J. (1998). Repressive coping and the directed forgetting of emotional material. *Journal of Abnormal Psychology, 107,* 141–48.

Nadel, L., and Moscovitch, M. (1997). Memory consolidation, retrograde amnesia and the hippocampal complex. *Current Opinion in Neurobiology, 7,* 217–27.

Neisser, U. (1982). Snapshots or benchmarks? In U. Neisser (Ed.), *Memory observed: Remembering in natural contexts* (pp. 43–48). San Francisco: W. H. Freeman.

Neisser, U., and Harsch, N. (1992). Phantom flashbulbs: False recollections of hearing the news about "Challenger." In E. Winograd and U. Neisser (Eds.), *Affect and accuracy in recall: Studies of flashbulb memories* (pp. 9–31). Cambridge: Cambridge University Press.

Newcomer, J. W., Selke, G., Melson, A. K., Hershey, T., Craft, S., Richards, K., and Alderson, A. L. (1999). Decreased memory performance in healthy humans induced by stress-level cortisol treatment. *Archives of General Psychiatry, 56,* 527–33.

Nijenhuis, E. R. S., Spinhoven, P., Vanderlinden, J., van Dyck, R., and van der Hart, O. (1998). Somatoform dissociative symptoms as related to animal defensive reactions to predatory imminence and injury. *Journal of Abnormal Psychology, 107,* 63–73.

Nijenhuis, E. R. S., Vanderlinden, J., and Spinhoven, P. (1998). Animal defensive reactions as a model for trauma-induced dissociative reactions. *Journal of Traumatic Stress, 11,* 243–60.

Norris, F. H., Weisshaar, D. L., Conrad, M. L., Diaz, E. M., Murphy, A. D., and Ibanez, G. E. (2001). A qualitative analysis of posttraumatic stress among Mexican victims of disaster. *Journal of Traumatic Stress, 14,* 741–56.

Ofshe, R., and Watters, E. (1994). *Making monsters: False memories, psychotherapy, and sexual hysteria.* London: Andre Deutsch.

Ogilvie, D. M. (1987). The undesired self—a neglected variable in personality research. *Journal of Personality and Social Psychology, 52,* 379–85.

Padesky, C. A. (1994). Schema change processes in cognitive therapy. *Clinical Psychology and Psychotherapy, 1,* 267–78.

Page, H. W. (1883). *Injuries of the spine and spinal cord.* London: J. A. Churchill.

Paivio, A. (1986). *Mental representations: A dual coding approach.* New York: Oxford University Press.

Pathé, M., and Mullen, P. E. (1997). The impact of stalkers on their victims. *British Journal of Psychiatry, 170,* 12–17.

Pendergrast, M. (1996). *Victims of memory: Incest accusations and shattered lives.* London: HarperCollins.

Perry, B. D., Pollard, R. A., Blakley, T. L., Baker, W. L., and Vigilante, D. (1995). Childhood trauma, the neurobiology of adaptation, and "use-dependent" development of the brain: How "states" become "traits." *Infant Mental Health Journal, 16,* 271–91.

Pezdek, K. (2001). A cognitive analysis of the role of suggestibility in explaining memories for abuse. *Journal of Aggression, Maltreatment, and Trauma, 4,* 73–85.

Pezdek, K., Finger, K., and Hedge, D. (1997). Planting false childhood memories: The role of event plausibility. *Psychological Science, 8,* 437–41.

Pillemer, D. B. (1984). Flashbulb memories of the assassination attempt on President Reagan. *Cognition, 16,* 63–80.

———(1998a). *Momentous events, vivid memories.* Cambridge, Mass.: Harvard University Press.

———(1998b). What is remembered about early childhood events? *Clinical Psychology Review, 18,* 895–913.

Pillemer, D. B., and White, S. H. (1989). Childhood events recalled by children and adults. In H. W. Reese (Ed.), *Advances in child development and behavior* (Vol. 21, pp. 297–340). Orlando, Fla.: Academic Press.

Pillemer, D. B., Desrochers, A. B., and Ebanks, C. M. (1998). Remembering the past in the present: Verb tense shifts in autobiographical memory narratives. In C. P. Thompson, D. J. Herrmann, D. Bruce, J. D. Read, D. G. Payne, and M. P. Toglia (Eds.), *Autobiographical memory: Theoretical and applied perspectives* (pp. 145–62). Hillsdale, N.J.: Erlbaum.

Pitman, R. K. (1989). Post-traumatic stress disorder, hormones, and memory. *Biological Psychiatry, 26,* 221–23.

Pitman, R. K., Orr, S. P., Lowenhagen, M. J., Macklin, M. L., and Altman, B. (1991). Pre-Vietnam contents of posttraumatic stress disorder veterans service medical and personnel records. *Comprehensive Psychiatry, 32,* 416–22.

Pitman, R. K., Shalev, A. Y., and Orr, S. P. (2000). Posttraumatic stress disorder: Emotion, conditioning, and memory. In M. S. Gazzaniga (Ed.), *The new cognitive neurosciences* (2nd ed., pp. 1133–47). Cambridge, Mass: MIT Press.

Poole, D. A., Lindsay, D. S., Memon, A., and Bull, R. (1995). Psychotherapy and the recovery of memories of childhood sexual abuse—US and British practitioners' opinions, practices, and experiences. *Journal of Consulting and Clinical Psychology, 63,* 426–37.

Pope, H. G., and Hudson, J. I. (1995). Can memories of childhood sexual abuse be repressed? *Psychological Medicine, 25,* 121–26.

Pope, H. G., Hudson, J. I., Bodkin, J. A., and Oliva, P. (1998). Questionable validity of "dissociative amnesia" in trauma victims: Evidence from prospective studies. *British Journal of Psychiatry, 172,* 210–15.

Pope, K. S. (1996). Memory, abuse, and science—Questioning claims about the false memory syndrome epidemic. *American Psychologist, 51,* 957–74.

Pope, K. S., and Brown, L. (1996). *Recovered memories of abuse: Assessment, therapy, forensics.* Washington, D.C.: American Psychological Association.

Porter, S., and Birt, A. R. (2001). Is traumatic memory special? A comparison of traumatic memory characteristics with memory for other emotional life experiences. *Applied Cognitive Psychology, 15,* S101–17.

Pynoos, R. S., and Nader, K. (1988). Psychological first aid and treatment approach for children exposed to community violence: research implications. *Journal of Traumatic Stress, 1,* 243–67.

Pynoos, R. S., Goenjian, A., Tashjian, M., Karakashian, M., Manjikian, R., Manoukian, G., Steinberg, A. M., and Fairbanks, L. A. (1993). Posttraumatic stress reactions in children after the 1988 Armenian earthquake. *British Journal of Psychiatry, 163,* 239–47.

Pyszczynski, T., Greenberg, J., and Solomon, S. (2000). Proximal and distal defense: A new perspective on unconscious motivation. *Current Directions in Psychological Science, 9,* 156–60.

Rachman, S. (1989). The return of fear: Review and prospect. *Clinical Psychology Review, 9,* 147–68.

Rauch, S. A. M., Hembree, E. A., and Foa, E. B. (2001). Acute psychosocial preventive interventions for posttraumatic stress disorder. *Advances in Mind-Body Medicine, 17,* 187–91.

Read, J. D., and Lindsay, D. S. (2000). "Amnesia" for summer camps and high school graduation: Memory work increases reports of prior periods of remembering less. *Journal of Traumatic Stress, 13,* 129–47.

Resick, P. A. (2001). *Stress and trauma.* Hove: Psychology Press.

Resick, P. A., Nishith, P., Weaver, T. L., Astin, M. C., and Feuer, C. A. (2002). A comparison of cognitive-processing therapy with prolonged exposure and a waiting condition for the treatment of chronic posttraumatic stress disorder in female rape victims. *Journal of Consulting and Clinical Psychology, 70,* 867–79.

Resick, P. A., and Schnicke, M. K. (1993). *Cognitive processing therapy for rape victims.* Newbury Park, Calif.: Sage.

Resnick, H. S., Yehuda, R., Pitman, R. K., and Foy, D. W. (1995). Effect of previous trauma on acute plasma cortisol level following rape. *American Journal of Psychiatry, 152,* 1675–77.

Reynolds, M., and Brewin, C. R. (1998). Intrusive cognitions, coping strategies and emotional responses in depression, post-traumatic stress disorder, and a non-clinical population. *Behaviour Research and Therapy, 36,* 135–47.

———(1999). Intrusive memories in depression and posttraumatic stress disorder. *Behaviour Research and Therapy, 37,* 201–15.

Richards, D., and Lovell, K. (1999). Behavioural and cognitive-behavioural interventions in the treatment of PTSD. In W. Yule (Ed.), *Post-traumatic stress disorders: Concepts and therapy* (pp. 239–66). Chichester: Wiley.

Rose, S., Bisson, J., and Wessely, S. (2002). Psychological debriefing for preventing posttraumatic stress disorder (PTSD) (Cochrane Review), *The Cochrane Library, Issue 1, 2002.* Oxford: Update Software.

Rose, S., Brewin, C. R., Andrews, B., and Kirk, M. (1999). A randomized trial of psychological debriefing for victims of violent crime. *Psychological Medicine, 29,* 793–99.

Rosen, V. M., and Engle, R. W. (1998). Working memory capacity and suppression. *Journal of Memory and Language, 39,* 418–36.

Rothbaum, B. O., and Foa, E. B. (1993). Subtypes of posttraumatic stress disorder and duration of symptoms. In J. R. T. Davidson and E. B. Foa (Eds.), *Posttraumatic stress disorder: DSM-IV and beyond* (pp. 23–35). Washington, D.C.: American Psychiatric Association.

Rows, R. G. (1916). Mental conditions following strain and nerve shock. *British Medical Journal, i*, 441–43.

Rubin, D. C., and Kozin, M. (1984). Vivid memories. *Cognition, 16*, 81–95.

Ruscio, A. M., Ruscio, J., and Keane, T. M. (2002). The latent structure of post-traumatic stress disorder: A taxometric investigation of reactions to extreme stress. *Journal of Abnormal Psychology, 111*, 290–301.

Sapolsky, R. (2000). Glucocorticoids and hippocampal atrophy in neuropsychiatric disorders. *Archives of General Psychiatry, 57*, 925–35.

Schacter, D. L., Kihlstrom, J. F., Kihlstrom, L. C., and Berren, M. B. (1989). Autobiographical memory in a case of multiple personality disorder. *Journal of Abnormal Psychology, 98*, 508–14.

Schooler, J. W. (1994). Seeking the core: The issues and evidence surrounding recovered accounts of sexual trauma. *Consciousness and Cognition, 3*, 452–69.

———(2001). Discovering memories of abuse in the light of meta-awareness. *Journal of Aggression, Maltreatment and Trauma, 4*, 105–36.

Schooler, J. W., and Engstler-Schooler, T. Y. (1990). Verbal overshadowing of visual memories: Some things are better left unsaid. *Cognitive Psychology, 22*, 36–71.

Schooler, J. W., Bendiksen, M., and Ambadar, Z. (1997). Taking the middle line: can we accommodate both fabricated and recovered memories of sexual abuse? In M. A. Conway (Ed.), *Recovered memories and false memories* (pp. 251–92). Oxford: Oxford University Press.

Schooler, J. W., Fiore, S. M., and Brandimonte, M. A. (1997). At a loss from words: Verbal overshadowing of perceptual memories. In D. L. Medin (Ed.), *The psychology of learning and motivation* (Vol. 37, pp. 291–339). New York: Academic Press.

Schwarz, E. D., Kowalski, J. M., and McNally, R. J. (1993). Malignant memories: Posttraumatic changes in memory in adults after a school shooting. *Journal of Traumatic Stress, 6*, 545–53.

Scott, M. J., and Stradling, S. G. (1994). Posttraumatic stress disorder without the trauma. *British Journal of Clinical Psychology, 33*, 71–74.

Segal, Z. V. (1988). Appraisal of the self-schema construct in cognitive models of depression. *Psychological Bulletin, 103*, 147–62.

Shalev, A. Y. (1992). Posttraumatic stress disorder among injured survivors of a terrorist attack: Predictive value of early intrusion and avoidance symptoms. *Journal of Nervous and Mental Disease, 180*, 505–09.

———(2002). Treating survivors in the immediate aftermath of traumatic events. In R. Yehuda (Ed.), *Treating trauma survivors with PTSD* (pp. 157–88). Washington, D.C.: American Psychiatric Press.

———(in press). Psycho-biological perspectives on early reactions to traumatic events. In R. Ørner and U. Schnyder (Eds.), *Reconstructing early intervention after trauma*. Oxford: Oxford University Press.

Shalev, A. Y., Peri, T., Canetti, L., and Schreiber, S. (1996). Predictors of PTSD in injured trauma survivors: A prospective study. *American Journal of Psychiatry, 153,* 219–25.

Shalev, A. Y., Sahar, T., Freedman, S., Peri, T., Glick, N., Brandes, D., Orr, S. P., and Pitman, R. K. (1998). A prospective study of heart rate response following trauma and the subsequent development of posttraumatic stress disorder. *Archives of General Psychiatry, 55,* 553–59.

Shapiro, F. (1995). *Eye movement desensitization and reprocessing.* New York: Guilford.

Shay, J. (1995). *Achilles in Vietnam: Combat trauma and the undoing of character.* New York: Touchstone.

Shephard, B. (2000). *A war of nerves: Soldiers and psychiatrists 1914–1994.* London: Jonathan Cape.

Shin, L. M., Kosslyn, S. M., McNally, R. J., Alpert, N. M., Thompson, W. L., Rauch, S. L., Macklin, M. L., and Pitman, R. K. (1997). Visual imagery and perception in posttraumatic stress disorder—A positron emission tomographic investigation. *Archives of General Psychiatry, 54,* 233–41.

Shin, L. M., McNally, R. J., Kosslyn, S. M., Thompson, W. L., Rauch, S. L., Alpert, N. M., Metzger, L. J., Lasko, N. B., Orr, S. P., and Pitman, R. K. (1999). Regional cerebral blood flow during script-driven imagery in childhood sexual abuse–related PTSD: A PET investigation. *American Journal of Psychiatry, 156,* 575–84.

Shobe, K. K., and Kihlstrom, J. F. (1997). Is traumatic memory special? *Current Directions in Psychological Science, 6,* 70–74.

Simpson, G. B., and Kang, H. (1994). Inhibitory processes in the recognition of homograph meanings. In D. Dagenbach and T. H. Carr (Eds.), *Inhibitory processes in attention, memory and language* (pp. 359–81). San Diego, Calif.: Academic Press.

Sloman, S. A. (1996). The empirical case for two systems of reasoning. *Psychological Bulletin, 119,* 3–22.

Smucker, M. R., Dancu, C., Foa, E. B., and Niederee, J. L. (1995). Imagery rescripting: A new treatment for survivors of childhood sexual abuse suffering from posttraumatic stress. *Journal of Cognitive Psychotherapy, 9,* 3–17.

Solomon, S., Greenberg, J., and Pyszczynski, T. (2000). Pride and prejudice: Fear of death and social behavior. *Current Directions in Psychological Science, 9,* 200–04.

Solomon, Z. (1995). Oscillating between denial and recognition of PTSD: Why are lessons learned and forgotten? *Journal of Traumatic Stress, 8,* 271–82.

Southwick, S. M., Morgan, A. C., Nicolaou, A. L., and Charney, D. S. (1997). Consistency of memory for combat-related traumatic events in veterans of Operation Desert Storm. *American Journal of Psychiatry, 154,* 173–77.

Spiegel, D., and Cardeña, E. (1991). Disintegrated experience: The dissociative disorders revisited. *Journal of Abnormal Psychology, 100,* 366–78.

Squire, L. R. (1994). Declarative and non-declarative memory: Multiple brain systems supporting learning and memory. In D. L. Schacter and E. Tulving (Eds.), *Memory systems 1994* (pp. 203–32). Cambridge, Mass: MIT Press.

Squire, L. R., and Alvarez, P. (1995). Retrograde amnesia and memory consolidation: A neurobiological perspective. *Current Opinion in Neurobiology, 5,* 169–77.

Steil, R., and Ehlers, A. (2000). Dysfunctional meaning of posttraumatic intrusions in chronic PTSD. *Behaviour Research and Therapy, 38,* 537–58.

Stone, A. A. (1993). Post-traumatic stress disorder and the law: Critical review of the new frontier. *Bulletin of the American Academy of Psychiatry and the Law, 21,* 23–36.

Strauman, T. J. (1990). Self-guides and emotionally significant childhood memories: A study of retrieval efficiency and incidental negative emotional content. *Journal of Personality and Social Psychology, 59,* 869–80.

Strauman, T. J., and Higgins, E. T. (1988). Self-discrepancies as predictors of vulnerability to distinct syndromes of chronic emotional distress. *Journal of Personality, 56,* 685–707.

Strauman, T. J., Lemieux, A. M., and Coe, C. L. (1993). Self-discrepancy and natural killer cell activity: Immunological consequences of negative self-evaluation. *Journal of Personality and Social Psychology, 64,* 1042–52.

Summerfield, D. (2001). The invention of post-traumatic stress disorder and the social usefulness of a psychiatric category. *British Medical Journal, 322,* 95–98.

Swan, S., and Andrews, B. (in press). The relationship between shame, eating disorders and disclosure in treatment. *British Journal of Clinical Psychology.*

Tarrier, N., Sommerfield, C., and Pilgrim, H. (1999). Relatives' expressed emotion (EE) and PTSD treatment outcome. *Psychological Medicine, 29,* 801–11.

Teasdale, J. D., and Barnard, P. J. (1993). *Affect, cognition, and change.* Hove: Erlbaum.

Terr, L. (1990). *Too scared to cry.* New York: Basic Books.

Treisman, A., and DeSchepper, B. (1996). Object tokens, attention, and visual memory. In T. Inui and J. L. McClelland (Eds.), *Attention and performance XVI: Information integration in perception and communication* (pp. 15–46). Cambridge, Mass.: MIT Press.

Treisman, A., and Gelade, G. (1980). A feature integration theory of attention. *Cognitive Psychology, 12,* 97–136.

Tromp, S., Koss, M. P., Figueredo, A. J., and Tharan, M. (1995). Are rape memories different? A comparison of rape, other unpleasant, and pleasant memories among employed women. *Journal of Traumatic Stress, 8,* 607–27.

Tulving, E., and Schacter, D. L. (1990). Priming and human memory systems. *Science, 247,* 301–06.

Ullman, S. E., and Filipas, H. H. (2001). Predictors of PTSD symptom severity and social reactions in sexual assault victims. *Journal of Traumatic Stress, 14*, 369–89.

Ursano, R. J., Fullerton, C. S., Epstein, R. S., Crowley, B., Vance, K., Kao, T. C., and Baum, A. (1999). Peritraumatic dissociation and posttraumatic stress disorder following motor vehicle accidents. *American Journal of Psychiatry, 156*, 1808–10.

Usher, J. A., and Neisser, U. (1993). Childhood amnesia and the beginnings of memory for 4 early life events. *Journal of Experimental Psychology: General, 122*, 155–65.

van der Hart, O., and Horst, R. (1989). The dissociation theory of Pierre Janet. *Journal of Traumatic Stress, 2*, 397–412.

van der Kolk, B. A. (1996). Trauma and memory. In B. A. van der Kolk, A. C. McFarlane, and L. Weisaeth (Eds.), *Traumatic stress* (pp. 279–302). New York: Guilford.

van der Kolk, B. A., and Fisler, R. (1995). Dissociation and the fragmentary nature of traumatic memories: Overview and exploratory study. *Journal of Traumatic Stress, 8*, 505–25.

van der Kolk, B. A., and van der Hart, O. (1991). The intrusive past: The flexibility of memory and the engraving of trauma. *American Imago, 48*, 425–54.

van der Kolk, B. A., van der Hart, O., and Marmar, C. R. (1996). Dissociation and information processing in posttraumatic stress disorder. In B. A. van der Kolk, A. C. McFarlane, and L. Weisaeth (Eds.), *Traumatic stress* (pp. 303–27). New York: Guilford.

Van Etten, M. L., and Taylor, S. (1998). Comparative efficacy of treatments for post-traumatic stress disorder: A meta-analysis. *Clinical Psychology and Psychotherapy, 5*, 126–44.

Van Velsen, C., Gorst-Unsworth, C., and Turner, S. (1996). Survivors of torture and organized violence: Demography and diagnosis. *Journal of Traumatic Stress, 9*, 181–93.

Weinberger, D. A., Schwartz, G. E., and Davidson, R. J. (1979). Low-anxious, high-anxious, and repressive coping styles: Psychometric patterns and behavioral and physiological responses to stress. *Journal of Abnormal Psychology, 88*, 369–80.

Weiner, B. (1986). *An attributional theory of motivation and emotion.* New York: Springer-Verlag.

Weiskrantz, L. (1995). Comments on the report of the working party of the British Psychological Society on "recovered memories." *The Therapist, 2*, 5–8.

Wells, A., and Hackmann, A. (1993). Imagery and core beliefs in health anxiety: Content and origins. *Behavioural and Cognitive Psychotherapy, 21*, 265–73.

Wenzlaff, E. M., and Wegner, D. M. (2000). Thought suppression. *Annual Review of Psychology, 51,* 59–91.

Wessel, I., and Merckelbach, H. (1994). Characteristics of traumatic memories in normal subjects. *Behavioural and Cognitive Psychotherapy, 22,* 315–24.

Wheeler, M. A., Stuss, D. T., and Tulving, E. (1997). Toward a theory of episodic memory: The frontal lobes and autonoetic consciousness. *Psychological Bulletin, 121,* 331–54.

Wheeler, M. E., and Treisman, A. M. (2002). Binding in short-term visual memory. *Journal of Experimental Psychology: General, 131,* 48–64.

Wild, J., Baxendale, S., Scragg, P., and Gur, R. C. (2002). Verbal memory predicts outcome in posttraumatic stress disorder. Manuscript submitted for publication.

Williams, L. M. (1994). Recall of childhood trauma: A prospective study of women's memories of child sexual abuse. *Journal of Consulting and Clinical Psychology, 62,* 1167–76.

——— (1995). Recovered memories of abuse in women with documented child sexual victimization histories. *Journal of Traumatic Stress, 8,* 649–73.

Wiltshire, H. (1916). A contribution to the etiology of shell shock. *Lancet (i),* 1207–12.

Winkielman, P., Schwarz, N., and Belli, R. F. (1998). The role of ease of retrieval and attribution in memory judgments: Judging your memory as worse despite recalling more events. *Psychological Science, 9,* 124–26.

Yapko, M. D. (1994). Suggestibility and repressed memories of abuse: A survey of psychotherapists' beliefs. *American Journal of Clinical Hypnosis, 36,* 163–71.

Yehuda, R. (2001). Are glucocorticoids responsible for putative hippocampal damage in PTSD? How and when to decide. *Hippocampus, 11,* 85–89.

Yehuda, R., and McFarlane, A. C. (1995). Conflict between current knowledge about posttraumatic stress disorder and its original conceptual basis. *American Journal of Psychiatry, 152,* 1705–13.

Yehuda, R., Resnick, H., Kahana, B., and Giller, E. L. (1993). Long-lasting hormonal alterations to extreme stress in humans: Normative or maladaptive? *Psychosomatic Medicine, 55,* 287–97.

Yehuda, R., Southwick, S. M., Krystal, J. H., Bremner, D., Charney, D. S., and Mason, J. W. (1993). Enhanced suppression of cortisol following dexamethasone administration in posttraumatic stress disorder. *American Journal of Psychiatry, 150,* 83–86.

Yerkes, R. M., and Dodson, J. D. (1908). The relation of strength of stimulus to rapidity of habit-formation. *Journal of Comparative and Neurological Psychology, 18,* 459–82.

Young, A. (1995). *The harmony of illusions: Inventing post-traumatic stress disorder.* Princeton, N.J.: Princeton University Press.

Young, J. E. (1990). *Cognitive therapy for personality disorders: A schema-focused approach.* Sarasota, Fla.: Professional Resource Exchange, Inc.

Yule, W. (2001). When disaster strikes—the need to be "wise before the event": Crisis intervention with children and adolescents. *Advances in Mind-Body Medicine, 17,* 191–96.

Yule, W., and Gold, A. (1993). *Wise before the event: Coping with crises in schools.* London: Calouste Gulbenkian Foundation.

Yule, W., Bolton, D., Udwin, O., Boyle, S., O'Ryan, D., and Nurrish, J. (2000). The long-term psychological effects of a disaster experienced in adolescence: I. The incidence and course of posttraumatic stress disorder. *Journal of Child Psychology and Psychiatry, 41,* 503–11.

Zoellner, L. A., Foa, E. B., and Brigidi, B. D. (1999). Interpersonal friction and PTSD in female victims of sexual and nonsexual assault. *Journal of Traumatic Stress, 12,* 689–700.

Index